LANDMARK BUILDINGS

ARIZONA'S ARCHITECTURAL HERITAGE

TEXT BY

ANN PATTERSON

AND MARK VINSON

PHOTOGRAPHY BY

ARIZONA HIGHWAYS MAGAZINE CONTRIBUTORS

ARIZONA HIGHWAYS
BOOKS

BOOK DESIGNER: Mary Winkelman Velgos

PHOTOGRAPHY EDITOR: Richard Maack

BOOK EDITORS: Bob Albano, PK Perkin McMahon

COPY EDITOR: Evelyn Howell

EDITORIAL ASSISTANT: Emily Lyons

ART ASSISTANT: Nathan Rice

ILLUSTRATIONS: Mark Vinson

MAP: Justin Velgos

Library of Congress Control Number 2003107042
ISBN 1-893860-21-3

First printing 2004. Printed in South Korea.

Published by the Book Division of *Arizona Highways* magazine, a monthly publication of the Arizona Department of Transportation, 2039 West Lewis Avenue, Phoenix, Arizona 85009. Telephone: (602) 712-2200
Web site: www.arizonahighways.com

Publisher: Win Holden
Managing Editor: Bob Albano
Associate Editor: Evelyn Howell
Associate Editor: PK Perkin McMahon
Art Director: Barbara Denney
Director of Photography: Peter Ensenberger
Production Director: Cindy Mackey
Production Coordinator: Kim Ensenberger

■ **Front Cover:** Desert View Watchtower at Grand Canyon National Park, Phoenix's historic City Hall, and Burton Barr Central Library in Phoenix.
■ **Title Page:** Details of Prescott's Hassayampa Inn, ASU's Nelson Fine Arts Center, and Tucson's Pima County Courthouse.

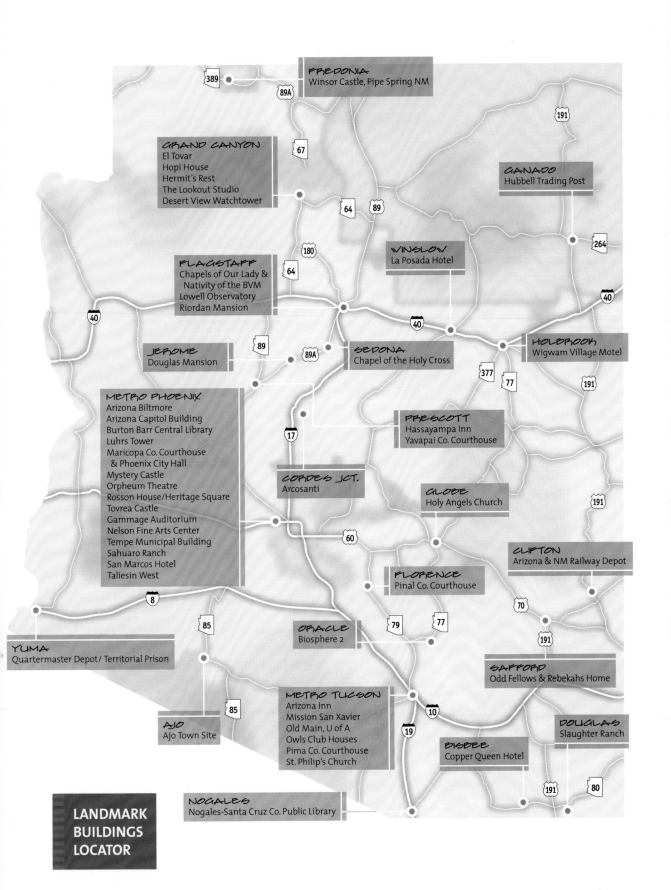

FREDONIA
Winsor Castle, Pipe Spring NM

GRAND CANYON
El Tovar
Hopi House
Hermit's Rest
The Lookout Studio
Desert View Watchtower

GANADO
Hubbell Trading Post

WINSLOW
La Posada Hotel

FLAGSTAFF
Chapels of Our Lady &
Nativity of the BVM
Lowell Observatory
Riordan Mansion

HOLBROOK
Wigwam Village Motel

JEROME
Douglas Mansion

SEDONA
Chapel of the Holy Cross

METRO PHOENIX
Arizona Biltmore
Arizona Capitol Building
Burton Barr Central Library
Luhrs Tower
Maricopa Co. Courthouse
 & Phoenix City Hall
Mystery Castle
Orpheum Theatre
Rosson House/Heritage Square
Tovrea Castle
Gammage Auditorium
Nelson Fine Arts Center
Tempe Municipal Building
Sahuaro Ranch
San Marcos Hotel
Taliesin West

PRESCOTT
Hassayampa Inn
Yavapai Co. Courthouse

CORDES JCT.
Arcosanti

GLOBE
Holy Angels Church

CLIFTON
Arizona & NM Railway Depot

FLORENCE
Pinal Co. Courthouse

YUMA
Quartermaster Depot/ Territorial Prison

ORACLE
Biosphere 2

SAFFORD
Odd Fellows & Rebekahs Home

METRO TUCSON
Arizona Inn
Mission San Xavier
Old Main, U of A
Owls Club Houses
Pima Co. Courthouse
St. Philip's Church

AJO
Ajo Town Site

DOUGLAS
Slaughter Ranch

BISBEE
Copper Queen Hotel

NOGALES
Nogales-Santa Cruz Co. Public Library

**LANDMARK
BUILDINGS
LOCATOR**

■ ■ ■ ■ ■ ■

ABOUT THE AUTHORS

Living in the Grand Canyon State, with its celebrated natural landmarks, both Ann Patterson and Mark Vinson find that Arizona's man-made environment is equally worthy of exploration.

Ann, who approaches architecture from a writer's perspective, is the former architecture critic for *The Arizona Republic*, the state's largest newspaper. She currently freelances for local and national publications, including *Phoenix Home & Garden* and *Art & Antiques* magazines, and enjoys international traveling with her husband. A founding member and loyal supporter of ASU's Faculty Wives Book Club, she recently was appointed to Tempe's Historic Preservation Commission.

Mark, a native of the Clifton-Morenci mining district who was Tempe's first historic preservation officer, currently serves Tempe as city architect/urban design manager. Previously, as chief designer for a Phoenix architectural firm, he specialized in commercial and medical buildings. A graduate of Arizona State University, where he received a master of science degree in building design, he lives in the Tempe-Chandler area with his wife and two sons and delights in hiking, golf, photography, sketching, and gardening.

■ ■ ■ ■ ■ ■
PREFACE AND ACKNOWLEDGMENTS

We began this project to encourage the public to recognize and appreciate a sampling of Arizona's landmark buildings. Also, we wished to explore varied facets of the state's rich architectural heritage in a single publication.

Several significant people and organizations helped us reach our goal. We are grateful to the Arizona Humanities Council and to the Rio Salado Architecture Foundation, a non-profit organization dedicated to educating professionals and the public about architecture and the built environment. Both organizations kindly supplied us with both encouragement and financial support. We also thank Bob Albano, managing editor of *Arizona Highways* Book Division, who agreed to publish the book to encourage people to visit the state's outstanding structures; and PK McMahon, associate book editor, who edited the manuscript, for her encouragement.

In selecting Arizona's built landmarks, we consulted with Arizona Humanities Council-approved scholars Dr. Douglas Kupel, author, consulting historian, and adjunct professor of history at Arizona State University, and Melissa Keane, author, archaeologist, consulting historian, and former chair of the Tempe Historic Preservation Commission. We owe them a debt of gratitude.

Also, Ann offers special thanks to her Kenny and Jennie, who took turns driving her from one end of the state to the other to visit sites and interview sources — as does Mark to his Linda, who introduced him to the value of non-published architecture.

DEDICATION

We dedicate this book with love
to our life mates, Bob Patterson and Linda Vinson,
and to our children, Rebecca and Kenneth and
Stephen Patterson and Jennifer Patterson Shick,
and Ken and Danny Vinson.

■ ■ ■ ■ ■ ■

CONTENTS

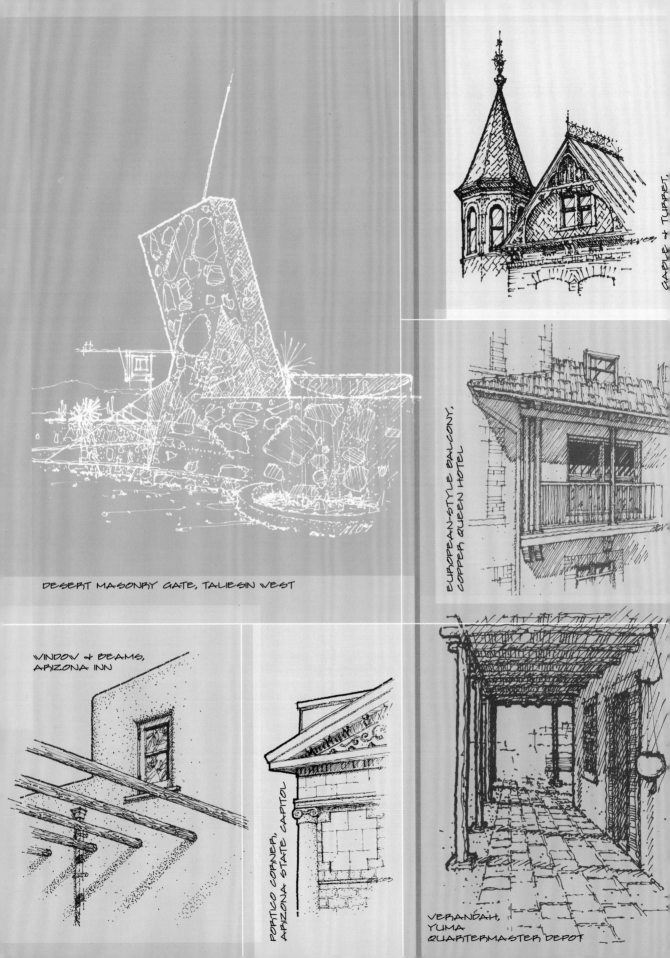

DESERT MASONRY GATE, TALIESIN WEST

GABLE + TURRET

EUROPEAN-STYLE BALCONY, COPPER QUEEN HOTEL

WINDOW + BEAMS, ARIZONA INN

PORTICO CORNER, ARIZONA STATE CAPITOL

VERANDAH, YUMA QUARTERMASTER DEPOT

INTRODUCTION

Who would guess that Tovrea Castle's tiered wedding-cake shape was meant to attract real estate investors?

Or that the design for Grady Gammage Auditorium began as a plan for an opera house in Baghdad, Iraq?

Arizona boasts extraordinary buildings revered for their architectural significance, but for most people, inanimate structures made of brick, glass, and steel come alive only when they learn the human stories behind their conception and construction.

Why didn't the Catholic fathers who built Mission San Xavier del Bac, the "White Dove of the Desert" near Tucson, finish the second tower of the graceful Spanish-style church? Historians speculate that the Franciscans may have truncated one tower to avoid paying taxes, or they ran short of cash, or they may have decided to leave the tower as a monument to a workman killed when he fell from the spire. (According to local Tohono O'odham legend, the unfortunate fellow transformed into a large rattlesnake that still resides in the area.) Scholars, however, can't say with certainty why the towers don't match. That's part of the mission's mystique.

Then there's the question of why those rustic stone buildings at the Grand Canyon appear so primitive. The answer is that Mary Elizabeth Jane Colter designed Hopi House, Hermit's Rest, the Lookout Studio, and Desert View Watchtower to resemble ancient Southwestern ruins. As one of America's most accomplished and yet little-known architects,

RICHARD MAACK

▲ The ancient Puebloans who constructed Lomaki (now part of Wupatki National Monument) created a design footprint for the organic architecture of today.

Colter designed hotels and train stations, mostly in a Southwestern mode, along the Santa Fe Railway line from Chicago to California for the Fred Harvey Company. A small, chain-smoking woman with piercing, violet eyes and hair she seldom combed, Colter was chastised for making a new structure appear aged. Crustily, she replied, "You can't imagine what it cost to make it look this old." Her impeccable taste, hard work, and single-mindedness allowed Mary Colter to define the look of America's national park architecture.

In addition to recounting the more repeatable anecdotes relating to Arizona's landmark buildings, we have attempted to discuss architectural styles as they evolved in Arizona.

We profile one of the state's oldest buildings, Tucson's Sonoran-style La Casa Cordova, a tiny, dirt-floored, adobe house built inside a fort in about 1848. And we look at Prescott's Yavapai County Courthouse, a crisp Greek Revival structure erected in 1918 to appease the tastes of that city's transplanted Midwesterners. Admittedly, assigning a style to a structure involves a degree of subjectivity, so we consulted the property inventory forms filed at the Arizona State Historic Preservation Office.

We profiled a number of buildings that are listed on the National Register of Historic Places. To qualify for listing, buildings, districts, sites, structures, and objects must meet certain criteria. They must be at least 50 years old and cannot have been remodeled beyond recognition. In addition, register candidates must have played a significant role in the community, state, or nation. And they must demonstrate an association with: an important historical event, like the migration of Mormon pioneers into Arizona via Pipe Spring's Mormon Fort; notable persons, such as Frank Lloyd Wright; noteworthy design trends or characteristics, like Paolo Soleri's futuristic Arcosanti; or local archaeology.

We reluctantly chose to exclude the notable remnants left behind by Arizona's earliest building cultures, the Anasazi (referred to as Ancestral Puebloans today), Sinagua, Salado, and Hohokam. Ruins of massive structures, such as Keet Seel, Wupatki, Besh-Ba-Gowah, and Casa Grande stand as silent testimonies to the skill, ingenuity, and climatic understanding of their unknown builders. Profiling these ancient structures of adobe and stone, however, would require a different approach and presentation. Therefore, we leave them for a future publication. We can only wish that we knew their stories with certainty. Their creative spirit lives on through the works of Mary Colter and other architects who found inspiration in the quiet majesty of these prehistoric marvels. A visit to the Lomaki Ruin at Wupatki, northeast of Flagstaff, sparked an epiphany for the architectural half of our team when Mark realized that the qualities of form, mass, material, and climatic response were not dependent on the whims of East Coast magazine editors, but were, in fact, the quintessential Arizona architecture.

Leaping forward to more recent centuries, our research revealed that the state's most prolific early architects remain largely unheralded in Arizona, though they leave behind large bodies of work, many still standing, throughout the state. The firm of Lescher and Mahoney completed more than 2,000 projects in Arizona, including the recently restored Orpheum Theatre in Phoenix. Tucson's Roy Place crafted at least a dozen buildings (now in the historic district) at the University of Arizona in Tucson, including the Humanities Building and Yuma Hall dormitory. Henry Trost created theaters, office buildings, and hotels in Arizona that remain landmarks, including the Hassayampa Inn in Prescott, two former Owls Club houses in Tucson, and the Luhrs Tower in Phoenix. Sadly, one of Trost's finest works, the Hotel Morenci, now exists only in the memories of that mining town's former residents and guests.

Arizona can rightfully claim association with Frank Lloyd Wright, the most famous architect of the 20th century, since he maintained a school, office, and home in Scottsdale. Wright also designed houses and public buildings here. Several of the striking structures about which we write were not designed by professional architects at all, but grew from some irrepressible yearning within dedicated amateurs. The buildings we chose are open to the public — at least some of the time — so readers can visit them, and our selections are spread throughout the state so that history and architecture fans can gain a sense of Arizona's scenic, cultural, and historical diversity while visiting them. Also, each structure that we profiled is specific to Arizona, that is, you're not likely to find something similar built anywhere else.

Buildings of major architectural importance to the state and its historical legacy have received full-length profiles. Other structures, we felt, lent themselves to vignettes; perhaps their building style is less absorbing or they no longer serve as active a role in their communities.

The story of Arizona is told in our buildings. As Frank Lloyd Wright once famously said, "The mother art is architecture. Without an architecture of our own we have no soul of our own civilization." We hope our readers have as much fun reading about and visiting Arizona's landmark buildings as we have had gathering and recounting their stories.

STONE ARCHES, EL TOVAR

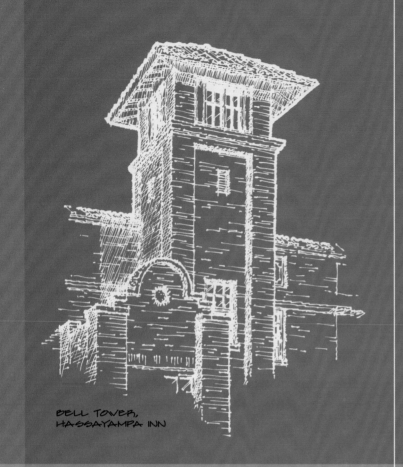

BELL TOWER,
HASSAYAMPA INN

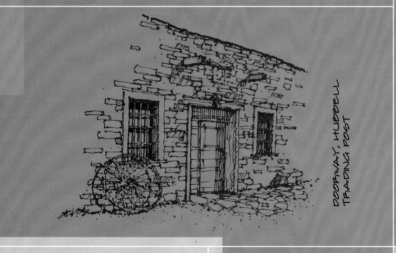

DOORWAY, HUBBELL
TRADING POST

PROFILED IN THIS SECTION

- ARCOSANTI (CORDES JUNCTION)
- CHAPEL OF THE HOLY CROSS (SEDONA)
- CHAPELS OF OUR LADY OF GUADALUPE & NATIVITY OF THE BLESSED VIRGIN MARY (FLAGSTAFF)
- DOUGLAS MANSION (JEROME)
- EL TOVAR (GRAND CANYON)
- HASSAYAMPA INN (PRESCOTT)
- HOPI HOUSE, HERMIT'S REST, THE LOOKOUT STUDIO, DESERT VIEW WATCHTOWER, ETC. (GRAND CANYON NATIONAL PARK, SOUTH RIM)
- HUBBELL TRADING POST (GANADO)
- LA POSADA HOTEL (WINSLOW)
- LOWELL OBSERVATORY (FLAGSTAFF)
- RIORDAN MANSION (FLAGSTAFF)
- WIGWAM VILLAGE MOTEL NO. 6 (HOLBROOK)
- WINSOR CASTLE AT PIPE SPRING NATIONAL MONUMENT (NEAR FREDONIA)
- YAVAPAI COUNTY COURTHOUSE (PRESCOTT)

GAZEBO, YAVAPAI CO.
COURTHOUSE SQUARE

TOWER + ENTRY,
LA POSADA

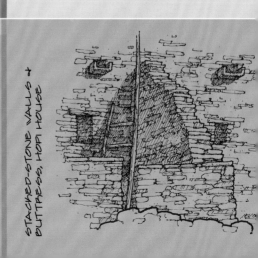

STACKED-STONE WALLS +
BUTTRESS, HOPI HOUSE

FLAGSTAFF AND NORTHERN ARIZONA

orthern Arizona beckons visitors from around the world with singular attractions like the Grand Canyon, Monument Valley, Canyon de Chelly, the Painted Desert, and the red rocks of Sedona. Add the grandeur of coniferous forests and alpine peaks, plus the cultural resources of several Indian reservations, and the region's allure becomes obvious.

Yet, during the early 1900s, few people actually settled in northern Arizona, a fact that persuaded Boston's Percival Lowell to establish the Lowell Observatory in Flagstaff, where astronomers could observe the heavens free of light pollution. Decades earlier, the same isolation had seemed threatening, spurring Mormon leader Brigham Young to build a fort at Pipe Spring to guard Mormon pioneers migrating south from Utah to take up farming in Arizona.

Over the years, the high country's splendid vistas have inspired architects to design unique travelers' accommodations in harmony with the surroundings — and their sometimes skewed interpretations of original cultures. Romanticized hostelries include El Tovar, a grandiose Norwegian hunting lodge-style log cabin on the Grand Canyon's South Rim; La Posada Hotel, a swank railroad stopover in Winslow; and the tepee-shaped Wigwam Village Motel in Holbrook, which carries over an icon of Plains Indian culture into the neighborhood of hogans and cliff dwellings.

Since so many northern Arizonans make a living by welcoming and providing for strangers passing through, it's not surprising the area's inns, dwellings, and public spaces add such diversity to the state's architectural repertoire.

DAVID ELMS, JR.

ARCOSANTI

■ **LOCATION**	Cordes Junction
■ **YEARS BUILT**	Construction on-going; ground broken in 1970
■ **STYLE**	Organic
■ **ARCHITECT**	Paolo Soleri
■ **SIGNIFICANCE**	Prototype town designed as an alternative to urban sprawl

For decades, Paolo Soleri's seemed a voice crying in the wilderness. Critics ignored, or worse, jeered, at his message that urban sprawl consumed too many of the Earth's limited natural resources — even as the world's rain forests, fisheries, and oil reserves grew seriously depleted.

Today on a wind-swept mesa at Cordes Junction, 60 miles north of Phoenix, Soleri speaks with the confidence of a prophet proven right. Arcosanti, the pedestrian-friendly prototype town that Soleri designed to conserve energy, raw materials, and land, teaches a lesson in economy that finally is gaining public attention.

The visionary architect stays a busy man. Wearing a collarless shirt, khaki pants, and rubber flip-flops, Soleri addresses TV cameras, adoring disciples, and news reporters with the aplomb of a man certain he's found a viable solution to the vexing problems of water and air pollution, traffic congestion, high crime rates, and disappearing desert and farm land. The octogenarian believes people are listening and repeats his philosophy, over and over again, in the same disarming, somewhat abstruse speaking style that charms his critics:

"The politician tells us day in and day out that the duty of a good American is to consume more and more to keep things rolling and humming; that is, to metastasize into an exurban landscape, the vast landscape of *muda* [waste]," Soleri says. "In that equation, exurbia equals the demise of the desert. . . .

"The American dream, physically embodied in the single-family house, has to be scrapped and reinvented in terms which are coherent with the human and biospheric reality. . . . It's the most expensive and wasteful of any kind of shelter for mankind. We have been

◀ **Although Arcosanti falls short of being the thriving metropolis envisioned by architect Paolo Soleri in the 1970s, the community continues to attract admirers of his ecology-conscious philosophy.**

trying to construct a lean alternative to hyper-consumerism at Arcosanti, our urban laboratory in Arizona's high country."

Set on approximately 4,000 acres of high desert remote from any real city, Arcosanti clusters a collection of rectangular and half-moon-shaped structures with the look of a housing development, or perhaps a monastery, established by extraterrestrials. Only about 10 percent complete so far, Arcosanti is Soleri's concrete statement expressing how the modern city could evolve without sprawl, alienation, or the rest of today's urban ills.

In Soleri's view, a successful city should 1) be densely populated to promote a sense of community while reserving surrounding space for agriculture and nature; 2) encourage citizens to live near their work to reduce their need for cars to commute; 3) be oriented so the sun can warm buildings in winter and be deflected in the heat of the summer; 4) include multiple-use structures, such as the five-story visitors center at Arcosanti, which holds living quarters, a bakery, cafeteria, offices, and a gallery; 5) combine frugality with beauty and functionality. Arcosanti's decorative roofs, for example, collect precious rainwater to use for irrigating plants.

Soleri teaches his students to make an apse by piling up a mound of earth, pouring concrete over the mound, removing the dirt and — *voila!* — an upside-down-bowl-shaped building. Workers decorate the ceilings of the apses by adding strips of wood, rope, or other items, as well as color, to the surface of the dirt mounds before pouring the concrete. "We can redesign inside the apse according to need," Soleri says.

The Italian-born architect and his followers began constructing Acosanti in 1970. Taking a leaf from the book of Frank Lloyd Wright, under whom he once studied, Soleri invites anyone over age 18 willing to pay for the privilege to help build Arcosanti and learn about "arcology." Soleri coined the word by combining the words architecture and ecology.

Soleri first intended that his model town would cover fewer than 25 acres of the land his foundation owns or leases at Cordes Junction, with the balance reserved for farming and as a nature preserve. He hoped the prototype city would house 5,000 to 7,000 residents who would walk to work and grow at least some of their food on-site or on the flood plains of the nearby Agua Fria River, which runs only seasonally. But Arcosanti's permanent population today numbers about 50.

Over the years, some 5,000 would-be architects, artists, educators, and others have attended Soleri's workshops at the demonstration site to practice his brand of construction techniques and landscaping, to study local history, and to attend cultural events, like the annual ethnic arts festival. The Cosanti Foundation, a non-profit, Scottsdale-based organization, sponsors the five-week workshops. The foundation and Soleri's business offices, a gallery, and a foundry operate out of Cosanti, which consists of 10 earth-cast concrete structures built in 1956 in what was then the middle of the desert near Phoenix. Soleri also lives at Cosanti.

So far, Arcosanti includes a visitors center; foundry; the Colly Soleri Music Center, named for his late wife; an apse filled with woodworking, metal, plumbing, and electrical workshops; a swimming pool; apprentice housing; and apartments for visitors. Since few workshop participants are professionals, the buildings have a rough-finished, Spartan look about them. Plans call for construction of a conference center for education and cybereducation and then a greenhouse, Soleri says.

Arcosanti operates on a pay-as-you-go plan. The foundation raises funds by selling handmade ceramic and metal wind-bells, by collecting fees from workshop participants and visitors, and from contributions.

Soleri, born in Turin, Italy, in 1919, took his Ph.D. in architecture with highest honors from Torino Politechnico in 1946. He then studied under Frank Lloyd Wright from 1947 to 1948. When a potential client asked Wright to do a very small house, the great man turned the commission over to Soleri. Thus Soleri met his future mother-in-law, Lenore Woods, for whom, in 1949, he designed and built a partially underground dome house near Cave Creek. In 1950, Soleri and his bride, Colly Woods Soleri, moved back to Italy where, as his first major commission, he designed a large ceramics factory. In the process, he learned to make wind-bells, now the financial life's blood of his projects. In 1956, Soleri returned to Arizona and began building Cosanti. Over time, he has designed several public buildings, among them a theater in Santa Fe (1966) and an amphitheater at Glendale Community College (1996). Mostly, though, he concentrates on Arcosanti, re-inventing it as construction moves slowly along. In addition, Soleri lectures, teaches, writes books, and assembles architecture exhibitions.

Shows expressing Soleri's ideas have appeared internationally, from New York City to Tokyo to Venice, and his honors include two Guggenheim grants and numerous prestigious awards.

Soleri notes that upscale condominium complexes are being built in city centers, that architects now take note of solar orientation and natural lighting to reduce energy costs, that some shop owners are choosing to live above their businesses, and that government officials are calling for limits on growth and are turning undeveloped land into parks or preserves. He has been urging these goals for more than 40 years.

■ **WHEN YOU GO** Arcosanti is near Cordes Junction, about 80 miles south of Flagstaff and about 60 miles north of Phoenix. Take Interstate 17 to Exit 262 and head east. Turn left at the first stop sign and follow the signs. Donations requested for admission and various specialized tours; self-guided tours always available. (928) 632-6217. Cosanti in Scottsdale is 1 mile west of North Scottsdale Road and 1 mile south of Shea Boulevard. (480) 948-6145.

CHAPEL OF THE HOLY CROSS

■ **LOCATION**	Sedona
■ **YEAR BUILT**	1956
■ **STYLE**	Modern
■ **ARCHITECT**	Anshen & Allen
■ **SIGNIFICANCE**	Contemporary chapel defined by its 90-foot-high, architecturally integrated cross

It was 1932. Leaving St. Patrick's Cathedral in New York City, Marguerite Brunswig paused to wonder why more churches weren't modern in styling, rather than copies of European cathedrals.

Later Brunswig passed the Empire State Building. "When viewed from a certain angle, a cross seemed to impose itself through the very core of the structure. What an idea for a church!" she thought.

▲ A yearning to see her faith expressed in modern architectural form led heiress Marguerite Brunswig to commission the design of Sedona's Chapel of the Holy Cross in the 1950s.

LARRY LINDAHL

Heiress to a fortune, Brunswig realized she had the funds to build such a church. Then, in 1941, Brunswig married businessman Tony Staude, and the two purchased the Doodlebug Ranch in Sedona, having fallen in love with the beauty of the red rocks overlooking Oak Creek Canyon. Now she had a place to build the church she envisioned. Sedona had a population of 300 at the time.

The couple contracted with San Francisco architects Anshen & Allen to design a chapel that would incorporate a large cross. Groundbreaking for the chapel, a non-denominational facility now owned by the Catholic Church, took place in 1954.

Construction presented a challenge. Fred Coukos, construction superintendent for contractor William-Simpson Construction Co., says he was appalled when he saw the site, a rock spur projecting 200 feet above the desert floor. "I took one look and thought, I better pack my bags and get out of here," he recalls.

But Coukos stuck it out. Crews dug a road to the site and poured concrete into foot-thick forms to make the walls. They had to import "tons and tons" of California beach sand to sandblast their surfaces because they couldn't find the right kind of sand locally.

The roof is 8-inch-thick concrete, protected by a waterproof membrane and covered with a 3-inch-thick concrete slab. Black steel frames support tinted glass panels that enclose the building ends. The front tubular aluminum doors stand 21 feet high, and the cross that Brunswig imagined so many years earlier dominates the opposite side of the church, rising 90 feet above solid rock within the building's spare framework. Almost 2,000 people visit the Chapel of the Holy Cross daily. Coukos says, "I didn't dream it would be so famous."

■ **WHEN YOU GO** The Chapel of the Holy Cross sits on a hillside above State Route 179, between Sedona and the Village of Oak Creek. From State 179, turn on Chapel Road and follow it to the chapel parking area at the end of the road. The chapel is a steep climb up a wheelchair-accessible ramp from there. Open 9 A.M. to 5 P.M. daily. Closed Thanksgiving, Christmas, Good Friday, and Easter. Special prayer service Monday at 5 P.M. Donations appreciated. (928) 282-4069.
www.diocesephoenix.com/parish/st_john_vianney_sed/chapel.htm

CHAPELS OF OUR LADY OF GUADALUPE AND NATIVITY OF THE BLESSED VIRGIN MARY

■ **LOCATION**	Flagstaff
■ **YEARS BUILT**	Our Lady, 1926-28; Nativity, 1929-30
■ **STYLE**	Gothic Revival, with variations
■ **DESIGNER/**	Father Edward A. Albouy (Chapel of Our Lady of Guadalupe);
ARCHITECT	Emmett G. Martin (Chapel of the Nativity of the Blessed Virgin Mary)
■ **SIGNIFICANCE**	Oldest existing Catholic churches in Flagstaff; built by parishioners / National Register of Historic Places, 1986 (both listed as part of the Flagstaff Multiple Resource Area North End Residential Historic District)

This tale concerns two chapels, built in the 1920s to serve quite different congregations, but which today welcome all worshippers, rich and poor, whatever their national origins. There's an adage in the Roman Catholic church that priests can be divided loosely into three types: pastoral fathers who concentrate on the emotional, physical, and spiritual needs of their parishioners; ecclesiastics who focus on the sacraments and the importance of a religious message in their homilies; and those destined to build.

"Father Edward A. Albouy was a builder," says Olivia Olivares, a librarian at Northern Arizona University and lay minister and translator for Flagstaff's chapels of Our Lady of Guadalupe and Nativity of the Blessed Virgin Mary. "Father Albouy came from France, was well-educated, very cultural. . . . He also decided there should be one [Catholic] church for whites and one for Mexicans [in Flagstaff]," she says.

Under Father Albouy, laborers built the Chapel of Our Lady of Guadalupe between 1926 and 1928 on Flagstaff's south side, a primarily Latino neighborhood. They were aided by sizable donations of materials from Flagstaff's Riordan family.

From 1929 to 1930, Albouy also directed construction of the Chapel of the Nativity of the Blessed Virgin Mary on the city's north side, where the town's prominent citizens lived.

Our Lady of Guadalupe church, an uncomplicated, two-story, rectangular building capped by a bell tower with a cross, has pointed, arched, beaded-glass windows suggesting familiarity with the Gothic Revival style, a favorite architectural look of the day. But the wood shingles on its pitched roof and the small attached and enclosed front entry area call to mind the California Bungalow style. Walls of stone support the white-painted, wood steeple. The bell inside the steeple no longer rings.

Carpeting covers the floor of the Chapel of Our Lady of Guadalupe, a flattened ceiling hides the rafters, and the basement contains a kitchen and an assembly hall. Over time, the simple design has been altered only by the additions in the 1960s of a ramp for the handicapped and a sacristy to the rear of the church.

Olivares, who researched the history of both churches for her parish, believes Albouy

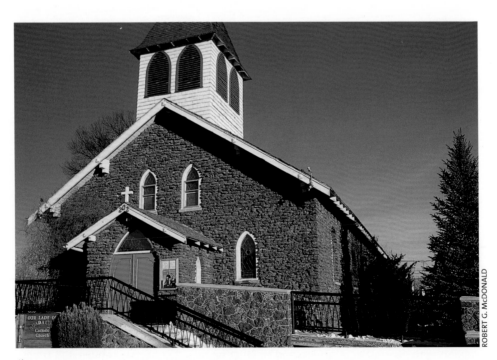

▲ Parishoners living on Flagstaff's primarily Latino south side built the Chapel of Our Lady of Guadalupe following Father Edward A. Albouy's simple design incorporating elements of Gothic Revival and California Bungalow styling.

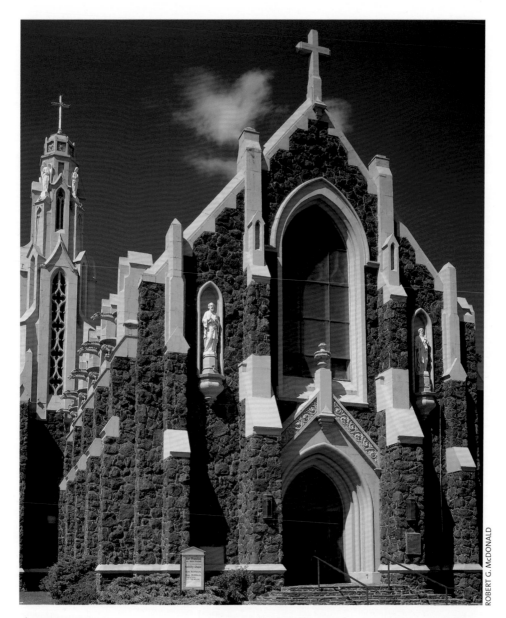

ROBERT G. McDONALD

▲ Gargoyles and mini flying buttresses garnish the Chapel of the Nativity of the Blessed Virgin Mary, originally a house of worship for Catholics living on Flagstaff's more affluent north side.

drew up a floor plan for Our Lady of Guadalupe but let southside parishioners carry out the design and construction.

By contrast, he hired Los Angeles architect Emmett G. Martin to create the Nativity of the Blessed Virgin Mary chapel. The two men worked closely to make Nativity a thing of splendor.

And it became just that, according to Flagstaff pioneer Michael J. Riordan, who wrote a glowing tribute to the church and its architect upon the building's 1930 completion. Riordan, with his brothers Matthew and Timothy, founded the Arizona Lumber and Timber Corporation, then Flagstaff's primary employer. In the tribute, Riordan stated the architect's purpose "was to produce a rugged, fortress-like structure with deep shadows that would fit

in and be a part of the bold mountain background, while embellishing it at the same time with the lightness of contrasting color and the effect of airiness produced by long lines, slender windows, and deep splays, and the remarkable noble tower."

Olivares says Nativity cost $105,000 to build, in 1930 dollars. No one knows what Our Lady cost, she says, in part because of the Riordans' generosity.

Laid out in crucifix form, Nativity shares many characteristics with Europe's Gothic cathedrals. Gargoyle rainspouts leer down from the concrete parapets; Munich stained glass infuses the pictorial windows with brilliant colors; and mottled, dark brown, exterior rock walls contrast dramatically with pink concrete embellishments. The structure features mini-flying buttresses; tall, narrow, pointed, arched openings; a soaring bell tower; exposed rafters; flagstone floors; and an overall vertical feeling — a church reaching toward the heavens.

The builders of both churches used the locally available malpais basalt rock. Parishioners scoured Flagstaff's mesas, collecting fieldstone from nearby lava flows and bringing back the basalt chunks in wheelbarrows, horse-drawn carts, and by hand.

In her book, *Stone Landmarks*, geologist Marie Jackson writes about Nativity: "One of the most distinctive features of the church's malpais basalt is the abundance of different kinds of lichens that have colonized its outer surfaces. Look closely along the surfaces of the tall basalt buttress on the west side of the church entrance and you'll see crustlike masses of white, deep yellow, pastel green, and copper-colored lichen attached to the pits and outer surfaces of the rock."

In dry weather, she observes, "The lichen appear obscure, almost as if they are shrinking into the rock, but when moisture returns they seem to swell and burst with color, giving the basalt stonework a lovely multi-colored hue." Some of the stone also features small, irregular holes, or vesicles, produced when volcanic gasses expanded in the fluid lava as it erupted 6 million years ago. According to Jackson, "Some chunks have so many vesicles that you can imagine the rock as a kind of solidified volcanic froth."

The rough stones cladding Nativity's walls, arranged randomly in a free-spirited way, achieve an over-all unity in the facade. At Our Lady, the rocks selected had at least one flat surface, and laborers stacked them in courses as a mason puts up bricks. "It took a lot more expertise to work the stone at Guadalupe than at Nativity," geologist Jackson writes.

According to Olivares, at the time, many southside Catholics felt slighted when the newspaper praised Nativity's churchgoers for their hard work gathering rock, while saying little about similar efforts at Our Lady. In addition, southsiders felt offended that Bishop Daniel Gercke of the Diocese of Tucson, then headquarters for Arizona's Catholic church, delayed laying the cornerstone at Our Lady until 1936, almost a decade after finishing the building. In contrast, the bishop had placed the cornerstone for Nativity upon its completion in 1930. "And those were only two examples of the church treating Latinos as second-class citizens," Olivares states.

Today, parishioners for the most part have "overcome the bad blood" of past decades, Olivares says. "Everyone comes together; everyone worships together. I'm very tied to this parish. We're very close."

In a strange way, this tale of Flagstaff's Catholic church buildings may still come full circle. Plans call for building a new church to provide sufficient space for everyone in the newly combined San Francisco de Asís Parish to worship, along with added classrooms and offices. The chapels of Our Lady and Nativity would be disposed of — leased, sold, closed, perhaps demolished.

To make this happen, the diocese may have to weigh the feelings of its lay members, like Olivares. Referring fondly to both Our Lady of Guadalupe and the Nativity of the Blessed Virgin Mary, she says, "These churches are really a labor of love. They show our extreme devotion to God and to the people of God."

■ **WHEN YOU GO** Chapel of Our Lady of Guadalupe: 224 S. Kendrick St. Follow Interstate 17, which becomes Milton Avenue, to Butler Avenue. Turn right on Butler to Kendrick, then left on Kendrick to the chapel. (928) 779-1341. Chapel of the Nativity of the Blessed Virgin Mary: 16 W. Cherry. Take Milton Avenue north until the road curves east and becomes Route 66/Santa Fe Avenue. From Historic Route 66, take Beaver Street north to the chapel. (928) 779-1341. Both churches are open Monday through Friday from 8:30 A.M. to 5 P.M. and Saturday from 12 P.M. to 5 P.M. Closed Sunday.

DOUGLAS MANSION

■ **LOCATION**	Jerome
■ **YEAR BUILT**	1916
■ **STYLE**	Territorial/Pueblo Revival
■ **ARCHITECTS**	(Royal W.) Lescher and (John Rinker) Kibbey
■ **SIGNIFICANCE**	One of the largest adobes in Arizona at time of construction / National Register of Historic Places, 1966

The following Arizona real estate advertisement appeared in the early 1960s:

> LOCATION: Near Jerome . . . Old mining town; population reduced to about 500 . . . PROPERTY: Approximately 5 acres . . . Magnificent views of every side. RESIDENCE: 23 rooms (9 bedrooms, 6 baths). 2-story Ranch style. Adobe construction, painted and plastered, 2' thick walls. Built about 1922 [sic] of finest materials available at that time . . . Attached 2 car GARAGE, heated, 4 rooms on ground floor. 2 Bedrooms and Kitchen above 2 Baths . . . OFFERED AT: $40,000.

Forty thousand dollars was not only a bargain-basement price for the property — the residence cost $150,000 to build — but the house known as the Douglas Mansion boasted a sterling provenance that ought to have increased the asking price.

The sellers were geologist James Douglas and his older brother, Louis W. Douglas, four-term U.S. Congressman from Arizona and budget director for President Franklin D. Roosevelt, vice chancellor of McGill University, and American ambassador to Great Britain during the Truman administration.

The Douglas brothers hoped to sell the family home after the death of their father, James Stuart Douglas. During a lifetime spent directing mining operations in Arizona and Sonora, Mexico, James S. Douglas had extracted some $125 million worth of gold, silver, and copper from the Little Daisy Mine near Jerome. In 1916, with some of the profits from his enterprises, the elder Douglas built his adobe mansion overlooking Jerome to host visiting mining executives and investors.

Despite its lowball price, the Douglas Mansion failed to sell, so the brothers donated the

▲ Positioned on a hill above the Little Daisy Mine in Jerome, the over-sized adobe built by mining executive James S. Douglas served as lodging for visiting mining officials and investors. The Douglas Mansion now is a state park.

8,700-square-foot residence and the two-story carriage house, along with its tack room, stable, hay loft, and bedroom suites, as well as the acreage, to the State of Arizona. The Douglas Mansion is now a mining museum and, since 1965, a part of Jerome State Historic Park.

A plaque at the mansion's entrance states the brothers' aim. They gave the house to Arizona "In memory of our grandfather Dr. James Douglas, our father James S. Douglas and our uncle Walter Douglas." All three Douglases played significant roles in the history of Arizona's mining industry.

The grandfather, Dr. James Douglas, was a Scottish physician and member of the Royal College of Surgeons who emigrated to Canada and became the founder and director of the Quebec Insane Asylum. On the side, the doctor invested in gold and copper mines, an interest which eventually ruined him financially.

The doctor's son, James Jr., commonly called "Professor," studied theology but stopped short of ordination as a Presbyterian minister. Instead, he switched to medicine and chemistry and then attempted to save his father's failing mining ventures. In the process, James Jr. developed a system for leaching copper ore called the Hunt and Douglas Process. (Thomas Sterry Hunt was a friend, chemist, and geologist.)

Unlike his father, James Jr. possessed the Midas touch. The Professor encouraged Phelps Dodge and Company to expand and convert itself into a mining conglomerate. On his recommendation, Phelps Dodge bought into Bisbee's Copper Queen Consolidated Mining Company. He was right on. By 1910, Bisbee's mines produced 3 million pounds of copper a month. Eventually, James Jr. became Phelps Dodge's first president and the namesake for the city of Douglas in the southeastern part of the state. Many people consider James Jr. the founder of Arizona's copper mining industry.

One of the Professor's sons, Walter, succeeded his father as president of Phelps Dodge.

Another son, James Stuart Douglas, at their father's request, oversaw Phelps Dodge operations in Bisbee, Douglas, and Prescott in Arizona, and Nacozari, Sonora, Mexico. He and others also founded the successful Bank of Bisbee and Bank of Douglas, later acquiring control of the Phoenix National Bank and Phoenix Savings and Trust Company.

In Jerome, James Stuart Douglas spent some four years rounding up investors and exploring the potential of Jerome's Little Daisy Mine, which many people thought had played out. He reorganized the United Verde Extension Company and became its president. In 1914, the company struck a rich copper vein. Soon the Little Daisy Mine was producing $700,000 worth of copper a month, and the mine's value was estimated at $60 million. Over time, Douglas repaid his initial $400,000 investment 300 times over.

James S. Douglas' nickname was "Rawhide Jimmy," although no one dared call him that to his face. The appellation reputedly came from the fact that Douglas used rawhide to shield the rollers of an incline — expensively neglected by previous managers — from cable scarring at a mine in Nacozari. "Rawhide" also seemed to suit his bluff, direct, often caustic personality.

He could have afforded a plush home in New York, Denver, or Chicago, but Douglas chose to build a few hundred yards from the Little Daisy Mine. He celebrated his 1916 bonanza by constructing a sprawling, mountaintop mansion overlooking the Verde Valley and the town of Jerome, which bustled with a population of 15,000. Jerome, situated at an altitude of about 5,400 feet, took its name from Eugene Jerome, the United Verde Copper Company's

▲ Fired-brick edging on the Douglas Mansion's roof parapet, a common element in Territorial style buildings, serves to protect the softer, underlying adobe brickwork.

chief investor, who was a cousin to Jennie Jerome, mother of Winston Churchill, Britain's prime minister during World War II.

The architects, the Phoenix firm of Lescher and Kibby, used mostly local building materials in constructing the home, including a core of 80,000 adobe bricks, plastered inside and out. Building contractor T.B. Stewart described the construction process this way:

"We blew the top off the hill and leveled the site off. To make the adobes [each measuring 11-1/2 x 17-1/2 x 3-1/2 inches] we brought in a crew of adobe men. These fellows mixed dirt, straw, and water together by hand, dumped it into a three-brick ladder-like frame, smoothed the surface, and sun-dried the bricks on site. They dried rather slowly, had to be turned on edge periodically, and occupied a tremendous amount of space. The same crew laid up brick mud for mortar."

James S. Douglas wrote thousands of letters during his lifetime, often on the back of envelopes to save writing paper. After completing his two-story Territorial/Pueblo Revival style home — one of the largest adobe buildings in Arizona at the time — he wrote his father, "It is an odd looking thing, but I think quite appropriate to the site, and it is going to be very comfortable."

In January 1917, James S. Douglas wrote his son a more definitive comment:

"I am writing this in the big room at the new house of which for tonight I am the sole occupant. The room is rather overpowering in its size but excepting for the fact that there is at least four times too much space in this house devoted to cupboards, cloakrooms, draperies, chests of drawer, & closets, & that the pantry is twice too big and the ice chest four times as large as may ever possibly be necessary, the 'tout ensemble' of the house . . . is a gigantic success, including its cost which . . . is the most gigantic thing about it."

The rooms in the Douglas Mansion are large, indeed. The living room, which Douglas called "overpowering," extends approximately 28 feet wide by 37 feet long, or at 1,406 square feet, the size of a small house. The living room contains a fireplace nearly big enough to walk into, six French doors, two segmented windows, light fixtures dangling from high ceilings, and poured concrete floors, once covered with area rugs.

A recreation room lies adjacent to the living room, equipped with a quarter-sawn oak pool table with maple and ebony veneer. A 5-foot-wide hallway, its floor originally laid with a 75-foot-long carpet, leads to what once were three bedroom suites and a library.

The living room, library, and a spacious upstairs bathroom are, today, the only rooms restored to anything like their original condition. Many of the interior walls have been removed, or reconfigured, to accommodate offices and exhibits of mining paraphernalia, Douglas family photographs, and fluorescent rocks. The entry to the museum, for instance, is cut into the former dining room, and the original front entry is sealed off. The public rest rooms occupy space where the pantry and a trunk storage room once stood. Hidden by a parapet, the flat roof wears a contemporary foam coating. The original central vacuuming system still works.

Fortunately, says Park Ranger Mike Rollins, most of the original doors, cupboards, sinks, porch screens, and hardware are stored on the premises, and indentations in the floors indicate where the walls were removed, in case some future official decides to restore the house as Douglas built it.

Copper production in Jerome peaked in 1929, then falling copper prices due to the Great Depression caused the Little Daisy Mine to shut down in 1938. During World War II, James Stuart Douglas retired to his native Canada and resumed his Canadian citizenship. He died there in 1949 at age 82. Jerome became a near ghost town, its population plummeting to fewer than 100 in the early 1950s. In the heyday of the Little Daisy Mine, the Douglas family sometimes gathered at their Jerome mansion to celebrate the Christmas holidays. Apparently no one stayed in residence long, though, except for a caretaker. According to James Stuart Douglas' letters, the polluted air caused by sulfur fumes from the smelter deterred lengthy visits. Nevertheless, guests enjoyed visiting the Douglas home. William F. Staunton, a mining engineer who worked in Jerome in the 1920s, told an interviewer, "[Douglas] was certainly a grand host. It made no difference whether he was there or not, the latch was always out for his friends, and usually they were a thirsty crowd. . . . sitting before blazing logs in the great fireplace, there was an air of peace and optimism."

■ **WHEN YOU GO** Jerome State Historic Park. Take Interstate 17 to the State Route 260 exit heading west. In Cottonwood, follow U.S. Route 89A south and turn off at Milepost 345 at the lower end of Jerome, then follow the paved road 1 mile. Open 8 A.M. to 5 P.M. daily except Christmas. Entrance fee. (928) 634-5381.
www.pr.state.az.us/Parks/parkhtml/jerome.html

EL TOVAR

■ **LOCATION**	Grand Canyon National Park
■ **YEAR OPENED**	1905
■ **STYLE**	Combination Swiss chalet and Norwegian hunting lodge
■ **ARCHITECT**	Charles E. Whittlesey
■ **SIGNIFICANCE**	Great lodge that helped open the Grand Canyon to tourism / National Register of Historic Places, 1974

Rooms without baths ran $4; rooms with baths cost $6. Lunch was $1, and a full-course dinner served by a comely, white-aproned Harvey Girl seldom exceeded $1.50. What a bargain that seems today.

El Tovar Hotel, 20 feet from the edge of the South Rim of the Grand Canyon, opened to Canyon tourists as a Fred Harvey Company hotel on Jan. 14, 1905; today, the elegantly rustic hotel still offers guests a million-dollar view of the Canyon, plus a wealth of American history.

Here, where reservations are taken more than a year in advance, prominent guests have included Ronald Reagan, George Bush, and Bill Clinton. The company now known as Xanterra Parks & Resorts, which purchased the Fred Harvey Company in 1968, considers El Tovar among its flagship properties.

Part of the charm of this cross between a Swiss chalet and a Norwegian hunting lodge goes back to its origins. In the 1870s, railroad travelers found the limited menus at rail-side eateries unappetizing and exorbitantly priced. Fred Harvey, an English immigrant then working as a railroad ticket agent in Leavenworth, Kansas, sold his idea for a chain of restaurants (and later, luxury hotels) to the Atchison, Topeka and Santa Fe Railway System in the 1870s. By 1916, Fred Harvey Company operations stretched west to Los Angeles and employed 2,100 people.

The Harvey Company's attention to detail is legendary: dining tables covered by linen tablecloths; hamburgers made of prime beef shipped from Kansas City feed lots; and attractive young women called Harvey Girls smiling fetchingly as they described menus featuring

▲ At El Tovar, a gable roof over the main entrance, a mansard roof pierced by dormer windows over the guest rooms, and a hip roof over the lobby and mezzanine, topped by a shingled turret, give the venerable lodge a distinctive look.

terrapin, antelope, quail, bluepoint oysters, fresh California-grown fruits and vegetables, and five different wines.

Fred Harvey wanted to lure tourists to travel by train, but his company accomplished much more than that. It opened up the West's natural wonders to wealthy travelers who sometimes resided an entire season in hotels like El Tovar and, returning home, spread the word about the grandeur of the scenery.

Over the years, dedicated managers have spent at least 25 times El Tovar's original $250,000 cost to preserve the hotel's woodsy ambience and to update its amenities.

The hotel's name is a variation on the spelling of Tobar, for Don Pedro de Tobar, a lieutenant with Francisco Vásquez de Coronado's party, which explored Arizona in 1540. Tobar never saw the Grand Canyon, but reputedly first told Coronado of its existence. Tobar's coat of arms hangs above the entrance.

Architect Charles E. Whittlesey, staff architect for the Santa Fe Railway, designed El Tovar to emulate Europe's "destination resorts" like The Park in Baden-Baden, Germany. The continent's grand hotels of the era tended toward the fussy Beaux Arts style. Usually located near train stations where the nobility and their entourages could disembark easily, the hostelries featured impeccably prepared gourmet food and encouraged guests to spend weeks, even months, taking the waters or breathing crystalline air in the mountains or by the seaside. By contrast, America's wilderness hotels tended to be simple, wood-frame buildings hung with Victorian gewgaws.

Whittlesey's mix of chalet and hunting-lodge styles advanced architecture a step beyond over-blown Victorian, while retaining the period's fondness for exotica.

▲ Log-slab paneling, dark-stained overhead rafters, and a number of animal head trophies in the entrance lobby perpetuate the architect's intent that El Tovar resemble a rustic hunting lodge. With the hotel's opening, visitors flocked to the Grand Canyon.

Constructed of Kaibab limestone boulders and Oregon Douglas fir, El Tovar rambles from three stories (on the south end) to four stories (on the north end). Hopi Indian builders spent two years constructing the 36,584-square-foot hotel, its first floor sheathed with log slab siding as a reminder of its log cabin precursors, and its upper stories covered with rough weatherboards. From the beginning, the hotel was equipped with electricity, powered by its own steam generator.

A wood turret wrapped with shingles gives El Tovar its distinctive alpine silhouette. The turret actually served a practical purpose, concealing a 10,000-gallon storage tank holding the hotel's water supply, which was hauled in daily by train, according to Mike Harding, rooms director for Xanterra's lodges at the Canyon. Today, El Tovar pumps its water from the North Rim of the Canyon, which sits approximately 1,000 feet higher than the South Rim's 7,000-foot elevation and receives more rain.

El Tovar's main entrance faces east toward Hopi House, an Indian craft shop. A verandah wraps the north and east ends of the building so guests can relax on straight-back, rush-bottom rocking chairs while viewing the comings and goings of visitors admiring the Canyon. The west wing contains a well-regarded dining room, newly remodeled kitchen, and utility wing. View windows flank two stone chimneys on the north and south sides of this wing.

Multiple wood-shingled roofs at several different levels add architectural interest to Whittlesey's design. A hipped roof with bracketed eaves shelters the central lobby and mezzanine portion of the building. The north and south wings feature mansard roofs pierced by dormers; the roofs step down by one and two stories to terraces connected to the most expensive suites, where kings and presidents sometimes stay overnight.

Dark-stained wood enriches the interior, with the heads of big game animals, like moose and elk, encircling the walls. The lobby features peeled-log posts, and the railings on the stairway leading to the mezzanine lounge, like the railings of the outdoor terraces and porches, have patterned balusters, saw-cut in the Swiss-chalet manner.

Originally, El Tovar contained 100 rooms, with a bathroom down the hall for those guests who paid extra. It long since has been remodeled to hold 77 rooms, each with its own bath.

Charles Whittlesey studied under the great American architect Louis Sullivan and practiced for a quarter of a century in Chicago before joining the Santa Fe Railway as its chief architect. Moving to Albuquerque in about 1900, Whittlesey quickly adopted the Mission Revival and Pueblo forms, crafting Albuquerque's Alvarado Hotel (since destroyed) in this manner before designing El Tovar. In 1906, Whittlesey moved to San Francisco after its great fire and earthquake, creating several commercial structures there, including the Pacific Building, which was made of reinforced concrete decorated with terra-cotta. In Arizona he also designed the Riordan Mansion in Flagstaff, giving it a rustic look similar to El Tovar's. Whittlesey died in 1941.

Over the years, El Tovar has undergone repeated renovations. In 1982, all the hotel's exterior wood was totally replaced with Douglas fir from Oregon. All the windows became double-paned, all the rooms had fire sprinklers added, a lightning suppression system was installed, and the furniture was updated at a cost of around $5 million. Many more millions of dollars have been poured into conserving the hotel since.

Architecturally, El Tovar's significance lies in its eclectic design, which bridged the gap between the staid, Victorian/European resort architecture of the late 19th century and the rustic look deemed appropriate for the scenic wonders of the Eastern United States. Along with South Rim landmarks designed by Mary E.J. Colter, El Tovar helped set the standard for national park architecture for years to come.

Also, creating El Tovar as a "destination resort" dramatically increased tourism, which helped the Grand Canyon become a national monument in 1908 and a national park 11 years later. Through the years, luminaries such as Albert Einstein, Greece's former King Paul and Queen Frederica, Richard Nixon and Dwight D. Eisenhower, Marlon Brando, and the Soviet cosmonauts have enjoyed the hotel's hospitality.

Today, some 4 million travelers visit Grand Canyon National Park annually. The lucky among them will include a stay at El Tovar in their Grand Canyon experience.

■ **WHEN YOU GO** The Grand Canyon's South Rim is 80 miles northwest of Flagstaff via U.S. Route 180. From the Grand Canyon National Park Service Headquarters/Visitors Center, travel less than 1 mile to El Tovar. (928) 638-2631.
www.cr.nps.gov/history/online_books/harrison/harrison5.htm

HASSAYAMPA INN

■ **LOCATION**	Prescott
■ **YEAR BUILT**	1927
■ **STYLE**	Mission Revival/Italian Renaissance Revival
■ **ARCHITECT**	Trost & Trost (Henry C. Trost, designer)
■ **SIGNIFICANCE**	Among the first hotels in the state built with automobiles in mind / National Register of Historic Places, 1976

By the 1920s, Prescott was having a hard time maintaining its economic base. True, gold had been discovered in the 1850s near Prescott, a fact that prompted President Lincoln to create the Arizona Territory in 1863 and to choose Prescott as its capital. Lincoln needed gold to fund the Union cause and hoped that designating Arizona a territory would aid that process.

Then, after the Civil War ended, Prescott lost the capital to Tucson in 1867. The town won the honor back in 1877, only to see the Territorial capital, with its jobs and prestige, move permanently to Phoenix in 1889.

Soon Prescott's gold mines played out. And on July 14, 1900, much of Whiskey Row, crowded with bustling bars and bordellos, along with some of the commercial district, burned to the ground.

The community rebuilt. But leaders began to seek another attraction to bring income into the mile-high city. They decided a resort hotel might entice Phoenicians and others to spend summers in Arizona's temperate central highlands. They proposed an inn, to be named for the nearby Hassayampa River, saying it should include swimming pools, roof gardens, sun parlors, tennis courts, and every imaginable amenity.

To accomplish their goal, the leaders formed the privately owned Hassayampa Hotel Company and tried, but failed, to secure financing for the project. After the plan had been downscaled to reasonable proportions, Prescott Mayor Morris Goldwater (uncle of the late U.S. Sen. Barry Goldwater) proclaimed June 26, 1925, as Prescott Hotel Day, asking for public donations in support of an inn.

Bill Otwell, a Prescott architect specializing in preservation, says, "At a dollar a share,

RICHARD MAACK

▲ Although architect Henry Trost's original plans called for Prescott's Hassayampa Inn to be a Pueblo Revival-style adobe building, townspeople forced him back to the drawing board once the foundation had been laid.

they raised $15,000 in one day." With the Prescott Kiwanis Club spearheading the drive, the community eventually contributed more than $200,000 by public subscription, enough to purchase a site on the northwest corner of Gurley and Marina streets and to start construction.

The respected architectural firm of Trost & Trost of El Paso, Texas, won a competition to design the facility, only to have their initial design rejected. Henry Charles Trost, who was best known for crafting Albuquerque's celebrated Pueblo Revival-mode Franciscan Hotel, wanted to do a Pueblo/Art Deco building in Prescott. But Prescottonians, mostly former New Englanders and Midwesterners, felt more comfortable with stone and brick and considered adobe unsuitable.

Over the Christmas holidays, Trost changed his scheme to a Mission Revival/Italian Renaissance Revival style. It was to be a flat-roofed, three-story structure made of wire-cut brick. The inn would be adorned by a molded cornice and three projecting bands separating the second and third story from the first-level store fronts. A four-story bell tower, capped with a pyramid-shaped roof, would add a focal point to the project.

The wings of the L-shaped building would hug the rear of the lot, leaving space for a garden and fountain on the sunny southeast corner. The plan also featured an avant-garde *porte cochere* with a covered driveway to protect passengers as they unloaded their luggage. According to architect Otwell, "The Hassayampa Inn was first envisioned when automobile tourists became fairly common on Arizona roads. The inn was one of the first hotels in the state designed with automobiles in mind."

The Hassayampa Inn opened Nov. 5, 1927, to much celebration. A headline in the *Prescott Journal-Miner* trumpeted, "New Hotel Pledges Prescott's Faith in Her Future." A reporter rhapsodized,

"The furnishings of the lobby and other rooms of the Inn would have delighted the artist soul of William Morris, the English artist who laid down the principle that there should be nothing in a house that could not be classed as either beautiful or useful and that so far as possible beauty and use should be combined."

Celebrities of the era like Tom Mix, Rudolph Valentino, Rudy Vallee, Mary Pickford, Douglas Fairbanks, and Will Rogers enjoyed the inn's spacious lobby with its taupe-and-blue wainscoting, matching floor tiles, beams hand-painted in floral and geometric motifs by itinerant artist C.H. Williams, and Peacock Alley — a wide hallway descending several steps to the dining room and to a bar featuring 14-foot ceilings. The small, hand-operated, Chinese-red passenger elevator off the lobby entrance, one of the oldest elevators in the state, is still operational.

Community ownership of the Hassayampa Inn ended during the 1930s, but the inn continued to function as a popular gathering spot for local people and tourists into the 1970s.

Then, declining revenues and a worn appearance caused some people to suggest its demolition.

In 1986, however, the Hassayampa's fortunes took a turn for the better. Experienced managers purchased the hotel and poured some $3 million into a five-month-long restoration. Otwell, along with Phoenix architects Allen & Philp, oversaw the installation of such practical necessities as a new central heating and cooling system and a fire sprinkler system. Crews cleaned and re-pointed the exterior red brickwork and replaced the fountain, which had disappeared. Artist Richard Schmit repainted the original images on the lobby ceilings. And workers renovated the dining room, bar, and guest rooms, creating new meeting rooms in the basement.

Originally, the inn contained 76 guest rooms, with baths at the end of the hall. Today the hotel offers 66 guest rooms, each equipped with at least a shower, sink, and toilet, and some boasting ball-foot bathtubs as well. A standard room contains two double beds, a three-drawer oak dresser, floor lamp, desk with a leather-and-tile top, ladder-back chair, in-room sink, and a closet. A shower and toilet fit into a space that probably accommodated a second closet at one time. One suite of rooms even holds a large whirlpool tub.

The most impressive renovation happened in the Peacock Dining Room, where etched glass Art Deco window panels now gleam under a handsome hammered-copper ceiling. The banquet room features 40-foot-long painted panoramas of Arizona, along with back-lit, stained-glass windows. Photomurals enhance some of the meeting rooms, and framed watercolor paintings of Prescott's historic homes add ambience to the hallways. Otwell says some public areas endured so many alterations over the years that it is almost impossible to decipher their original condition.

Nonetheless, the hotel's nominating papers for the National Register of Historic Places declare, "Construction of the hotel in 1927 introduced a new style of architecture to Prescott, one which was considered modern and fashionable. Today the Hassayampa Inn remains relatively unchanged and is the best preserved and largest local example of its style [Mission Revival/Italian Renaissance Revival] in the community."

■ **WHEN YOU GO** 122 E. Gurley St. Entering Prescott on State Route 89, the highway intersects with Gurley Street. Turn right onto Gurley, going west to the hotel. Coming into town on State 69, the highway becomes Gurley Street when it reaches Prescott; follow Gurley about five blocks west to the hotel. (928) 778-9434, (800) 322-1927.

HOPI HOUSE, HERMIT'S REST, DESERT VIEW WATCHTOWER, ETC.

- **LOCATION** Grand Canyon National Park
- **YEARS BUILT** 1905-1937
- **STYLE** Rustic
- **ARCHITECT** Mary Elizabeth Jane Colter
- **SIGNIFICANCE** Structures blend with natural setting and recall prehistoric dwellings; influenced national park architecture / National Register of Historic Places, 1987

Hermit's Rest looks as if a hoary mountain man had used the logs and rocks he wrested from a jumble of stones and tumbled trees to build a primitive shelter. The structure appears poised to slide from the South Rim into the Grand Canyon's abyss.

And that's the impression architect Mary Elizabeth Jane Colter hoped to create: a rustic look in its natural setting.

The rest stop consists of unplaned logs, only their bark and limbs lopped off, and contains furniture carved from twisted tree stumps. A dilapidated mission bell suspended from piled-up rocks welcomes guests to the site. Visitors warm themselves beside a blackened fireplace nestled inside an enormous rock dome. Hermit's Rest was meant to accommodate tourists traveling the 8-mile service road west from the Santa Fe Railway Station to an old trailhead. Horse-drawn carriages (or later, Harveycars) transported the adventurous travelers.

The Fred Harvey Company wanted to evoke the Old West's majesty and mystery in its stores and hotels built near Santa Fe Railway stations. Mary Colter interpreted this vision with verve.

RICHARD MAACK

▲ Builders completed Hopi House, the first Mary Colter-designed structure to grace the Grand Canyon's South Rim, a few days before adjacent El Tovar opened.

▲ A blazing fire at Hermit's Rest invites visitors to pause and contemplate the local materials used in the fireplace construction; the Desert View Watchtower perches thrillingly close to the Canyon's abyss.

Born April 4, 1869, to Irish immigrants in Pittsburgh, Pennsylvania, Colter studied at the California School of Design (now the San Francisco Art Institute) and apprenticed with a California architect. But employment opportunities were scarce for architects — never mind a woman architect — so she took a job teaching mechanical arts in a St. Paul, Minnesota, high school, where she remained the next 15 years. She also lectured in history at an extension university and attended classes in archaeology.

A chance acquaintance led to an offer in 1901 to arrange the interior of an Indian arts and crafts store next to the Alvarado Hotel, which the Harvey Company operated in Albuquerque, New Mexico. Arriving in New Mexico, Colter fell in love with the Southwest and Southwestern design. Her gift shop displays at the Alvarado Hotel became an instant hit.

Colter, a strong-willed woman, was utterly committed to her calling. The Harvey Company valued her because she had an eye for high quality Indian art and because she understood how to make architecture complement the Western landscape.

Harvey executives quickly hired her to work at the Grand Canyon, where they were building a hotel to be called El Tovar. This time, she would design an entire Indian gift shop as well as organize its displays.

The result was Hopi House, completed Jan. 1, 1905, just a few days before El Tovar opened. Interestingly, Charles E. Whittlesey, El Tovar's architect, also had designed Albuquerque's Alvarado Hotel, site of the Indian crafts shop Colter had decorated earlier.

Colter modeled Hopi House after the Hopi Indian dwellings she visited in Oraibi, Arizona, using stone and wood native to the region. The three-story structure features ter-raced roofs, each rooftop acting as a courtyard for the apartment above. Tree-limb ladders and stone steps connect one level to the next. Hopi House has small windows, low door-ways, and ceilings made in typical Hopi fashion, with beams covered by layers of sticks topped with a mud mix.

Hopi craftsmen helped construct the building and, at first, some even lived there. Later, artisans employed to demonstrate pottery-making or rug-weaving took up residence on the third floor of Hopi House, while the first two floors featured Colter's tasteful arrangements of Indian pottery, blankets, jewelry, and other items. In this way, the traveling public became acquainted with some of Arizona's Indian art and culture.

In 1910, the Fred Harvey Company offered Colter a permanent position designing and decorating their hotels, restaurants, and train stations across the Southwest. At 41, Colter began a new career.

In all, Colter designed eight buildings in Grand Canyon National Park. In addition to Hopi House (1905) and Hermit's Rest (1914), they include: The Lookout Studio (1914), Phantom Ranch (1922), The Watchtower at Desert View (1932), Bright Angel Lodge (1935), and men's and women's dormitories at the South Rim (both 1937). Colter also decorated El Tovar's cocktail lounge, but her work there is no longer apparent.

Elsewhere in Arizona, Colter designed La Posada Hotel in Winslow (1930) and decorated the Painted Desert Inn in Apache County (1947). All these facilities still stand. And all of Colter's buildings at the Grand Canyon claim a place on the National Register of Historic Places as contributing to the Grand Canyon Village Historic District.

Probably the high point of Colter's architectural efforts at the Grand Canyon is The Watchtower at Desert View, 25 miles east of Grand Canyon Village. Not only are the views spectacular from that location — visitors can see the muddy Colorado River carving the depths of the Grand Canyon, the Painted Desert, and the Kaibab National Forest — but the tower itself is an architectural gem.

During her years with the Harvey Company, Colter continued to collect the best of local Indian art — beautiful pottery, baskets, rugs, and jewelry — purchased at cost through the company's auspices. She befriended Indian artists, and she regularly visited cliff dwellings throughout the Southwest. All this prepared her well to design The Watchtower at Desert View.

When she was past 60, Colter took the unusual, and at that time dangerous, course of chartering a small airplane to locate the ruins of prehistoric Indian towers, sites she later visited by car, and then photographed and sketched the remains to better understand their forms and means of construction.

The Watchtower consists of a one-story, circular tower, known as the Kiva Room, that contains a gift shop and small fireplace, linked to a hollow tower reaching five stories, or 70 feet, high. The Kiva Room is notable for its ceiling made of logs salvaged from the Grand View Hotel and laid in a stepped formation frequently used in Indian structures.

Exquisite murals cover the plastered walls in the taller tower. Some murals, painted by Fred Greer, replicate prehistoric Indian pictographs and petroglyphs, and others,

▲ The Lookout Studio functions as a gift shop and a station for photo opportunities.

created by Hopi artist Fred Kabotie, illustrate Hopi mythology and religious ceremonies.

Visitors can climb the stairs to the top of the tower, which is built with local stones applied to a steel framework attached to a concrete foundation. The tower's smooth surface of carefully articulated stones is broken every so often by irregular protruding rocks to provide texture. Bands of different-colored rocks and windows in varying sizes contribute to the architectural interest.

As a building material, stone dominates Colter's Grand Canyon designs. In the History Room at Bright Angel Lodge, for example, Colter ordered the fireplace constructed in layers of rocks to resemble the Canyon's geologic strata. Colter's simple cabins at Phantom Ranch pile one river rock on top of another to form the walls. A short walk from El Tovar, The Lookout Studio, also known as The Lookout, seems almost integral to the Canyon because of the way its rubble masonry meshes with the edge of the South Rim. Her first building at the Canyon, Hopi House, consists entirely of stone. (In 1998, Phoenix architect James Woodward supervised a restoration of that exterior rock, replacing the crumbling stones from 1905 with new ones.)

Of course, Colter also liked wood, but, again, it had to appear rustic. She preferred peeled log, log slabs, rough-sawn boards, or board and batten to using smooth two-by-fours. The men's dormitory for employees in Grand Canyon Village features exterior boards laid in a herringbone pattern, and the women's dormitory, now called Colter Hall, combines stone and wood in an interesting manner.

Mary Colter died in Santa Fe, New Mexico, in 1958 at the age of 88.

Having abandoned European styling early in her career, Colter made her mark by showcasing local materials in dramatic constructions strongly rooted in America's past and paying tribute to the richness and vitality of the Southwest's Indian and Spanish heritage.

■ **WHEN YOU GO** On the Canyon's South Rim, Grand Canyon Village lies 80 miles northwest of Flagstaff, via U.S. Route 180. Obtain a free map as you enter the park. Open 365 days a year. Canyon View visitors center open 8 A.M. to 5 P.M.; Desert View visitors center open 9 A.M. to 5 P.M. Entrance fee to park. (928) 638-7888. www.nps.gov/grca

HUBBELL TRADING POST

■ **LOCATION**	Ganado
■ **YEARS BUILT**	1883-1920
■ **STYLE**	Vernacular
■ **ARCHITECT**	John Lorenzo Hubbell
■ **SIGNIFICANCE**	Oldest continuously operated trading post in Navajoland / National Historic Site, 1965 / National Register of Historic Places, 2002

Indian trading posts played as basic a role in the commerce and culture of the Southwest in the late 1800s as did corner drugstores in Middle America.

At the trading posts, Indians exchanged wool, sheep, corn, and piñon nuts for domestic staples like flour, cloth, seed, and canned goods. Savvy traders encouraged the Indians to weave blankets in patterns that were likely to sell and to hammer out silver jewelry and weave baskets that would meet the growing demand for handmade Indian crafts, a demand that the traders helped create.

▲ Built to last by Indian trader John Lorenzo Hubbell, the trading post at Ganado bears witness to the interwoven cultures found in Navajoland.

Hubbell Trading Post, built amidst northeastern Arizona's vast piñon-and-juniper high-lands at an elevation of about 6,400 feet, remains the oldest continuously operated trading post in Navajoland. America's largest Indian reservation, the Navajo Nation spreads over 25,000 square miles of Arizona, New Mexico, and Utah, an area approximating the size of West Virginia. In this region, pelting rain can transform dusty roads into impassable quag-mires, and winter storms sometimes threaten the Indians' pastoral livelihood — their herds of sheep.

The trading post sits near a streambed by the shade of large cottonwood trees. John Lorenzo Hubbell, known to the Navajo as Nak'ee Sinili (Man Wearing Spectacles) began trad-ing at the site in the late 1870s after buying the business from William Leonard (Leonard's buildings were razed in the 1920s.) In 1883, Hubbell began building a store, starting with the jewelry and rug rooms, and adding a grocery room and warehouse in 1889. In 1893, he built a barn, and between 1897 and 1910, he constructed an adobe home for his family, installing electricity and running water in the 1920s. The trading post originally lay outside the boundaries of the Navajo Nation, but later was made part of the reservation.

Hubbell was born in November 1853 in Pajarito, New Mexico, his father a Connecticut Yankee and his mother the granddaughter of one of the first governors of New Mexico under Mexican rule. As a child, Hubbell spoke both English and Spanish, plus a little Navajo. A risk-taker with a sense of fair play, Hubbell learned the art of the deal as a clerk in a Mormon trading post in Kanab, Utah. Also in Utah, he was shot and seriously wounded. (Some say he was caught dallying with another man's wife.) Local Paiute Indians nursed him back to health.

Hubbell harbored political ambitions, serving as sheriff of Apache County and as part of the Territorial government and running unsuccessfully for the U.S. Senate. In 1879, he married Lina Rubi of Cebolleta, New Mexico, and they had four children: Adela, Barbara, John Lorenzo Jr., and Roman.

A born diplomat, Hubbell expressed his customer-based trading philosophy in 1907:

"The first duty of an Indian trader, in my belief, is to look after the material welfare of his neighbors; to advise them to produce that which their natural inclinations and talent best adapt them; to treat them honestly and insist upon getting the same treatment from them. . . . This does not mean that the trader should forget that he is to see that he makes a fair profit for himself, for whatever would injure him would naturally injure those with whom he comes in contact."

When Hubbell arrived in Ganado, the Navajos were still recovering from losses suffered in what became known as the Long Walk. During the bitterly cold winter of 1863, Col. Kit Carson and his men had forced thousands of men, women, and children to march some 300 miles to Fort Sumner in eastern New Mexico. Historians estimate that 2,000 Navajos died from starvation, illness, or exhaustion while making the arduous journey. When the Navajos agreed to sign a treaty with the United States in June 1868, they were permitted to return to the reservation. Many discovered the government had destroyed or confiscated their crops, herds, homes, and belongings during their four-year absence.

Hubbell extended credit to the Navajos, advised them on improving their silver-smithing and rug-weaving operations, explained federal regulations to them, and hired Navajo workers to erect his buildings, freight merchandise to and from the trading post, install an irrigation system to water his fields, and clerk in his store. Hubbell even donated a small portion of his land for a Navajo school.

Over time, Hubbell and his family prospered; he and his sons eventually operated 30 trading posts, wholesale warehouses, ranches, and farms. He became fluent in the Navajo language and made friends with tribal leaders.

Some have charged that Anglo traders took advantage of Indians, under-valuing or selling pawn without their customers' permission. Pawn is the turquoise and silver jewelry the Navajo offered as collateral for loans. But Hubbell seems not to have succumbed to such greed, instead handing out free snacks to mothers and children, as well as providing overnight accommodations to his customers in need.

The trader's six-bedroom mud-adobe house, with its 16- to 18-inch-thick walls, screened porch, and root cellar, sits on a shallow stone-and-mud-mortar foundation. Appropriately, his home is filled with a collection of beautiful rugs and finely woven baskets the Navajos brought him in trade, as well as with Indian artwork and artifacts. Covering the home's walls are red crayon Indian portraits by Eldridge Ayer Burbank, one of the many artists Hubbell knew and entertained. Dozens of Indian baskets decorate the hand-hewn log ceiling above the tongue-and-groove wood flooring. The family took particular pride in the tiger-eye oak table and a dozen hand-carved, straight-back chairs with leather seats that grace the dining room. The kitchen, with its high ceiling and linoleum-covered floor, has a large window facing toward an outdoor oven where cooks once baked 400 to 500 loaves of bread a week.

Hubbell built the store in phases, starting with the jewelry and rug rooms, which today are still packed with a fortune in both commodities. The adobe walls are faced with local sandstone and mortar on the outside, painted and plastered on the inside. Stone parapets edge the roof, now tarred, which tops board-and-beam ceilings. The wood-plank floor in the "bullpen," or main trading room, creaks loudly to signal that someone is entering. The U-shaped bullpen features shelves loaded down with coffee, flour, sugar, calico, pocketknives, and canned goods, visible behind tall, glass counters. The post still sells soft drinks, soap, newspapers, bags of dog food, work gloves, and moccasins of all sizes.

Other structures at the site include a two-story barn with horse stalls and a hay loft; a chicken coop still housing chickens; a guest hogan built in the 1940s as a memorial to Hubbell; the National Historic Site visitors center; and a root cellar, bunkhouse, manager's residence, corrals, and miscellaneous sheds. Hubbell's last addition to the store was the laundry room, which fire destroyed in 1966.

John Lorenzo Hubbell died Nov. 12, 1930, at age 77. Hubbell and his wife, along with three of their children (Barbara, Adela, and Roman), and his Navajo friend Bi'lii Lani (Many Horses), lie buried on Hubbell Hill, the cone-shaped hill overlooking the trading post. Following Navajo tradition, Hubbell's grave has no marker.

After Hubbell's death, his daughter-in-law, Dorothy Hubbell — Roman's wife — ran the trading post. The National Park Service took over in 1967, continuing to operate one of the West's most successful and influential trading posts in the tradition of fair and honorable trade started more than a century ago.

■ **WHEN YOU GO** Hubbell Trading Post is 1 mile west of Ganado on State Route 264. From Interstate 40, take U.S. Route 191 north to Ganado. Open winter hours 8 A.M. to 5 P.M.; summer hours 8 A.M. to 6 P.M. Closed Thanksgiving, Christmas, and New Years Day. From April through October the Navajo Nation operates on Daylight Savings Time, while the remainder of the state of Arizona does not. During this period, Arizona time is one hour behind Navajo Nation time. No entrance fee. (928) 755-3475. www.nps.gov/hutr/home.htm

LA POSADA

■ **LOCATION**	Winslow
■ **YEARS BUILT**	1928-30
■ **STYLE**	Spanish Colonial Revival
■ **ARCHITECT**	Mary Elizabeth Jane Colter
■ **SIGNIFICANCE**	Architect Colter's favorite design; rehabilitation has sparked community pride / National Register of Historic Places, 1992

Imagine you're visiting one of the great ranches of the old Southwest, a gracious hacienda owned by a wealthy Spanish don and his family. The main house is large, rambling, and romantic. It features lustrous red-tile roofs, airy balconies with exotic wrought-iron railings, dramatic circular stairways, and grand halls, decorated to the tastes of its affluent, sophisticated, and educated owners.

Inside, the furniture either has been crafted with painstaking care locally or consists of rare antiques and fine art collected during the don's extensive travels. Outside, the estate contains acres of fragrant fruit trees, flowering gardens, and a lovely wishing well.

Architect Mary Elizabeth Jane Colter envisioned just such a fantasy setting when she designed the 75-room, Spanish Colonial-style La Posada, a luxury hotel in Winslow now undergoing careful rehabilitation. Colter believed buildings should not only reflect their physical surroundings but also should conjure up the legends and local history of the region they inhabit. Working for the Fred Harvey Company as an architect and interior designer, she designed and furnished La Posada to welcome travelers crossing the West by rail.

As it turned out, La Posada, which opened May 15, 1930, was the last of the great Fred Harvey Company resort hotels built by the Santa Fe Railway between Chicago and Los Angeles. Allan Affeldt, the "white knight" many Winslow residents credit with rescuing the hotel from the ravages of time and adversity, says of La Posada, "Colter was in her prime [age 60] when she did this. It was her favorite design."

Sadly, Mary Colter lived long enough to learn that La Posada and its adjacent railroad station were to be closed in the late 1950s and the furnishings auctioned off. Rail passenger traffic had declined to the point that the Santa Fe Railway decided to cease operations in Winslow. Colter lamented a few months before her death (on Jan. 8, 1958, at the age of 88), "There's such a thing as living too long."

Today Colter's ghost can rest in peace. La Posada, which means "resting place" in Spanish, has been snatched from the jaws of the demolition crew. The rooms are returning to their former glory and, more gratifying, the hotel's refurbished restaurant, lobby, and ballroom are attracting appreciative crowds.

"When I first heard that we might lose it," says Marie LaMar, whose parents once worked for the Fred Harvey Company, "The grass [at the hotel] was as brown as corn flakes." The ensuing rehabilitation, she adds, "was a community effort, by the grace of God and the spirit of Mary Colter. Now the hotel is a living history hotel . . . "

In its heyday, as many as a thousand people a day arrived by train to eat in the hotel's dining areas. The tracks and depot stand just south of La Posada's lush front lawns.

While the trains stopped in Winslow to take on water and unload supplies, their passengers enjoyed meals served by white-aproned Harvey Girls, who were made famous by a movie starring Judy Garland.

▲ A grand hallway and graceful staircase lead to La Posada's Route 66-oriented courtyard.

▲ Just as architect Mary Colter had envisioned, guests arriving at La Posada by rail could easily imagine themselves staying at the estate of a wealthy Spanish landowner.

Early La Posada guests included Clark Gable, Carole Lombard, Douglas Fairbanks, Mary Pickford, Gary Cooper, Jimmy Durante, and John Wayne, as well as the reclusive Howard Hughes, Charles and Anne Morrow Lindbergh, humorist Will Rogers, and Franklin D. Roosevelt and Harry S. Truman.

Affeldt says that trains continue to rush by the hotel every 12 minutes or so, but that the building is so well engineered that little is heard when they pass. LaMar says, "People don't realize the heft of it [the La Posada structure]."

Colter designed La Posada in the shape of the letter *E*, its three wings intended to defeat the blustery winds sweeping in from the Painted Desert. Built at the then-exorbitant cost of $2 million, the hotel once offered 70 guest rooms and five suites. Decor in each guest room featured a Spanish or Navajo rug and homespun draperies with large, boldly colored floral patterns, as well as a picture of San Ysidro, the patron saint of the inn, a drawered chest, and a decorative tin mirror from Mexico. Flooring consisted of oak cut in random widths and pegged and grooved. Colter ordered the poplar doors sandblasted to make them look old.

In the public lounge, two high-backed divans upholstered in tapestry stood near the spacious fireplace. Tall, wooden candlesticks copied from those in a Mexican church flanked the fireplace. A bearskin rug added a homey touch.

Benches and chairs, some of them replicas and some of them antiques dating to the 1800s, furnished the lobby and corridors. Painted window glass in the hallway filtered the light. Wrought-iron ashtrays shaped like jackrabbits standing upright interjected a bit of whimsy, while linoleum tiles, laid in a distinctive mosaic pattern in the guest room corridors, helped absorb the sound of the trains rushing by.

Today, guests usually arrive by car, rather than by rail. They enter what was once the hotel's back door, which faces onto Historic Route 66.

Once inside, visitors often hear the strains of orchestral music echoing from the lobby's polished flagstone floors and 2-foot-thick, plastered, cast-in-place concrete walls. They see wide, arched openings; a long, brick corridor; massive overhead beams; and huge painted portraits filling nearly every wall. After checking in, they discover that the guest rooms look almost like the original spaces, except for black and white photos showing the hotel as it once was.

Affeldt was working on a doctorate in cognitive sciences and serving as chairman of an architectural think tank in Irvine, California, in 1993, when he first heard that La Posada had become an endangered building.

He phoned the Winslow Chamber of Commerce, which directed him to LaMar and Janice Griffith, curator of the town's Old Trails Museum. The women explained to Affeldt that the Santa Fe Railway had consigned Mary Colter's masterpiece to its "disposal list," a decision that amounted to La Posada's death sentence. They told Affeldt that, on the positive side, they and other local supporters organized the La Posada Foundation and had succeeded in getting the hotel listed on the National Register of Historic Places. And they reported applying for a $500,000 matching grant from the U.S. Department of Transportation, which they later received.

But a complete restoration would cost upwards of $11 million, they said, and they had no idea how to raise that kind of money.

Affeldt knew that Mary Colter had designed the interior of the rail passenger depots in Chicago, St. Louis, Kansas City, and Los Angeles, as well as the La Fonda Hotel in Santa Fe, and that she had served as architect for Hopi House, Hermit's Rest, The Watchtower, and Bright Angel Lodge at the Grand Canyon, among others. But until then he hadn't known about La Posada.

It was love at first sight. Soon he and his wife, artist Tina Mion, arrived in Winslow.

Affeldt set up a closely held corporation to purchase the 72,000-square-foot hotel and 6,000-square-foot depot and grounds, including giant cottonwood, elm, and juniper trees, broad lawns, and the remains of a rose garden. In 1997, La Posada Hotel, LLC, gained clear title to the property; then Affeldt set to work in earnest. He added new plumbing and room air conditioners, rebuilt the heating system, painted the hotel two tones of creamy beige (it had been desert pink), and began rehabilitating the rest of the building. "Fortunately, it was structurally perfect," he says.

Meanwhile, the Santa Fe Railway decided, after all, that it would remain in Winslow. It now rents office space from Affeldt and his group.

Gradually, some of La Posada's original furniture found its way back to the hotel, including four magnificently carved, Colter-designed, oak double benches.

Once again, the gift shop offers Indian crafts and Colter-designed dinnerware. Tina

Mion discovered that the hotel's high ceilings, smooth walls, and indirect lighting make an excellent gallery for displaying her artwork.

In the dining room, furnishings fashioned after the original round tables and carved-wood chairs complement the log-beamed ceiling. The kitchen, for which Colter specified the most advanced electric equipment in 1930, features industrial-grade ovens and stainless-steel fixtures. A vanished wishing well was recently reconstituted in the sunken garden, and an on-site carpentry shop is restoring or replicating the furniture.

La Posada's rehabilitation has helped jump-start Winslow's return to self-confidence. The town, which in 1948 boasted Arizona's largest commercial airport, had been languishing. Now, a large outdoor mural draws visitors to Take It Easy Park, which commemorates a 1972 hit song by the classic country rock group The Eagles that includes the lyrics, "... standing on a corner in Winslow, Arizona ..." Route 66 fans can visit both attractions handily, as the park is within easy walking distance of La Posada.

"La Posada," says local historian Janice Griffith, "was once the fanciest small hotel in the Southwest. But it seems like it went to sleep in the 1940s and never woke up. Restoring La Posada does two things for Winslow. It gives us back our badly needed community sense of pride. And it gives us hope."

■ **WHEN YOU GO** 303 E. Second St. From Interstate 40, take Exit 253; follow North Park Drive south. It becomes Berry Avenue. Turn east on Third Street, then south on Apache Avenue to Historic Route 66 and La Posada. (928) 289-4366.

LOWELL OBSERVATORY	
■ **LOCATION**	Flagstaff
■ **YEARS BUILT**	1894-1929
■ **STYLE**	Rustic, Modern
■ **ARCHITECTS**	Guy Lowell (Slipher Building); Johnson-Walzer Associates (Visitors Center)
■ **SIGNIFICANCE**	Site of the planet Pluto's discovery; buildings used local volcanic rock and lumber / National Register of Historic Places, 1966

Clyde Tombaugh, a 23-year-old Kansan and amateur astronomer, was thrilled when, in December 1928, the Lowell Observatory in Flagstaff invited him to help search for "Planet X," Earth's theorized, but as-yet-undiscovered, ninth planet.

Tombaugh knew the task would be tough. He would have to manipulate a heavy dome, direct the cumbersome 13-inch telescope, expose and develop 14- by 17-inch glass photographic plates, and do it all in Flagstaff's freezing cold. He would be looking for a tiny, moving object — hopefully a planet — hidden among millions of stars in the Milky Way.

To that end, he worked 12-hour days, seven days a week — weather permitting — for almost a year.

On Feb. 18, 1930, the young scientist saw a dot of light move. "That's it!" he cried. Tombaugh had discovered Pluto near where Percival Lowell, the observatory's founder, had predicted it would be located.

Lowell was a Boston aristocrat and a brilliant mathematician whose sister, Amy Lowell, and cousin, James Russell Lowell, ranked among America's great poets of the day. A brother,

The plaque on the mausoleum reads:

ASTRONOMY NOW DEMANDS BODILY
ABSTRACTION OF ITS DEVOTEES.
TO SEE INTO THE BEYOND RE-
QUIRES PURITY — AND THE BEING
DOING IT MAKES HIM PERFORCE A
HERMIT FROM HIS KIND.
HE MUST ABANDON CITIES AND
FOREGO PLAINS. ... ONLY IN
PLACES RAISED ABOVE AND ALOOF
FROM MEN CAN HE PROFITABLY
PURSUE HIS SEARCH. HE MUST
LEARN TO WAIT UPON HIS OPPOR-
TUNITIES AND THEN NO LESS TO
WAIT FOR MANKIND'S ACCEPTANCE
OF HIS RESULTS. FOR IN COM-
MON WITH MOST EXPLORERS HE
WILL ENCOUNTER ON HIS RETURN
THE FINAL PENALTY OF PENETRA-
TION THE CERTAINTY AT FIRST
OF BEING DISBELIEVED.

MARS AND ITS CANALS
PERCIVAL LOWELL

▲ Fittingly, Percival Lowell's observatory-themed mausoleum sits on Mars Hill, overlooking
Flagstaff, within an active community of astronomers.

Abbott Lawrence Lowell, headed Harvard University. Although Percival Lowell had taken on the task of running the family's cotton mills, electric companies, and trust funds in Lowell, Massachusetts, he soon grew bored. What really intrigued him was the study of planets, particularly Mars, the so-called "red planet." Believing that Mars showed evidence of intelligent life, he decided to build his own observatory to learn more about it. After investigating potential sites in Algeria, the Swiss Alps, Mexico, and California, he settled on a 7,000-foot-high mesa in Flagstaff, where the air was clear and calm, for his observatory.

Construction began on Mars Hill in 1894. Flagstaff, anxious to attract a research facility, donated five acres and built a wagon road up the hill. A variety of structures occupies the campus, ranging from researchers' homes and community water towers to telescope domes and an instrument shop. Almost all of the materials used to construct the observatory's buildings were indigenous — mostly rough chunks of volcanic rock and trees from the adjacent forests.

The Clark Dome, which was set in place permanently in 1896, is the first structure tourists see as they approach the observatory from the east. It holds a 24-inch refracting telescope and was designed so that the upper portion would turn on steel rollers to point the telescope toward different parts of the sky. When the dome proved reluctant to roll, an elevated trough filled with water was substituted for the rollers. In theory, the dome should have circled by flotation through the water. Unfortunately, high winds caused the dome to rock and slosh brine down the dome's interior, making stains visible even today. In 1900, astronomers tried mounting the dome on steel wheels. Then, in 1959, they placed car tires in a track. To this day, the dome rolls gently on tires to the desired position.

The Pluto Telescope Dome, dating from 1929, houses the 13-inch-wide field search telescope that Tombaugh used to discover Pluto. The building has a concrete foundation, an exterior of malpais rock, and a metal roof that rotates.

Percival Lowell's third cousin, Guy Lowell, a graduate of the Ecole des Beaux Arts in Paris, designed the Slipher Building, which commemorates the work of brothers Vesto and Earl Slipher. In 1912, Vesto Slipher discovered "the red shift," indicating that the universe continues to expand, a major coup in the astronomical field. The one-story building with a prominent rotunda was constructed in 1916. However, when the roof leaked, a second floor with a pitched roof to shed rainwater was added in 1927.

In 1923, a granite mausoleum honoring Lowell (1855-1916) was built on site. More recent buildings include the 1965 Planetary Research Center and the Steele Visitors Center, built in 1994.

Henry Giclas, associated with Lowell Observatory since the late 1920s and now an emeritus astronomer, says much has changed since Percival Lowell's days, when astronomers worked in freezing weather and retreated to a "warm room" to thaw out before returning again to the chilly telescopic eyepiece to unveil the mysteries of the night sky. In those days, calculating an object's position mathematically often took weeks by hand. "But now we work in a warm room and control the telescope by computer. We see the image on a screen. And we punch in numbers on the computer and get the answer right away," Giclas says. Some things haven't changed, though. "We still have to stay up all night, although now it's a lot more comfortable."

■ **WHEN YOU GO** 1400 W. Mars Hill Road. Lowell Observatory is 1 mile west of downtown Flagstaff. Take Santa Fe Avenue (Historic Route 66) up the hill to the observatory. (928) 774-3358. www.lowell.edu

RIORDAN MANSION

- **LOCATION**   Flagstaff
- **YEAR BUILT**   1904
- **STYLE**   Arts and Crafts
- **ARCHITECT**   Charles E. Whittlesey
- **SIGNIFICANCE**   Among the state's best examples of Craftsman-style architecture / National Register of Historic Places, 1979

If you operated a lumber company at the turn of the last century, it stood to reason you'd build a wood home — and you wouldn't use today's spindly two-by-fours. You'd build it using full-dimension two-by-sixes, log-slab siding, maple for the hardwood floors, and hand-split wooden shingles. Flagstaff's Riordan brothers, Timothy and Michael, owners of the Arizona Lumber and Timber Company, completed such a mansion just south of town in 1904.

The residence, considered among the best examples of Craftsman-style architecture in Arizona, boasts a large collection of original Arts-and-Crafts-style furniture.

In the early 20th century, the Arts and Crafts movement swept the United States, popularized by *The Craftsman* magazine, which was founded in 1901 by New York cabinetmaker Gustav Stickley. Arts and Crafts design emphasized simplicity, economy, and naturalistic local materials — exactly what the Riordans sought.

Educated and ambitious, the Riordan brothers hired architect Charles E. Whittlesey to

RICHARD MAACK

▲ Having made a fortune in lumber, Flagstaff brothers Timothy and Michael Riordan built a duplex mansion, the halves identical except for dining rooms and roof lines.

RICHARD MAACK

▲ Touches of Arts and Crafts décor embellish the Whittlesey-designed living room in Elizabeth and Timothy Riordan's half of the manse.

create their combined homes, incorporating the best furnishings and latest design. At the time, Whittlesey was designing El Tovar Hotel at the Grand Canyon.

Essentially an elaborate duplex connected by a Rendezvous Room, or "cabin," the structure housed the Riordan brothers, their wives (who also were sisters), and their eight children.

Caroline and Elizabeth Metz, daughters of a Cincinnati merchant, came to Flagstaff to visit their cousins, the Babbitts, also Arizona pioneers. The sisters met the Riordan brothers, and Timothy and Caroline were married in 1889, followed by Michael and Elizabeth in 1892.

Whittlesey's design features beamed ceilings, custom-designed lighting fixtures, and bathrooms upstairs and downstairs. The 40-room house has easy-clean linoleum flooring in the kitchens, built-in shelves and cabinets, multiple fireplaces, wainscoting, window seats, and inglenooks. The inglenook, a hallmark of the Arts and Crafts style, is a cozy nook composed of built-in benches flanking a fireplace.

Tim and his family occupied the east wing of the mansion; Michael and family, the west wing. Differences in the nearly identical homes include an upstairs sleeping porch in the west wing only, a rectangular dining room on the west wing versus a striking, elliptical dining room in the east wing, and a combination skylight/ventilation system in the east wing. The two-story wings, each a commodious 6,000 square feet in size, connect via the one-story Rendevous Room, which contains a fireplace, billiards table, and huge windows uniquely illustrated with photographs layered in the glass.

Strong Catholics, the Riordans nurtured family togetherness. Fun-loving Timothy kept over-sized birch-bark moccasins in the Rendezvous Room, telling guests they were the mythical lumberjack Paul Bunyan's baby shoes. The more scholarly Michael harbored an artistic streak demonstrated by two totem faces carved on the log ends of his wing and by the colorful stained glass windows he helped design.

Even though their livelihood kept them in a small logging town in Territorial Arizona, the Riordans' capacious combined homes show that they sacrificed little in the way of style and convenience.

■ **WHEN YOU GO** 409 Riordan Road. In Flagstaff, follow Milton Road (State Route 89A) to Riordan Road. Turn east on Riordan Road to Riordan Mansion State Park, adjacent to the Northern Arizona State University campus. Open 7 days a week May through October, 8:30 A.M. to 5 P.M.; November through April, 10:30 A.M. to 5 P.M. Closed Christmas. Entrance fee. (928) 779-4395.

WIGWAM VILLAGE MOTEL NO. 6

■ **LOCATION**	Holbrook
■ **YEAR BUILT**	1950
■ **STYLE**	Pseudo-vernacular
■ **ARCHITECT**	Frank Redford
■ **SIGNIFICANCE**	Symbolizes the kitschy automobile culture of U.S. Route 66 / National Register of Historic Places, 2002

Originally a wagon road, later a railroad route, and then a two-lane highway serving motorists with wanderlust, U.S. Route 66 wound its way into American history and lore. Dubbed the "Mother Road" by author John Steinbeck, celebrated in song by Nat King Cole, and featured on 1960s television as Martin Milner and George Maharis searched for adventure in their Corvette convertible, the 2,400-mile ribbon of blacktop connected Chicago with Santa Monica.

Along the way, pioneers, dust bowl refugees, and tourists passed through such exotic locales as Carthage, Missouri; Shamrock, Texas; Two Guns, Arizona; and Needles, California.

Once motorists reached Arizona, the Grand Canyon, Meteor Crater, Petrified Forest, and untold numbers of rock gardens, curio shops, and other attractions lay within easy reach, while giant figures of concrete, fiberglass, and metal — cowboys, Indians, lumberjacks, astronauts, jackrabbits, and dinosaurs — beckoned to the curious. Weary travelers could tow their own Airstream trailers and pull into a roadside camp or choose to spend the night in a "log cabin," "pueblo," or "wigwam."

Even today in Holbrook, one can bypass the generic chain restaurants and express hotels at the freeway interchange and, instead, as the slogan goes, "Get Your Kicks on Route 66" — whether it's shopping for mementos at Western Junk Gallery & Curios or the Pow Wow Trading Post; visiting the Petrified Rock Gardens or Courthouse Park; wetting your whistle at the Empty Pockets Saloon; getting beautified at Elsa's Premiere Hair Salon; eating at the Hilltop House Restaurant or Joe & Aggie's Cafe; or staying at the Sun 'n Sand or the Wigwam Village — where a neon sign asks, "Have you slept in a wigwam lately?"

The idea for Holbrook's Wigwam Village occurred to Chester E. Lewis shortly after the close of World War II. While passing through Cave City, Kentucky, he saw a motel with a filling station, lunchroom, and store in the form of a village of Indian tepees. Lewis decided he could build one back in his hometown of Holbrook, on a plot of land he owned along Hopi Drive, the town's main drag — which happened to be U.S. Route 66.

▲ Holbrook's Wigwam Village gives motorists driving the "Mother Road" a chance to experience unadulterated kitch.

With automobiles and gasoline readily available and affordable for the first time in years, Americans of all walks of life took to the highways, especially Route 66, in increasing numbers. Eschewing the railroad-oriented downtown hotels of the past, this new generation of travelers responded instead to the convenience and fantasy of unique roadside accommodations like those Lewis had seen in Kentucky.

The enterprising Lewis located the tepees' designer/builder, Frank A. Redford, and arranged for the purchase of a license and a set of plans. Lewis did most of the construction on the motor court himself, with help from family and friends.

Architect/builder/entrepreneur Frank Redford's original wigwam opened as a filling station and cafe on U.S. Highway 31E in Horse Cave, Kentucky, in 1933. The main building, a 60-foot-tall steel, frame, and stucco wigwam, had two smaller versions housing restrooms on either side. The design, actually more representative of the tepees of the nomadic Plains Indians, was inspired by a tepee-shaped, short-order restaurant the well-traveled Redford had seen in California, as well as by the real thing on a Sioux reservation in South Dakota. Redford calculated the overall effect of his wigwams would appeal to tourists.

By 1936, Redford had a U.S. government patent on his design, and he added six cabins, forming what he called a Wigwam Village. In 1937, Redford and his wife Vera built and opened their second village on the more rapidly developing U.S. Highway 31W in neighboring Cave City, this time with 15 guest units arranged in a semicircle around another large gas station/lunchroom/souvenir-store wigwam, again flanked by two smaller restroom structures. Coordinated staff uniforms, menus, stationery, decor, and souvenirs reinforced the tepee theme. The couple emphasized cleanliness and decency.

Conceptually, Wigwam Villages grew out of the old tourist camp model, which appealed to travelers seeking neighborly accommodations. The idea caught on. Over the next 16 years, Redford licensed the construction of four more villages and built another himself. The villages never operated as a chain but rather as an association of independent owners that depended on word-of-mouth advertising and mutual referrals. Numerous unlicensed imitations, including the Wigwam Lodge on East Apache Boulevard (now an Arizona State University parking lot) in Tempe, also sprang up.

The Redfords sold their Kentucky holdings after World War II and moved to California, building the last "official" Wigwam Village in San Bernardino.

By now divorced, Frank and Vera operated the village as partners, with Vera greeting visitors in a beaded buckskin outfit. The village was sold after Frank's death in 1958.

When it opened on June 1, 1950, Holbrook's Wigwam Village No. 6 was the last of the independently owned and operated villages to be completed. Chester Lewis' village featured 15 guest wigwams numbered 1 through 16 (there was no No. 13), arranged in the shape of the letter *C* at the perimeter of the rectangular site. The gas pumps, office/store, and restrooms were at the open end of the *C*, facing the highway. Regularly spaced around a gravel auto court, the guest units alternated with juniper trees, seating areas, and an occasional concrete dinosaur or actual petrified log. Unit No. 6 was the first completed.

Built of stucco over building paper on a wood frame, each identical unit stands about 25 feet high, not including faux tent poles, and spreads to 20 feet in diameter at the base. All have 16 sides, and guests enter through an inset door in one side. Plaster "tent flaps" folded back on either side of the door welcome you to your "little home on the plains." The original gas heater and electric lights remain, as do the two 18- by 24-inch windows, positioned for viewing at sitting height. Each unit also has a small bathroom containing a sink, toilet, and shower.

MARK VINSON

▲ Whether termed a tent, tepee, or wigwam, designer Frank Redford's steel, frame, and stucco adaptation of a Plains Indian abode fares well with tourists seeking fantasy accommodations.

Coin-operated radios were installed in each unit, as agreed to in the contract with Redford. A guest could enjoy a half-hour of drama or music for a dime. At the end of each month, Lewis and his sons collected the coins to pay the licensing fee. Molds purchased from Redford were used for making tepee-shaped ashtrays and lamp bases.

When Texaco started requiring standardized filling stations in the late 1950s, Lewis demolished the original filling station/office/store wigwam. He replaced it with a faintly Pueblo Revival structure with a canopy over the gas pumps.

Then, in April 1974, Interstate 40 replaced U.S. Route 66, bypassing Holbrook. Business immediately began to suffer. Lewis closed the motel, although he kept the gas pumps open a while longer. The village sat deserted for the next dozen years.

After Lewis' death in 1986, family members unlocked the doors of the wigwams and discovered little had changed since the 1950s, down to the pink color scheme and rustic hickory-stick-and-wicker furnishings. The family decided to begin renovation in 1987. They reopened a few units the next year, with the entire village hosting guests again soon after that.

The main building now houses a souvenir shop and museum in addition to the office. The gas pumps are gone, but the canopy serves as a porte cochere for arriving guests. The flanking wigwam restrooms now provide storage. In keeping with the tradition of offering modern amenities in a rustic setting, cable TV and refrigerated air conditioning have been added to the units.

A '52 Chevrolet DeLuxe, '54 Buick Special, '56 Ford Ranch Wagon, '57 Ford Coupe, and a '38 Ford (formerly used for Lewis family petrified-wood hunting forays) are parked permanently in the auto court, contributing to the retro atmosphere at the village.

Today, the vision of Redford and Lewis to attract tourists by offering the unexpected in a clean, orderly setting with modern conveniences lives on in Holbrook. Elinor and Clifton Lewis, Chester's daughter and son, operate the Wigwam Village with help from other family members.

Travelers from across the country and as far away as Europe stop, intrigued by the idea of sleeping in a wigwam. Meri Anderson, a recent guest, typifies many who, having seen the wigwams as children, return as adults. Born in Holbrook, Anderson moved away with her family when she was 5. She recalls that when she was little, "I used to wish I didn't live in Holbrook so I could come and visit and stay in the wigwams."

■ **WHEN YOU GO** 811 W. Hopi Drive. Holbrook is 90 miles east of Flagstaff, via Interstate 40. Take Exit 285 east onto West Hopi Drive (Historic Route 66). (928) 524-3048.

WINSOR CASTLE

■ **LOCATION**	14 miles southwest of Fredonia
■ **YEARS BUILT**	1870-72
■ **STYLE**	Vernacular
■ **BUILDERS**	Brigham Young, Joseph W. Young, Anson Perry Winsor
■ **SIGNIFICANCE**	Fort/ranch house built to protect Mormon families / National Register of Historic Places, 1966

Mormon Church leader Brigham Young himself traveled to the remote, tall-grass country of the Arizona Strip to step off the boundaries for a fort and ranching headquarters at Pipe Spring, 14 miles southwest of Fredonia.

The president of the Church of Jesus Christ of Latter-day Saints took time to visit Pipe Spring in the fall of 1870, convinced that a fort enclosing a reliable water source was needed to protect Mormon families crossing the Colorado River at Lee's Ferry and moving into Arizona Territory and, potentially, Mexico, to settle.

Young also sought grazing land for the Mormons' growing herds of cattle and sheep acquired when members tithed — or donated a portion of their profits to the church — in the form of animals instead of cash. He had heard that the nourishing grasses in the Arizona Strip were "belly high to a horse" and hoped the Pipe Spring outpost would become a joint church/citizen ranching venture.

But first, settlers had to feel safe. Four years earlier, Indians had raided the claim of Dr. James Whitmore, a Mormon who began raising longhorn cattle there. Whitmore had taken title to 160 acres at Pipe Spring in 1863, building a dugout and corrals and planting an orchard and vineyard. But the raiders killed Whitmore and his brother-in-law, Robert McIntyre, as they rode to recover their missing livestock. Now Young aimed to make friends of the local Kaibab Paiute Indians and Navajo tribal elders.

Young envisioned the fort as twin, two-story stone houses separated by an open courtyard. If an attack was anticipated, the 10-by-12-foot gates at either end of the courtyard could be closed and barred. Otherwise, the gates would remain open, allowing wagons to enter the space. A ranch manager and his family would live in the north house, built over a spring, with the south building housing a dairy processing center downstairs and accommodations for workers and/or guests upstairs. Young also planned to use the meat, butter,

▲ Wide-swinging gates at both ends of the Winsor Castle compound allowed wagons to enter and load up with cheese and butter destined for St. George, Utah, 55 miles away.

and cheese produced at the ranch to feed workers building an imposing half-million-dollar Mormon Temple (under construction from 1871 till 1877) in nearby St. George, Utah.

Setting the enterprise in motion by buying the Pipe Spring ranch from Whitmore's widow for $1,000, the church president appointed his nephew, Joseph W. Young, to supervise construction. Anson Perry Winsor, who was already on hand, served as ranch manager from 1870 to 1875 — which explains the fort's name: Winsor Castle.

When Brigham Young first walked off the fort's footprint, the project measured 66 by 152 feet. But David Lavender, author of *The History of Arizona's Pipe Spring National Monument*, speculates in his book that the cost of such a large structure, and the effort required to excavate a slope behind the north house, led to scaling down the plan to 40 by 68 feet.

As many as 30 laborers, including blacksmiths, carpenters, and cabinetmakers, worked on the fort. Excavating behind the north house proved so arduous, the men stopped digging when the floor level of the north house was still 5 feet higher than the southern building's floor. This created a distinctive jog in the building's profile.

Stone for the structures came from large boulders of red sandstone found northwest of the site. Workers cut the boulders to the right dimensions using a technique as old as Egypt's pyramids. The men drilled holes along the natural fracture lines of the stone, drove in wooden pegs, soaked the pegs with water, then waited till the swelling pegs split the rocks apart. Mules and oxen dragged the slabs to the building site, where they were shaped, faced, and hoisted to form the substantial 20-inch-thick walls of the fort.

Ponderosa pine trees from Mount Trumbull, 60 miles away, were cut down, milled into boards, and hauled by wagon to Pipe Spring. Laborers nailed the boards for the first floor to juniper joists laid directly on the ground. Planks forming the second level rested on great beams 12 inches wide and 2 inches thick.

Viewed from the outside, the fort's most striking feature is its lack of windows. Only small rifle ports — 15 on the south building and eight on the northern house — pierce the thick, exterior stone walls. Daylight enters the buildings through windows and doors opening onto the courtyard. Upstairs, porches with painted wood railings allowed families to watch the activities happening in the dirt yard below.

A small, wooden lookout tower crowned the shingled roof on the north house. At first, residents climbed the tower to scout for Indians. Later, Mormons used the tower to watch for federal marshals searching for polygamists.

By the time the fort was finished in 1872, the threat to Mormon settlers from Indian attack had diminished significantly: The fort was never used defensively. Meanwhile, the ranch prospered. In 1879, the Winsor Stock Growing Company, its shares owned by the Mormon Church and influential individuals including Brigham Young and Winsor, reported successfully running 2,269 head of cattle on the Arizona Strip.

However, by the 1880s a different issue consumed the church's attention. The federal government began vigorously enforcing an 1862 law abolishing polygamy, and Mormon leaders realized they must outlaw polygamy to gain statehood. They did so, and Utah became the 45th state on Jan. 4, 1896. For Mormons in multiple marriages, the Arizona Strip, just across the Arizona border from Utah, seemed to offer them a chance to maintain their lifestyle, remote from those enforcing the law. By the early 1890s, a number of women and their children were living at Pipe Spring to prevent the arrest of their husbands and fathers for polygamy. When someone spotted approaching federal authorities, says Andrea Bornemeier, Chief of Interpretation and Resource Management at Pipe Spring National

Monument, "They sent the kids to the hills, the women hid, and the men ran. A woman [in a polygamous relationship] might be out here for a few weeks or four or five years."

In 1895, the church, faced with the confiscation of church property as punishment for having endorsed polygamy and suffering from a decline in its rangelands because of over-grazing, decided to disengage itself from a losing operation and sold the Pipe Spring ranch. The property remained in private hands until May 31, 1923, when President Warren G. Harding designated the then 40-acre site as Pipe Spring National Monument.

Northern Arizona's hauntingly beautiful Arizona Strip country, consisting of nearly 8,000 square miles of isolated, high-desert terraces and forests situated north of the Grand Canyon, has been peopled successively by nomadic hunter-gatherers, prehistoric Ancestral Puebloans (the Anasazi) living in pit houses and pueblos, and the Southern Paiute tribes, who reside there still. Spanish missionaries and explorers, such as the priests Francisco Dominguez and Silvestre Escalante, visited the area in the 1700s, and John Wesley Powell stopped at Pipe Spring between trips down the Colorado River.

Pipe Spring's name reputedly came from an 1858 feat of marksmanship. Mormon mis-sionary Jacob Hamblin camped at the spring while leading a party to visit the Hopi Indians. Someone bet Hamblin's brother William, known as "Gunlock Bill," that he could not hit a silk handkerchief tied to a bush 50 yards away. Bill's first shot appeared to miss the target, but he claimed the air stirred up by the bullet flicked the handkerchief aside so no bullet hole was visible. Taking a second shot, Bill then plugged the bottom out of the bowl of a pipe from 50 paces away, proving his skill and giving Pipe Spring its name.

Some 55,000 visitors stop at the monument annually. They come to see a fortified ranch house as it would have been in the 19th century. A butter churn and cream separator occupy the dairy room, where rounds of cheese once were packed in barrels filled with flour to keep the cheese from growing rancid. In the north house, with its 8-foot ceilings and plas-tered walls, a crocheted antimacassar covers a family Bible. Fixtures include an iron cook stove, braided rugs, and bottles and jugs, with pretty curtains framing the windows. Upstairs, visitors find a cradle that converts to a youth bed, a treadle sewing machine, bed-springs made of rope, a wash basin, slop jar, and handmade quilts.

Additional attractions at Pipe Spring include two rustic cowboy cabins, a corral holding real longhorn steers, and relics of the first telegraph station established in Arizona, its lines strung in 1870 by the Deseret Telegraph Company from St. George to Kanab, Utah, through Pipe Spring. Upon completion of the Mormon temple in St. George in 1877, travel increased between Arizona and Utah as couples went to St. George to marry in the temple. The route they followed became known as the Honeymoon Trail.

Today, the tall grasses of the Arizona Strip are long gone. A spring no longer gushes under the Mormon fort. But a visit to Winsor Castle at Pipe Spring National Monument makes it easy to imagine life in the time of Brigham Young.

■ **WHEN YOU GO** Pipe Spring National Monument is in the far north of Arizona, 14 miles southwest of Fredonia and 21 miles southwest of Kanab, Utah. From Flagstaff, take U.S. Route 89 north to Bitter Springs, then take U.S. 89A across the Colorado River to Fredonia and swing west on State Route 389 to the monument. Open June through September, 7 A.M. to 5 P.M.; tours every 30 minutes from 8 A.M. to 4:30 P.M. Open October through May, 8 A.M. to 5 P.M.; tours every 30 minutes from 9 A.M. to 4 P.M. Closed Thanksgiving, Christmas, and New Years. Entrance fee (no charge for ages 16 and under). (928) 643-7105. www.nps.gov/pisp/

YAVAPAI COUNTY COURTHOUSE

■ **LOCATION**	Prescott
■ **YEAR BUILT**	1916-18
■ **STYLE**	Greek Revival
■ **ARCHITECT**	William N. Bowman of Denver
■ **SIGNIFICANCE**	Example of Eastern town planning transplanted to Arizona Territory / National Register of Historic Places, 1976

Outsiders often think of Arizona as a monolithic desert — a giant outdoor sandbox, if you will. In fact, two-thirds of the state is high country blessed with coniferous forests, cliffs that tower over deep chasms in the Earth, crystalline lakes, and alpine meadows.

Mile-high Prescott, surrounded by ponderosa pine trees and favored with a mild, healthful climate, is among the larger urban centers in Arizona's uplands. When it came time for Prescott to build its third county courthouse in 1916, the citizens looked back with nostalgia to the courthouses of their Midwest and New England hometowns. Prescottonians also wanted to reflect the pride they felt in Prescott having served twice as the Territorial capital (1863-1867 and 1877-1889), and in its designation as the county seat for one of Arizona Territory's original four counties.

Surveyors laid out the Prescott town site in 1864 in a grid pattern. Citizens at the time set the courthouse site in the middle of the town's grid, to be surrounded by the lawns, park benches, and shade trees they were used to. They hoped that citizens would interact with their county government in the respectful fashion that was traditional at home and not in the rough, rowdy manner that sometimes characterized the West.

Since the laying out of the town site, Prescott has had three courthouses. Today's courthouse dominates the block-square Courthouse Plaza, with stately elm trees; well-tended, grassy plots rimmed by concrete curbs; and an antique bandstand. The granite blocks used to construct the courthouse were hand-cut from a local quarry and put in place by Italian stonemasons. Standing four stories tall, the substantial, rectangular building measures 90 by 150 feet. In the Greek Revival Neoclassical style, it features a symmetrical arrangement of classic Doric columns, decorative cornices, and Greek pediments. Visitors enter either by climbing the broad stairways located on all four sides of the building or through the ground-level basement doors.

The courthouse succeeds in conveying feelings of substance, stability, rock-solid integrity, decency, and propriety.

Denver architect William N. Bowman won a nationwide competition to design and build Yavapai County's third courthouse. Construction took two years and cost $223,753. The use of solid granite block — rather than a veneer — added considerable expense, but the community felt the monumental effect warranted the extra expenditure. Since adjacent Whiskey Row had already endured a decimating fire, Prescott also required that the structure be fireproof, so the interior walls and floors are built of reinforced concrete, with steel trusses supporting the roof.

Like Midwestern courthouses, which tend to be flanked by statues of uniformed Civil War officers riding horseback, the Courthouse Plaza features two heroic figures. The best-known artwork shows a mounted soldier, sculpted in 1907 by artist Solon Hannibal Borglum, which honors local Rough Rider William "Buckey" O'Neill and his comrades who

▲ A mounted likeness of local hero Bucky O'Neill, sculpted by Solon Borglum, makes an unending charge through Prescott's Courthouse Square.

were killed in the Spanish-American War (The popular O'Neill had served Prescott in many capacities, holding office as mayor and as Yavapai County sheriff.) A 1990 sculpture portrays a cowboy and his horse to recognize Prescott's ranching heritage.

Prescott's first courthouse, built in 1865-66, housed a jail and sheriff's office on the first floor and a courtroom/meeting space upstairs. Public hangings took place on the grounds. The building later became the Bellevue Hotel.

The second courthouse, done up in pink brick and striped awnings, replaced the first courthouse after judges and employees complained of overcrowded courtrooms. The squarish, two-story structure, built in 1878 on the site of the current facility, cost $60,000, and according to a 1976 published history of the building, the public both "cussed and discussed" its landscaping. "The people wanted grass, trees, and fences. The fence was built, but didn't keep out the livestock. Instead of grass, the people got rocks," an observer said. "The gardener, Mr. J.A. Kutsche, was finally hounded out of town, and grass and trees, a fountain and $200 bandstand were all built and things settled down again until July 1892, when the courthouse caught on fire."

The damage to the second courthouse was quickly repaired, but the building was later razed because it "was unsanitary and reeks with foul smells," according to a July 15, 1914, issue of *Yavapai Magazine*. "If it should catch fire, practically all the records would be destroyed, since the building does not even approximate being fireproof.... It is in such bad condition that the cupola sways in a strong wind and might cause damage if it should fall."

Prescott historian and preservationist Elisabeth Ruffner recalls that the second courthouse became the scene of the hanging of outlaw Fleming "Jim" Parker by Sheriff George C. Ruffner (the uncle of her late husband, Lester Ward "Budge" Ruffner). Parker had shot and killed a deputy county attorney on the courthouse steps, she says, then stole Sheriff Ruffner's white Arabian stallion, Sureshot, and attempted to escape. "We [the Ruffner family] have a wonderful, hand-tinted portrait of Sureshot," Elisabeth Ruffner says.

No story about Prescott's Courthouse Plaza would be complete without mentioning the July 14, 1900, fire. The conflagration caused more than $1 million in losses and nearly destroyed Montezuma Street's Whiskey Row — a block of gambling halls, brothels, and saloons where drinks sold for 12 1/2 cents each — across from the courthouse. According to one account, "The scene during the fire was beyond all power of description. Wagons and buggies, men on horseback, men, women, and children afoot were scurrying hither and thither, the human part of it being more or less excited."

Locals soon rebuilt Whiskey Row, and in later years it served as the colorful backdrop for movies, commercials, and TV shows, including the film *Junior Bonner*, starring Steve McQueen, Robert Preston, and Ida Lupino.

Yavapai County Manager James Holst says employees are trying to maintain the building as it once was, except that the jail has been removed to accommodate more courtrooms. Meanwhile, renovation has been ongoing for years. "So when you go through it, hopefully, it looks pretty much like when it was constructed. We don't want to turn it into a museum. We've tried to avoid that," he says.

The building is "the focal point for the whole court system for the county," says Patrick Kirshman, the courthouse's facilities director. "There's just an on-going calendar of events that happens there. I think that's what the big draw is."

The Courthouse Plaza — bounded by Gurley, Montezuma, Cortez, and Goodwin streets — anchors Prescott's thriving downtown commercial district, which includes antique malls, clothing boutiques, craft stores, restaurants, banks, and hotels. Many of the old buildings facing the plaza have been renovated and are designated as part of the Yavapai Courthouse Plaza Historic District.

Among the historic buildings facing the Courthouse Plaza are the old Knights of Pythias Hall, now a shoe store; the Masonic Temple, now professional offices; and the Palace Hotel, a saloon and restaurant.

On Sept. 1, 1964, Sen. Barry M. Goldwater of Phoenix, the second Republican since statehood to represent Arizona in the U.S. Senate, chose the courthouse's north steps to launch his presidential campaign. Goldwater lost the election, but he must have enjoyed the symbolism of announcing his candidacy in an Arizona town that looks so comfortably all-American. As Prescottonians like to say, "It's everybody's hometown."

■ **WHEN YOU GO** 120 S. Cortez St. State Route 89 becomes Gurley Street when it enters Prescott. Follow Gurley to the Courthouse Plaza, which is bounded by Gurley, Montezuma, Cortez, and Goodwin streets. (928) 445-2000 or (800) 266-7534 (Chamber of Commerce).

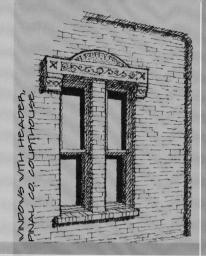

WINDOWS WITH HEADER, PINAL CO. COURTHOUSE

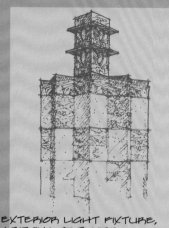

EXTERIOR LIGHT FIXTURE, ARIZONA BILTMORE

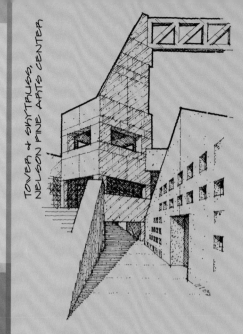

TOWER & SKYTRUSS, NELSON FINE ARTS CENTER

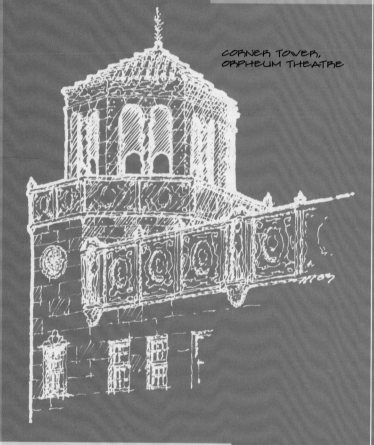

CORNER TOWER, ORPHEUM THEATRE

PROFILED IN THIS SECTION

- ARIZONA BILTMORE (PHOENIX)
- ARIZONA CAPITOL (PHOENIX)
- BURTON BARR CENTRAL LIBRARY (PHOENIX)
- GRADY GAMMAGE MEMORIAL AUDITORIUM (TEMPE)
- LUHRS BUILDING & LUHRS TOWER (PHOENIX)
- MARICOPA COUNTY COURTHOUSE/PHOENIX CITY HALL (PHOENIX)
- MYSTERY CASTLE (PHOENIX)
- NELSON FINE ARTS CENTER (TEMPE)
- ORPHEUM THEATRE (PHOENIX)
- PINAL COUNTY COURTHOUSE (FLORENCE)
- ROSSON HOUSE/HISTORIC HERITAGE SQUARE (PHOENIX)
- SAHUARO RANCH (GLENDALE)
- SAN MARCOS HOTEL (CHANDLER)
- TALIESIN WEST (SCOTTSDALE)
- TEMPE MUNICIPAL BUILDING (TEMPE)
- TOVREA CASTLE (PHOENIX)

PACKING SHED, SAHUARO RANCH

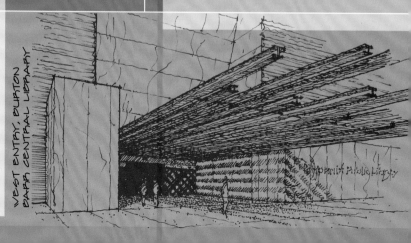

WEST ENTRY, BURTON BARR CENTRAL LIBRARY

PHOENIX AND CENTRAL ARIZONA

The city of Phoenix takes its name from the mythical phoenix bird that rose from its own ashes to fly once more.

Founded on the banks of the Salt River in 1867, Phoenix began its dynamic rise to national prominence by building on a site where, well before the 1400s, prehistoric Hohokam Indians developed a sophisticated irrigation system to water their corn, beans, and squash.

Central Arizona's Territorial-era buildings reflect the region's development of rural farming, as exemplified by Glendale's Sahuaro Ranch. More recently, the "Valley of the Sun," the metropolitan Phoenix area, is developing a distinctive design style all its own. The new architectural look in buildings such as Phoenix's Burton Barr Central Library celebrates this still-young state's optimism and unquenchable enthusiasm and responds successfully to the region's challenging desert climate.

With the population of metropolitan Phoenix approaching 4.5 million, the capital city and its surrounding neighbors play a central role in the state's burgeoning business and cultural activities. As the state's largest city, Phoenix naturally contains the greatest concentration of striking structures. Historic buildings weathering well over time include the tastefully restored Orpheum Theatre, a rare example of a 1920s atmospheric theater, and the funky Mystery Castle, hand-built from found objects and cast-offs, like casserole dishes and railroad ties. Outstanding building complexes include Frank Lloyd Wright's architectural school, Taliesin West in Scottsdale, and Antoine Predock's lavender-hued Nelson Fine Arts Center at Arizona State University in Tempe.

Other communities in the region boast equally impressive architectural creations — for example, the oft-remodeled Pinal County Courthouse in Florence and a Romanesque church in Globe that is adorned with fleurs-de-lis in deference to the French-born priest who oversaw its construction.

RICHARD MAACK

ARIZONA BILTMORE

■ **LOCATION**	Phoenix
■ **YEAR BUILT**	1928
■ **STYLE**	Late Prairie
■ **ARCHITECT**	Albert Chase McArthur
■ **SIGNIFICANCE**	Grande dame of Phoenix's luxury resorts; sparked growth of local hospitality industry

The 730-room Arizona Biltmore at 24th Street and Missouri in Phoenix has hosted a who's who among business leaders, politicians, and entertainment personalities since it opened in February 1929 — just months before the October stock market crash signaled the start of the Great Depression.

Yet, despite being an oasis of apparent tranquility with its freshly clipped lawns and flowering gardens, the elegant hotel continues to stir debate eight decades after its dedication. The question is, who actually designed the structure?

All agree that the architect of record is Albert Chase McArthur. But as far as anyone knows, McArthur did not design a building of equal importance either before or after the Biltmore, while in his later years, Frank Lloyd Wright, acknowledged as America's greatest 20th-century architect, wrote McArthur's widow that, "I have always given Albert's name as architect . . . and always will. But I know better and so should you."

Wrightian trademarks include repeated geometric motifs in the concrete-block façade and stained-glass windows, dramatic spatial relationships, and the use of locally available construction materials.

The story of the controversy begins with Charles and Warren McArthur persuading their older brother, Albert, an architect who once worked for Wright as a draftsman, to design a resort hotel 8 miles northeast of what were then Phoenix's outskirts.

Charles and Warren McArthur had moved to Phoenix from Chicago and were operating a Dodge dealership when they decided to build a winter haven in sunny Arizona for wealthy visitors fleeing the Midwest's snow and slush. In 1925, they recruited Albert, a commercial architect from the East, to help realize their ambition.

Albert Chase McArthur agreed to join the enterprise. And, in an ironic role reversal, McArthur offered Frank Lloyd Wright a job as his draftsman. McArthur believed that Wright owned the patent for a knitlock cast-concrete block, also called textile block, which McArthur intended to apply to the hotel facade.

Almost 60 at the time, Wright felt threatened by more than his usual number of financial and marital difficulties: The bank had foreclosed on his home in Spring Green, Wisconsin, and auctioned his belongings; he had just concluded a bitter divorce from his second wife; and he was about to wed Olgivanna Lazovich Hinzenberg, a 26-year-old Montenegro native.

McArthur offered Wright $10,000 to lease the patent and acquire Wright's expertise in installing the block system. Wright immediately came to Phoenix.

Only later did McArthur discover that Wright did not own the block's patent. Meanwhile, Wright, well-known for his autocratic and sometimes tempestuous personality, succeeded in alienating McArthur's associates. As a result, Wright was asked to leave after only four months at the building site. Decades later, Wright's widow, Olgivanna, observed, "It was very difficult for him [McArthur] since my husband, as we all know, was never famous as a man who willingly made any compromises."

Wright left for other prospects in California, but in 1930 wrote a letter stating, "Albert McArthur is the architect of that building — all attempts to take the credit for that performance from him are gratuitous and beside the mark. But for him Phoenix would have had nothing like the Biltmore, and it is my hope that he may be enabled to give Phoenix many more beautiful buildings as I believe him entirely capable of doing so."

But the great architect was far less complimentary in his off-the-cuff remarks. Toward the end of construction, McArthur had asked Wright what he thought of the Biltmore. McArthur said that Wright told him, "It was far from being a great work of art . . . and that it lacked even the most primitive elements of good design."

Over the years, though, Wright's association with the Biltmore has added a certain cachet.

Movie stars and assorted celebrities have always flocked to the hotel, now known as the Arizona Biltmore Resort & Spa. Clark Gable, a regular, once lost his wedding ring on the golf course, though it later was found. Marilyn Monroe swam in the yellow-and-blue-tiled Catalina Pool. Frank Sinatra, Sammy Davis Jr., and Liza Minelli performed an impromptu concert in the lobby.

More recently, famous guests have included actors Tom Cruise, George Clooney, and Alec Baldwin; model Christie Brinkley; news anchor Tom Brokaw; and sports superstar Michael Jordan. Every American president since Herbert Hoover has patronized the Biltmore at some time in his life, including Ronald Reagan, who honeymooned there with wife Nancy.

A three-day gala, starting Feb. 23, 1929, marked the formal grand opening of the four-story hotel, with its green copper roof and decorative Biltmore Block. Set against the backdrop of Squaw Peak [now known as Piestewa Peak], the hotel complex included 15 small cottages.

Highlighting the opening ceremonies, a Ford trimotor airplane flew over, and the pilot released a bouquet of roses attached to a large gold key. Although the flowers and key missed their target and landed on the Biltmore's roof, an agile onlooker scaled the building, retrieved the key, and presented it to the manager, who opened the doors to the waiting elite.

Guests entered a 200-foot-long hotel lobby, its high ceilings glittering with real gold leaf. In the Aztec Room, a maze of copper-filigreed beams supported an elegant domed ceiling, also covered in gold leaf. Waitresses in the dining room changed uniforms three times a day to present a constantly neat appearance. A sunroom and alcoves provided secluded spaces in which to read, chat, and take afternoon tea, and the hotel featured gift shops and a stockbroker's office with a direct wire to the New York Stock Exchange.

A "men's smoker," later called "The Mystery Room," allowed men a place to purchase bootleg whiskey and to gamble. The hotel opened during Prohibition, when buying or selling liquor was illegal. To avoid prosecution, the McArthur brothers installed a liquor cabinet that could convert to a bookcase in the event of a police raid.

The Arizona Biltmore embodies a belief shared by Albert McArthur and Wright that buildings succeed best if they harmonize with their locale's forms and patterns.

The sculpted blocks in the Biltmore's facade make a case in point and introduce a second mystery: What does the design on the blocks represent? Hopi sculptor Emry Kopta created the distinctive image, described in the resort's promotional materials as "a geometric pattern inspired by a palm tree." Olgivanna Wright called it "abstracts inspired by cacti." Warren McArthur III, Albert and Charles' nephew, says, however, that the pattern artistically represents Albert's theories on light frequencies and musical tones. It surely looks desert-inspired. The standard Biltmore Block, made of cement and sand and erected horizontally, measures 18 by 13-1/2 inches. A makeshift factory set up on-site produced more than 250,000 blocks during the resort's construction.

The Arizona Biltmore represented a crowning achievement for two salesmen from Chicago. But the financial collapse in October 1929 wiped them out. Chewing-gum magnate William Wrigley Jr., one of the Biltmore's original investors, took ownership. And the three McArthurs left for California, Warren later moving to New York, where he made a second fortune. But Albert suffered a heart attack and spent the rest of his life in Los Angeles, designing small homes and park structures and researching color theories and metaphysics. He died in 1951. Wright would outlive him by eight years.

Wrigley began his dominion over the Biltmore by adding the colorful Catalina Pool with its daffodil yellow and cobalt blue ceramic tiles. At first, he opened the luxurious main hotel only to upper-crust society members whom he knew, relegating their children to the cottages. By 1931, however, Wrigley had constructed his own 18,000-square-foot home — known locally as "The Wrigley Mansion" — on a 5-acre hilltop site overlooking the Biltmore. After that, he abolished the "invited guests only" rule.

When Wrigley died in 1932, his son Philip took over. Under the Wrigleys, the hotel gained nationwide fame as a luxury resort where the well-heeled could relax, sometimes for months at a time, with their privacy assured.

In May 1973, the Wrigleys sold the Biltmore to Talley Industries. Two weeks later, with the hotel closed for remodeling, a welder's torch sparked a fire that destroyed the fourth floor

▲ Sunlight heightens the effect of the gold leaf ceiling in the Biltmore's Gold Room, circa 1992.

and significantly damaged the lower ones. Losses reached $2.5 million — the hotel's original cost. Turning to Taliesin West, Frank Lloyd Wright's Arizona architectural school, Talley hired Taliesin Associated Architects to reconstruct the hotel, and the Biltmore reopened 82 days later.

The Taliesin team installed a bold geometric decor of yellow, mint green, orange, and blue. Workers reapplied 38,000 square feet of 4-inch-square gold leaf to the ceilings, and concrete blocks cast on site replaced those damaged by fire. One of Wright's graphic designs, originally used on the cover of an anthology of lectures he gave at Princeton in 1930, was rendered in glass and became the focal point of the new entry area. Some question remains whether the mural, entitled "Sahuaro Forms and Cactus Flowers," is installed right side up or upside down.

Control of the Biltmore changed several times after that, the complex selling for ever-escalating sums, with a recent price estimated at $240 million.

Amenities now include seven lighted tennis courts, eight swimming pools, a 16,000-square-foot conference center/meeting area, full-service indoor-outdoor spa, beauty salon, shops, several restaurants, access to two golf courses, and condominium rentals. The resort and spa now fills all the available land. "Every orange grove is gone," says Debora Bridges, director of public relations for the resort.

According to its own Web site, The Arizona Biltmore is "the only existing Frank Lloyd Wright-inspired hotel in the world. . . . The resort's design was inspired by consulting architect Frank Lloyd Wright, who collaborated with former student Albert Chase McArthur."

Taliesin West spokesman Bruce Pfeiffer speaks wearily of the long-lived conflict. "We keep clear of the argument to avoid trouble with the McArthur family," he says, adding, "Mrs. Wright felt he did most of it."

Having written a book about the issue, Warren McArthur III says unequivocally, "Wright really made very little contribution."

Architectural historian Bernard M. Boyle, retired Arizona State University professor of architecture, studied Albert Chase McArthur's letters, papers, and drawings relating to the Biltmore. Boyle says, "If there was a Wright influence, it was only secondarily. Wright's influence came from the years McArthur had known him. McArthur was not the greatest of architects. But this was his greatest building."

■ **WHEN YOU GO** 2400 E. Missouri Ave. From 24th Street and Camelback Road in Phoenix, take 24th Street north to Missouri Avenue; turn east on Missouri and follow the road, crossing over the canal and turning left to the hotel entrance. Tours depart Tuesday, Thursday, and Saturday at 2:30 P.M. Afternoon tea is served November through May, 2:30 P.M. to 4:30 P.M. in the lobby. (602) 955-6600 (concierge).

ARIZONA CAPITOL

■ **LOCATION**	Phoenix
■ **YEAR BUILT**	1898-1900, plus additions in 1919, 1939, 1956, and 1974
■ **STYLE**	Neoclassical Revival (early additions; later additions are Modern)
■ **ARCHITECT**	James Riely Gordon
■ **SIGNIFICANCE**	Housed both Territorial and State Legislatures / National Register of Historic Places, 1974

In 1889, after moving Arizona's capital between Prescott and Tucson, the Territorial government finally settled on the growing town of Phoenix as the governing body's permanent home. A new capitol made of Arizona stone would honor this choice and the Territory's rich store of natural resources. The resulting domed structure was grand enough to endure as the Arizona State Capitol when statehood finally arrived and, after state offices expanded into more modern digs, to be preserved as a museum in 1981.

Most spectacularly, 15 tons of copper now gleam on the Capitol dome, showcasing the state's copper mining industry. (Arizona produces two-thirds of the nation's copper and about 10 percent of the world's copper supply.) Additional native materials include the cutface granite on the first floor walls, taken from the mountains near Phoenix; tuff from Prescott on the upper walls; and white oak, brought from the state's northern forests, for the interior woodwork.

"What's unusual about this building," says Michael Carman, the museum's director and author of *Under the Copper Dome*, "is that: a) it has a copper dome; b) the building materials are local; and c) it was both a Territorial and a State Capitol; I don't know of any others like that." Built between 1898 and 1900, the building has classical proportions, columns, pilasters, porticos graced with pediments, rotundas topped with domes, and acanthus leaf motifs reminiscent of ancient Greece and Rome.

Selecting an architect to design the Capitol followed a nationwide competition. James Riely Gordon of San Antonio, Texas, won over 15 other competitors by recycling a variation of his earlier rejected concept for the Mississippi State Capitol. (While "Riely" may seem like a misspelling, museum director Carman confirms it is the correct version, but the name *was* misspelled on the museum's plaque.)

▲ Holding symbols of victory and enlightenment, the rooftop statue of "Winged Victory" further ennobles the stately Arizona Capitol building.

Gordon's design called for a grand staircase rising to a second-floor entry, but Territorial officials nixed the scheme as too expensive. While some tour guides say this may explain why three double doors on the second floor appear to lead nowhere, according to Carman, the doors actually open onto a narrow balcony from which Arizona's governors sometimes deliver their inaugural speeches.

For his trouble, Gordon received $2,250, or approximately 1.5 percent of the $135,774 cost of the 49,760-square-foot building. (Today, the usual architect's fee is 6 to 10 percent of the building's cost.) Gordon returned the "compliment" by visiting Arizona just long enough to meet with the Capitol commission; then he returned to Texas, leaving behind a contractor to supervise construction.

Gordon intended that the Capitol dome should be roofed with copper to honor the Territory's copper mining industry. However, the legislature parsimoniously settled for terne, a lead-and-tin alloy, camouflaged with copper-colored paint. Architect Gerald A. Doyle

▲ Wooden balustrades in the Capitol building rotunda echo the circular theme established by the copper dome overhead.

discovered this fakery during a 1970s restoration of the Capitol. Fortunately, the Arizona Mining Association rose to the occasion, and member mining companies donated enough copper to roof the dome as originally intended. Before the building opened, an anonymous artist created a 16-foot zinc "Winged Victory" weathervane to top the dome. The figure, which rotates in the wind, weighs 600 pounds and cost the Territory $175.

When Doyle examined it in the 1970s, he found it full of bullet holes. Rumor has it cowboys once used the weathervane for target practice. In the 1950s, some legislators, annoyed that prevailing winds caused them to be greeted each day by the statue's backside, had a caretaker shackle it permanently to face the entrance. During the 1970s restoration, Doyle freed the figure to rotate again.

The Capitol finally was ready for occupancy in August 1900. But with the hot, humid Phoenix summer — and no air-conditioning — legislators delayed the dedication until cooler weather. On Feb. 25, 1901, Territorial officials celebrated the Capitol dedication with parades, songs, and fruit punch.

Today, the Arizona Capitol Museum's restored rooms and colorful displays illustrate the mix of brilliance and bloopers that make Arizona's history so absorbing.

While striving for statehood, members of the 1910 Arizona constitutional convention met in the Capitol's assembly chamber (later home to the House of Representatives) to write a state constitution. The porthole-like windows set high up on the walls vented the hot air that rose toward the ceiling. However, the windows swiveled on their central axes, rather than simply opening in or out, which prevented the installation of screens. So birds flew into the chamber and perched on the chandeliers, with unpleasant results for the convention-eers below. Appropriately dignified furnishings in the room included oak desks, spindle-back chairs, and graceful, dual-energy chandeliers. The novel light fixtures used either gas or electricity. If the globes faced up, gas fueled the lights; if down, they ran by electricity.

Visitors still can see the offending windows, replicated light fixtures, and a reproduction of the original carpeting on the third floor of the Capitol.

Incidentally, President William Howard Taft vetoed the first constitution that Arizona submitted because it permitted the recall of judges. Approval came when citizens eliminated this clause, and on Feb. 14 — Valentine's Day — 1912, Arizona became the 48th state to join the Union. Shortly thereafter, Arizona's feisty leaders reinstated judicial recall and, on Nov. 5, 1912, granted women the right to vote. (The United States did not pass the 19th Amendment to the Constitution granting suffrage to women until 1920.)

A tile mosaic of the state's great seal inlaid in the Capitol rotunda floor reveals an early blooper. Arizona has long been known for five major industries, often promoted as the five Cs: copper, climate (essentially, the hospitality industry), cotton, cattle, and citrus. All five Cs appear in the state's official great seal.

The mosaic in the Capitol, however, lacks several elements, including the cow and the citrus orchard, while the miner inexplicably wears a bowler hat and cuffed pants. No respectable copper miner would don a bowler hat, and cuffed pants were a no-no for safety reasons and to prevent workers from smuggling out any turquoise they found in the copper ore.

The story goes that the Ohio company hired to create the mosaic sent legislators a sketch of their final concept for approval. The Legislature, which met only six weeks every other year, refused to take the time to proof it. After the work's installation, legislators recognized the errors, but when looking into the cost of correcting the mistakes, they felt the $8,000 repair price was too high. As a result, the flawed version of the great seal still greets visitors entering the museum.

Among the more interesting exhibits is the governor's office, with its partner's desk, chandelier with dangling electrical cords, and noted Arizona artist Lon Megargee's large painting of Canyon de Chelly. Here sits a surprisingly life-like wax figure of George W.P. Hunt, the new state's first governor. The nearly bald Hunt sported a walrus-like mustache and weighed more than 300 pounds. He took a special interest in the Capitol's landscaping, reportedly sometimes mowing the lawn and tending the roses himself. Hunt served seven terms as governor, although not consecutively, and he now rests eternally in a white pyramid in Phoenix's Papago Park.

Governors continued to serve from this office until the executive tower's completion in 1974.

Another popular display is the ceremonial silver service from the *USS Arizona*. State symbols, like a saguaro cactus and a cowboy, adorn the set. Japan sank the battleship on Dec. 7, 1941, during its Pearl Harbor bombing raid, killing 1,177 men on the *Arizona*. But, following naval tradition, the ship had been stripped for battle the preceding January because of turmoil in Europe, and the silver was not aboard.

Today, the old Capitol forms the centerpiece of a state government complex on 10.23 acres at the western terminus of Washington Street. Planted with tall trees and colorful flowers, the Capitol grounds extend east across 17th Avenue to Wesley Bolin Memorial Plaza, a lushly landscaped memorial garden and amphitheater filled with monuments honoring diverse aspects of Arizona's proud history, a sight the Territorial legislators would have relished.

■ **WHEN YOU GO** 1700 W. Washington St. From Central Avenue and Washington Street in downtown Phoenix, follow Washington west to the Capitol Museum. Find public parking east of the museum at Wesley Bolin Plaza. Open Monday through Friday, 8 A.M. to 5 P.M. Closed holidays. Guided group tours at 10 A.M. and 2 P.M.; self-guided tours at other times. (602) 542-4675. http://azcapitol.lib.az.us/capitol_home.

BURTON BARR CENTRAL LIBRARY

■ **LOCATION**	Phoenix
■ **YEAR BUILT**	1995
■ **STYLE**	High-tech modern
■ **ARCHITECTS**	William Bruder in association with DWL Architects & Planners
■ **SIGNIFICANCE**	Arizona's first major public building designed by a local architect with an international reputation.

If you want to see how a building is put together, try touring downtown Phoenix's Burton Barr Central Library. You'll see the structure's nuts and bolts, its textured concrete walls, pillars, and flooring out in the open as the inherent sculptural design. Working elements, like elevator cables and computer-guided shade louvers, proudly proclaim the building's technological premise.

The sleekly modern municipal library helped its designer, local architect William P. Bruder, earn an international reputation for innovation and high-tech spectacle.

"I like to think I build for the common man," says Bruder, who crafted the design for the $28-million modern library in collaboration with Wendell Burnette and DWL Architects & Planners. Visually stunning inside and out, the library showcases the architectural theories and detailing that Bruder has spent a lifetime developing.

Most of the building materials originate locally, a Bruder hallmark. Structural elements and their connections appear boldly — no marble veneer or dropped ceilings hide this building's functionality. And the design fits into and respects the city's desert climate, helping to conserve energy.

Above all, the design is honest. What you see is what you get: Witness the unpainted concrete columns and the steel cables and pulleys. Visitors usually catch their first glimpse of the library from Central Avenue, where the five-story building and its shining copper skin might look a little like a sophisticated warehouse. But then, many observers note the vertical, polished-steel panels pointing to entrances defined by I-beam canopies cantilevered over recessed doorways, and they conclude that this is no warehouse.

Patrons enter the building through tunnels complete with low ceilings of perforated metal illuminated to sparkle like heavenly constellations. Sky-blue walls contain inspirational sayings, like "There is nothing like a dream to create the future: Victor Hugo," mixed in with the names of donors.

▲ By placing copper cladding on the Burton Barr Central Library, architect Will Bruder
acknowledged the state's copper mining legacy.

Giant fabric sails shade the building's all-glass north skin from the summer sun. On the glazed south facade, giant aluminum louvers — like huge venetian blinds — adjust automatically to reduce heat gain and glare, helping to transform the building into an energy miser, yet both north and south window walls admit natural light so that during the day patrons can read without artificial light. At the same time, readers can look up from their books to enjoy framed views of downtown Phoenix and distant mountain ranges. And where the hot summer sun might intrude most brutally — striking the east and west walls of the structure — concrete slabs, corrugated copper cladding, and steel shade the 280,000-square-foot library and its contents. Bruder says the library uses a third of the energy engineers had anticipated, though the building contains 10,000 square feet of exterior glass.

The rules of classical architecture dictate that a long, low entry should explode into a voluminous open space, a strategy used to create drama. In 1986, Bruder won the prestigious Rome Prize to study in Italy where he observed this device in its place of origin. Bruder made the library's tunnels open out into an impressive 48- by 24-foot atrium bathed with the light from skylights five stories overhead. A black reflecting pool "grounds" the lobby floor, while glass-encased elevators rise and fall noiselessly, emphasizing the large area between the floor and the distant ceiling.

Many of Bruder's design details unfold as practical solutions to common problems. For example, baffled light bars jut from the metal-mesh bookshelving so readers can read the titles easily. The steel-top desks where the librarians sit are identified with light-box bases, signaling where help is available. Room dividers double as art exhibition surfaces. The visual warmth of wood paneling and oak shelves breaks up a regimen of sleek, metallic surfaces and rough, pock-marked concrete.

The library's decor blends utilitarian blue carpeting with the dull gray of the formed concrete. Here and there, however, walls finished in elegant venetian plaster, colored apple-green or mustard-yellow, contrast with the ubiquitous gray. Primary red, blue, and green distinguish the directional signs, while yellow arrows add more punch to the color palette. Study lights come equipped with yellow shades. And colorful computer stands and children's furniture provide touches of whimsy.

In another clever architectural treatment, the interior lights render the thin, perforated exterior copper cladding translucent at night, exposing the building's stairwells, stacks, and study desks to the view of drivers cruising the area.

The designer achieves an architectural *tour de force* on the fifth floor. Here the corrugated, galvanized-steel roof appears to float high above the main reading room. Actually, a series of tensile cables and stainless steel struts supports the roof decking by connecting to a forest of concrete columns. Shaped like candlesticks, the columns taper from 2 feet in diameter at their base to a 10-inch diameter at the metal tips, ending just beneath translucent skylights, glacial blue and 6 feet across. A small aperture punctures each skylight so that, at exactly solar noon during the summer solstice, sunlight pierces the openings and "lights" the candlestick columns, seemingly setting them on fire. Meeting to watch this phenomenon has become a community event, the architect says.

Bruder has designed several other major facilities, including the Cholla and Mesquite branches in the Phoenix Public Library system, the Deer Valley Rock Art Center, and the Scottsdale Museum of Contemporary Art. Early in his career, he supervised a number of design-build houses, with clients contributing sweat equity to the projects.

Educated as a sculptor, Bruder studied design with visionary architects Paolo Soleri and Gunnar Birkerts. In person, he is voluble in his dedication to architecture as an art form. The architect, who lives in central Phoenix, says his ambition is "to contribute buildings that enhance the urban sense in the city of Phoenix."

■ **WHEN YOU GO** 1221 N. Central Ave. From Central Avenue and Van Buren streets in downtown Phoenix, take Central north to the library. Open Monday through Thursday, 10 A.M. to 9 P.M.; Friday and Saturday, 10 A.M. to 6 P.M.; Sunday, 12 P.M. to 6 P.M. (602) 262-4636. www.phoenixpubliclibrary.org

GRADY GAMMAGE MEMORIAL AUDITORIUM

■ **LOCATION**	Tempe
■ **YEARS BUILT**	1962-1964
■ **STYLE**	Organic
■ **ARCHITECT**	Frank Lloyd Wright
■ **SIGNIFICANCE**	Frank Lloyd Wright's last major public design / National Register of Historic Places, 1985

This is a tale of two men who shared a dream that would come true only after the men died.

One man was Dr. Grady Gammage, for 27 years the president of Arizona State College, later changed to Arizona State University. Gammage, a reserved, dignified scholar, burned with a passion to transform the small Tempe liberal arts college into a great university. His vision included building an auditorium worthy of what he considered the school's grand future prospects.

The second man was Gammage's friend Frank Lloyd Wright. During Wright's long life (92 years) and distinguished career, the architect designed such notable projects as the Johnson Wax Administration Building in Racine, Wisconsin, and the Guggenheim Museum in New York City.

Luckily for Gammage, Wright wintered at Taliesin West, Wright's Arizona home and architectural school in Scottsdale. There, Wright and his wife, Olgivanna, often entertained Gammage and his wife, Kathryn, at black-tie dinners and recitations.

Gammage believed the college needed a landmark structure of the sort only Wright could design. But when Gammage suggested an auditorium-classroom-office structure, Wright observed realistically about Gammage and the possibility of an auditorium on campus, "What a charming fellow — but he has no money."

Then in 1958, Gammage and others engineered a statewide initiative to change the college's name to Arizona State University. Voters approved by a 2-1 margin despite fierce opposition from the legislature and the Arizona Board of Regents, filled mostly with graduates of ASU's arch-rival, the University of Arizona.

The name change cleared the way for Gammage to proceed with his dream of building an auditorium at ASU.

Wright finally agreed to tour the campus and examine possible sites. Wearing his trademark navy blue cape and carrying a cane, Wright stopped at the sweeping curve on the southwest side of the ASU campus, where Mill Avenue and Apache Boulevard meet, and declared that this location should be the place for the auditorium. The projected structure should be circular to mirror the bend in the street, he said, and the plan should

▲ Even the ramp leading to Frank Lloyd Wright's Grady Gammage Memorial Auditorium, a popular venue for musical performances, sets the stage for entertainment.

"with outstretched arms bid 'Welcome to Arizona!'"

As it happened, Wright had already conceptualized an opera house for another desert city, Baghdad, Iraq. With the Baghdad opera house as a starting concept, Wright designed a totally new, multi-purpose auditorium with only some similarities to the earlier design. The drawings delighted Gammage, and he forwarded them to a skeptical board of regents. The regents, however, fretted over Wright's idea, thinking it too extreme and too costly. One legislator called the design, "Frank Lloyd Wright's little joke on Arizona."

Then, on Apr. 9, 1959, Wright unexpectedly died. Suddenly, Wright's plan for a performing arts auditorium assumed special significance because it would become the great architect's last major design.

Gammage worked diligently to line up political and financial support for the plan, enlisting, among others, Walter Bimson, president of the Valley National Bank, the state's largest bank, and influential civic leader Lewis Ruskin. On Dec. 12, 1959, Ruskin delivered an eloquent speech to the regents, praising Wright's concept.

Ten days later, Gammage, worn out by his battles on behalf of ASU, died at the age of 67.

The entire university community went into mourning. Gammage's body lay in state in the Capitol rotunda, an honor reserved for only the highest-ranking dignitaries.

At this point, Wright's trusted aide, William Wesley Peters, guaranteed that the proposed auditorium would be completed on time and within budget, if the legislature accepted it. Reluctantly, lawmakers approved the plan, more than anything as a tribute to Gammage, who had meant so much to Arizona education. (He also had served as president of Flagstaff's Arizona State Teachers College, now Northern Arizona University.)

The Grady Gammage Memorial Auditorium opened on Sept. 18, 1964, with a gala performance by the Philadelphia Orchestra under the baton of Eugene Ormandy. Construction of the 3,017-seat auditorium had, indeed, come in on time and under budget, with the cost a low $3.5 million. According to David Dodge, a former Wright apprentice who now has his own firm, "Taking into account the cost-of-living index, this theater building cost less per seat than any large theater built in America since colonial days."

Gammage Auditorium now is known worldwide for its near-perfect acoustics; its easy-access seating uninterrupted by aisles or pillars; its floating balconies providing "surround sound" to listeners; and its twin "flying buttress" exterior pedestrian bridges, each 200 feet long, which connect the upper floors to the parking area so patrons can leave the building within minutes.

Basically, the structure marries two circular forms, one an audience hall with its lobbies and promenades encircled by a lofty colonnade; the second element housing the stage and working areas as well as four floors of classroom and rehearsal space used by the school of music — the legislature having insisted that the building serve an educational purpose.

Unlike the Baghdad opera house, which was to have been concrete, the auditorium consists of a steel interior framework covered with an unusually heavy (2-inch-thick) surface of cementitious plaster. On the outside, the plaster integrates blown-on marble chips, a mixture called Marblecrete, and in some areas, the exterior is brick veneer. Dodge says, "The building is built like an eggshell. It is a very lightweight structure but, like a violin, it serves music perfectly. In many people's minds this is the finest hall for music in the world."

The orchestra shell, conceived by the Taliesin team and designed by Yale University Professor George Izenour, contributes mightily to the fine sound quality in the auditorium. In recent years, however, it had been a logistical obstacle when Gammage presented Broadway musicals like *Phantom of the Opera* and *Showboat* to increase ticket receipts. Such giant productions require a greater stage depth than Gammage provided. This meant the orchestra shell had to be either moved or abandoned in order to stage the large shows.

The university determined to preserve the shell and hired Taliesin Associated Architects to devise a "garage" in which to store the shell when a larger stage is required. Today, in the space of just a morning, the 100,000-pound, 32-foot-tall telescoping shell of steel, along with its large pipe organ and screen weighing thousands of pounds, can be scooted along with air casters guided by overhead rails into a partially underground storage area. With the shell on stage, the performance area measures 32 feet deep; with the shell removed, the stage expands to a depth of 40 feet. The garage measures 80 feet long and 10 feet thick and appears next to the box office, where its exterior wall displays notices of coming events.

Phoenix attorney Grady Gammage Jr., Dr. Gammage's only child, expresses the reluctance many people felt about altering a Frank Lloyd Wright building, even slightly. "The garage was a compromise that I was supportive of and willing to live with," he says. "First of all, it's reversible. And second, the little garage is sort of innocuous. It was more okay than losing the shell, which was part of the original building."

Gammage Auditorium hosts grand opera and dramatic performances, organ recitals, chamber music and symphony concerts, lectures, and solo performances, as well as Broadway extravaganzas.

Even regular Gammage-goers continue to marvel at features in the building they fully discover only after visiting multiple times. "The hall is just filled with ideas," Dodge says.

Wright's justly famous detailing appears on all levels. For example, heavily scored mortar joints between each row of bricks gives a horizontal look to the building. Cast-concrete shapes atop the exterior pillars resemble drawn stage curtains. Curved phone booths, ticket receptacles, and water fountains echo the circular form of the building. The carpeting's colorful motif echoes a silk fabric designed by Wright. And 57 varieties of rust red dominate the overall color scheme. However, the exit signs, at the request of Frank Lloyd Wright's widow, are green and not regulation red, to harmonize with the green accenting the interior light globes.

Technical innovations include a fore-stage lift which, when raised, adds 11 feet to the front of the stage, and, when recessed, provides an orchestra pit large enough to accommodate 60 musicians. When raised only partway, it adds three rows of seating to the hall.

The American Classic pipe organ has approximately 3,000 pipes, and the newly installed handicapped seating is removable.

"This auditorium," Dodge says, "has held up very well over the years. And it's largely due to the many wonderful people at the university who value and understand the vision this building adds to the cultural life of the community."

■ **WHEN YOU GO** Gammage Memorial Auditorium sits at the southwest edge of ASU's main campus, where Apache Boulevard meets Mill Avenue in Tempe. The ASU campus is southeast from downtown Phoenix and about 2 miles south of State Loop 202. Surface parking surrounds the auditorium; there is a parking garage east of the building. Guided tours start most days (except weekends) at 1:00 P.M., 2:00 P.M., and 3:00 P.M., unless an event is in progress. (480) 965-3434 (tickets for performances); (480) 965-4050 (information). www.asu.edu.tour/main/ggma

HOLY ANGELS CHURCH

■ **LOCATION**	Globe
■ **YEAR BUILT**	1918
■ **STYLE**	Romanesque Revival
■ **ARCHITECT**	James S. Pigott
■ **BUILDER**	Father Virgil Genevrier with Albert Altweis
■ **SIGNIFICANCE**	Embodies the aspirations of an ambitious priest and his copper camp congregation / National Register of Historic Places, 1983

French-born Father Virgil Genevrier was assigned to Globe's newly established Sacred Heart Parish in October 1915. Said to be fluent in nine languages and an accomplished musician, Father Genevrier arrived in the mining town by way of Cairo, Egypt; Pueblo, Mexico; and East Orange, New Jersey. Possessed of an iron will and inexhaustible energy,

▲ Dedicated to the Holy Angels of Heaven, the historic Romanesque Revival church in Globe displays a façade of locally quarried tufa stone with marble columns at the entry portico.

▲ Wall-hung stations of the cross and Emil Frei-crafted stained glass windows infuse the interior of Holy Angels Church with palpable spirituality.

Father Genevrier determined that the existing Sacred Heart facilities were woefully inadequate and embarked on an ambitious fund-raising campaign to remedy the situation. No one — Catholic or not — was immune from a request to contribute. Father Genevrier asked New Jersey architect James S. Pigott to create a plan for the new church in the imposing Romanesque Revival style, a popular design for churches in his native France. Workers broke ground in September 1916, with Father Genevrier acting as general contractor, assisted by congregation member Albert Altweis, who actually *was* a contractor. The dedication of Holy Angels Church took place Sept. 29, 1918. Tufa, a volcanic rock quarried on the nearby San Carlos Apache Indian Reservation, served as the primary building material. The poured-in-place concrete foundation walls were formed to resemble cut stone. Delicate stained glass windows by Emil Frei of St. Louis, the premier glass artist of the day, punctuate the massive walls. A single corner tower rises above the structure, and a gabled parapet caps the west-facing main facade, which shows a hint of the Mission Revival style. Also on the west, in contrast to the rough-cut stone used elsewhere in the walls, smooth-surfaced stone suggests a central arch, within which a fleur-de-lis stained glass window is set. An entry portico featuring four engaged marble Corinthian columns frames three pairs of copper-clad doors, and a pitched metal roof completes the composition. The equally impressive interior includes a nave defined by a flattened barrel vault. Carved wood fixtures, a recessed confessional, and a faux marble altar built in Italy enrich the simple, yet elegant space. Deacon Jim Gersitz, in pointing out the fleur-de-lis motif repeated in the windows, woodwork, and even the gold-finished *saboreum* (the Communion service set) theorizes that use of the design was symbolic of Father Genevrier's French roots and reflects his involvement in all aspects of the church's planning and construction. Fulfilling the ambitious priest's aspirations, Holy Angels Church, far from being a relic of days gone by, continues to be a touchstone in the lives of its congregation.

■ **WHEN YOU GO** 201-231 S. Broad St. From U.S. Route 60 eastbound through Globe, veer left onto Broad Street at the railroad underpass and proceed east. The church is located two blocks past the Cobre Valley Center of the Arts. Weekdays, stop at the parish office, 143 S. Broad St., to pick up a key. Tours available upon request. (928) 425-3137.

LUHRS BUILDING & LUHRS TOWER

■ **LOCATION**	Phoenix
■ **YEAR BUILT**	1923-24 and 1929
■ **STYLE**	Second Renaissance Revival and Moderne
■ **ARCHITECT**	Henry Charles Trost, Trost & Trost
■ **SIGNIFICANCE**	Longtime focal points of downtown business square

Just as Phoenix grew from a cow town to a metropolis in the space of a century, Block 64 of the original town site, at Jefferson Street and Central Avenue, developed from horse corrals and a livery stable to a major business and financial center in the same time period.

Immigration fueled Phoenix's growth, and George H.N. Luhrs was among the early newcomers who worked to ensure that Phoenix would grow commercially, transforming from a small town into a thriving city.

Born in Germany, Luhrs moved to the United States in the late 1860s, arriving in Phoenix in 1878 at age 31. Trained as a wheelwright, he had heard that the town was a hay-growing center, so Luhrs and a partner joined in a blacksmithing and wagon-making enterprise. In 1882, they purchased an entire city block for $2,000.

Like Phoenix, Luhrs had limited foresight at first. The sleepy town practically gave away land in its central city in the 1870s, it was so desperate to attract residents. The partners' goal was to convert Block 64 into a campground. Later, they built a corral and livery stable, but soon afterwards they dissolved the partnership.

By the early 1900s, Luhrs found himself caught up in the excitement of the town's turn-of-the-century population/business boom. Phoenix succeeded Prescott as the Arizona Territorial capital and became the state capital in 1912.

Luhrs began his real estate empire, modestly enough, by building the two-story Luhrs Central Building at 132 S. Central Ave. in 1913-14. The Neoclassical Revival structure remains as one of Phoenix's few terra-cotta buildings.

In 1923-24, Luhrs added the 10-story Luhrs Building at 11 W. Jefferson St., for a time the tallest structure in Phoenix and the largest commercial building between El Paso and Los Angeles.

Five years later, Luhrs and his son, George Jr., erected the 13-story Luhrs Tower at 45 W. Jefferson St., which was finished in 1929.

When Luhr's health began to fail in the 1920s, George Jr. started managing his father's business ventures. An attorney and bachelor, George Jr. once confessed that he was "married" to the Luhrs properties.

Luhrs Sr. chose well-known architect Henry Charles Trost of El Paso, Texas, to design both the Luhrs Building and the Luhrs Tower. During his career, Trost crafted a prodigious number of buildings in Arizona, New Mexico, and west Texas — 300 in El Paso alone. The architect won commissions for all sizes and types of buildings, from bungalows to libraries, in styles ranging from Victorian to Art Deco. Trost once lived and worked in Tucson, and admirers recognize him today as one of the region's first architects to consciously adapt buildings to their desert environment. He referred to the Southwest as "Arid America."

The Luhrs Building and Luhrs Tower illustrate Trost's virtuosity.

The red-brick Luhrs Building represents the Second Renaissance Revival architectural style. The design employs a classical three-part massing, with a separate base, shaft, and

▲ The 10-story Luhrs Building and the 13-story Luhrs Tower, foreground, stand on land originally occupied by an early Phoenix corral and livery stable.

cornice, and cast-concrete detailing. Above the first floor, the L-shaped building offers every office a window. It rests on concrete-and-steel piers with footings 15 feet square, excavated to a depth of 18 feet below ground level, and the lower portion of the exterior pillars is granite. The Luhrs Building cost about $553,000 to construct.

The style of the cast-in-place concrete Luhrs Tower, on the other hand, is Moderne — also called Art Deco or, regionally, Pueblo Deco — with Spanish Colonial Revival elements. The tower seems to soar to great heights due to its vertical piers and window panels, along with its stepped-back top floors. Art Deco chevron motifs mix with floral patterns at the apex of the tower. At street level, cast iron grilles and marble facings adorn the storefronts. The reinforced-concrete tower employs both an inner and an outer wall, which trap air between the walls as insulation. Inside, the surprisingly small lobby has imported French marble wainscoting, brass elevator surrounds, and an elaborately stenciled Spanish Colonial-style ceiling. Some say that the mustachioed face above the main entrance is a Trost self-portrait. The project cost around $400,000.

Both buildings played a strategic role in Phoenix's commercial development.

For nearly a half-century, the Luhrs Building housed the all-male Arizona Club, a refuge for the elite to which most of Phoenix's business and policy leaders belonged at one time or another. The building's top four floors accommodated members' special needs. The seventh and eighth floors held bedrooms, most equipped with a bath or a shower; the ninth floor featured an office, lounge, library, billiards room, and, for a time, slot machines; and the 10th floor boasted an elegant, 22-foot-high arched ceiling; crystal chandeliers; a kitchen; and dining rooms. Partitions between the dining rooms could be removed for large, formal dinner parties or to form a ballroom for dancing. Magnificent views of the city spread out below.

Many tales have been told about the high jinks of Arizona Club members in the Luhrs Building. Members built a boxing ring on the roof and applauded as Luhrs business manager Adam Diaz won an unofficial decision over John Henry Lewis, later proclaimed official Light Heavyweight Champion of the World.

On another occasion, club members decorated for a Western-themed dance using hay and live barnyard fowl. Boisterous guests threw chickens out the windows, as well as a chair, which landed on a car parked in the street below. And, in the 1930s, the Prohibition Department, a tenant in the building, occasionally siphoned off confiscated liquor into containers that somehow fell into the hands of appreciative Arizona Club members.

The Luhrs complex seldom suffered vacancies. The Luhrses believed in affordable rents. When the Luhrs Building opened, offices went for $15 to $45 a month. Luhrs Jr. claimed the family barely broke even with the Arizona Club's rent — $1,950 a month for all four floors.

Initial tenants in the Luhrs' properties included a harness and saddle company, doctors, lawyers, and dentists. Later came credit unions, brokerages, and insurance agents. Today, attorneys predominate because of the buildings' proximity to the Maricopa County Courthouse. Other current occupants include a barbershop, men's clothing store, bail bondsman, snack bar, art gallery, and flower shop.

Wandering through the Luhrs complex resembles negotiating a rabbit warren. In addition to the tower, Luhrs Building, and Central Building, the complex includes: the Luhrs U.S. Post Office Station/Arcade at 45 W. Jefferson St.; the Luhrs Tower Annex, a 1950 extension of the tower's first two floors that copies the tower's style and extends along First Avenue south to the alley; and the Luhrs Parking Center, an undistinguished 1,000-car garage completed in 1958. Beginning in 1923 as a look-alike to the Luhrs Building and serving as a post office until 1980 and as an Army induction center during World War II, the station/arcade has been altered into a labyrinth of zigzagging corridors, staircases, and a tunnel between the Luhrs Tower and Luhrs Building.

Luhrs Jr. sold the entire city block to investors in 1976, but the family name remains with the downtown complex.

George Luhrs and his son changed the Phoenix skyline with the Luhrs Building and the Luhrs Tower. Successful completion of the Luhrs complex introduced Phoenix to the world as a bustling commercial center with local entrepreneurs capable of executing large-scale construction projects — an impressive legacy for an immigrant wheelwright to leave his adopted city.

■ **WHEN YOU GO** 11 and 45 W. Jefferson St. Luhrs Tower is located on Jefferson Street, west of Central Avenue, between Central and First avenues.

MARICOPA COUNTY COURTHOUSE / PHOENIX CITY HALL

■ **LOCATION**	Phoenix
■ **YEARS BUILT**	1928-29
■ **STYLE**	Neoclassical and Spanish Colonial Revival with Art Deco (Pueblo Deco) influences
■ **ARCHITECTS**	Lescher and Mahoney (city side); Edward Neild (county side)
■ **SIGNIFICANCE**	Building's rich exterior ornamentation represents the coming of age of local governments / National Register of Historic Places, 1989

How can a building express optimism and excitement? Downtown Phoenix's historic city/county building virtually shouts out that the city and Maricopa County anticipated a prosperous future in the pre-Depression years 1928-29.

Note the cheery scrolls around the top of the building. Catch the regionally-influenced Art Deco motifs — chevrons, wave patterns, stylized birds, floral and geometric shapes — all symbolic of a positive outlook.

The architecture declared in concrete what Mayor Fred Paddock and City Manager W.C. LeFebvre boasted at the building's dedication: "Everybody knows that Arizona is the best place on the face of the earth to live. . . . The greatest service that can be rendered to mankind is for more people to take up their residence in this most delightful place."

The impressive edifice was built for a mere $1.2 million, with both governments retaining the best architects available. Edward Neild of Shreveport, Louisiana, crafted the county's eastern two-thirds of the structure, while Lescher and Mahoney of Phoenix designed the city's westward-facing portion.

Neild designed most of the exterior in a mix of Neoclassical, Spanish Colonial Revival, and Art Deco styling, while Lescher and Mahoney contributed the city hall's ornate interiors and the sculpted phoenix birds guarding the west entrance.

Constructed of poured-in-place, reinforced concrete augmented by pink granite, bronze doors, cast-iron window surrounds, and granite steps, the building has rusticated terra cotta, sandstone-like exterior panels capped by a hipped roof in seven shades of red clay tile. The courthouse has been the easily recognized backdrop for more than one sensational case. Tried here were Ernesto Miranda, whose conviction for rape, kidnapping, and robbery the U.S. Supreme Court overturned in 1966, subsequently requiring police to read suspects their

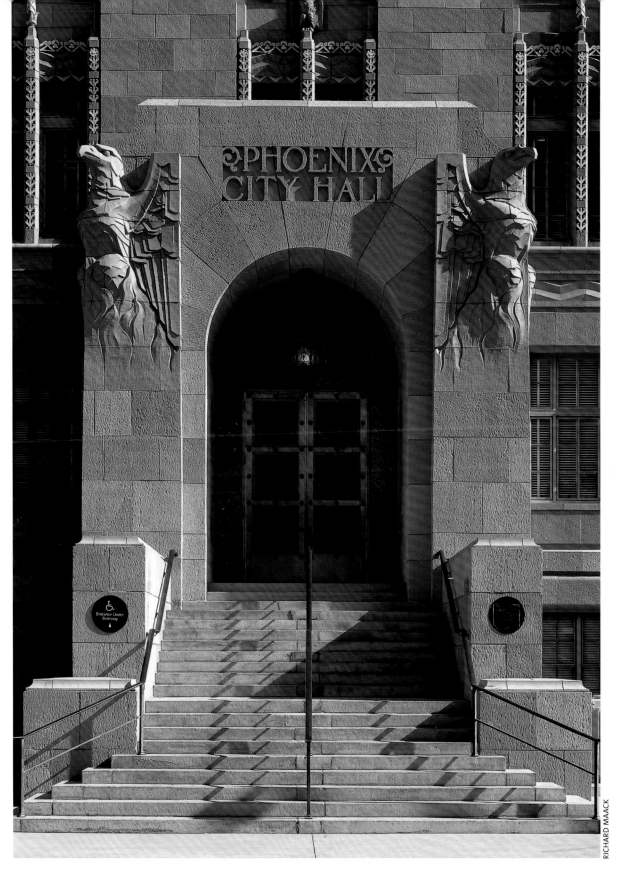

▲ The buoyant Art Deco façade of Phoenix's Historic City Hall reflects the confident outlook shared by area leaders in the late 1920s before the Depression.

Miranda Rights; and Winnie Ruth Judd, charged with shooting two of her friends to death, dismembering one, and taking both corpses to California in two trunks and a suitcase.

In 1987, a mechanical failure led to a $1.8 million renovation of the old city hall by the Orcutt-Winslow Partnership. Most city services moved across the street to a glamorous, 20-story city hall, completed in 1994, with Historic City Hall now containing the headquarters for Phoenix's sister city program and various meeting rooms.

The north-facing "Old Courthouse," which is being rehabilitated by Gerald Doyle & Associates and Swan Architects Inc., includes 13 courtrooms and their support facilities. Marriage licenses and passports are also issued here. Since 1987, new air-conditioning, electrical, and fire sprinkler systems have been installed, many courtrooms have been brought back to their original condition, and new offices and reception areas added to some courtrooms. The marble borders were cleaned, as were the colorful ceramic tiles on the risers in the entry's circular staircase. Deputy court administrator Hugh Gallagher expects the refurbishment of the top floor and installation of a museum to be completed in 2004.

Water-conserving xeriscaping now dapples the walkways surrounding the monumental structure with shade, inviting visitors to linger for a while and contemplate the building's message, first communicated so optimistically in June 1929, when Phoenix and Maricopa County believed the sky was the limit — just before the stock market crashed in October and put such illusions to rest for a very long time.

■ **WHEN YOU GO** The building is on the southwest corner of Central Avenue and Washington Street in downtown Phoenix. 125 W. Washington St. (courthouse entrance, north side), (602) 506-3912 (deputy court administrator). 17 S. Second Ave. (city hall entrance, west side).

MYSTERY CASTLE

■ **LOCATION**	Phoenix
■ **YEARS BUILT**	1929-1945
■ **STYLE**	Eclectic/Organic/Vernacular
■ **BUILDER**	Boyce L. Gulley
■ **SIGNIFICANCE**	Eccentric fantasy built of rocks and recycled treasures

Boyce Luther Gulley, a Seattle businessman with two years' training in architectural engineering, delighted in creating elaborate, mysterious sand castles for his 5-year-old daughter, Mary Lou. But, at the end of their Sundays at the seashore, the tide would roll in and sweep away his fanciful constructions, making her cry.

Gulley tried to explain that Father Neptune needed the sand castle in the ocean. But Mary Lou would exclaim rebelliously, "To heck with Father Neptune. Let him make his own." And she begged her dad to build a sand castle for her in the desert where no waves would destroy his efforts.

Boyce Gulley apparently took her message to heart, although his little girl wouldn't know this until she was grown and her father had died.

The story goes that in 1927 doctors diagnosed Gulley with tuberculosis — virtually a death sentence then. Saying nothing to anyone, Gulley disappeared — leaving behind his wife, Frances, and little Mary Lou.

▲ **Using detritus of the desert and castoffs of civilization, Boyce Gulley crafted a recycler's dream castle in the foothills south of Phoenix.**

Two years later, Gulley turned up at the base of South Mountain, south of Phoenix, living in an abandoned boxcar, probably trying to recover his health in the Arizona sunshine. There he began building one of the strangest, most bizarre and, in some ways, farsighted constructions his neighbors — or anyone else, for that matter — had ever seen.

His "sand castle" in the desert gradually grew into an 18-room, 8,000-square-foot rambling residence. Gulley worked until he died in 1945, crafting a marvel of imaginative enterprise in which he recycled everything — from prehistoric stone *metates,* used for hand-grinding grain, to fragile Venetian glass fruit bowls — in a house set against the mountain, 450 feet above Phoenix.

One lucky day, his daughter says, Gulley happened upon a carload of Pyrex dishes at a swap market. He bought the lot for just $7.50 and used the square containers — like glass block — in the walls, sidelights, floors, and ceilings of the structure, introducing light and protecting those inside from the prying eyes of neighbors. The translucent casserole dishes work especially well in the ceiling of the castle's underground chapel, where they collect daylight from the patio above and bathe the chapel below with natural illumination.

Accompanied only by a mule named Jackson, Gulley scrounged for used brick, old telegraph poles, abandoned railroad tracks and ties, leftover tiles, saguaro cactus skeletons, spent shell casings, rejected lumber, damaged wagon wheels, coal clinkers, discarded furniture, and rocks, rocks, and more rocks, hauling everything back to the structure he spent years building, in fits and starts, apparently as the spirit moved him.

Gulley arranged the rocks in artistic assemblages, sometimes sprinkling small and larger pebbles between the pieces of flagstone flooring. Using a mortar incorporating goats' milk, he fixed the rocks in place, a technique he reputedly learned from local Indians. He framed an opening for a large, round window with oval river rocks. Rocks mortared into

▲ **Whimsical and romantic, the Mystery Castle contains 18 rooms and 13 fireplaces, with stairways, hallways, doors, and trapdoors of varying sizes.**

raised platforms and niches displayed his collectibles. He incorporated semi-precious stones, like green malachite and blue azurite, hand painted tiles, and even gold nuggets, into his colorful compositions. The more dramatic rocks feature prehistoric petroglyphs.

"My father loved the Southwest. He was a real desert buff," says Mary Lou Gulley, now all grown up. "But this house also is a tribute to the state of Arizona."

Among Boyce Gulley's most startling architectural creations is a half-spiral stairway seemingly held up by nothing, one of 14 outside stairways that appear to float between the ground and roof.

Apparently, judging from the way the house meanders up and down over five different levels, Gulley started building without a preconceived plan. Some describe his style as stream-of-consciousness architecture: It grew and developed as the builder dreamed up possibilities and adapted his imaginings to the imperatives of brick-and-mortar construction in a desert environment. "I think artists are born, not made," his daughter says.

Nearly every room unveils another version of Gulley's droll whimsy: The brass bed in the guest room is literally a "roll-away" bed. It rolls on railroad tracks into a storage space when it's not in use. An underground bar comes with an antechamber containing what Mary Lou calls "bunks for drunks." Some of the beds are shorter than others, which must have been unsettling to the inebriated.

Local couples often marry in the castle chapel, the service accompanied by music from a pedal organ, circa 1870. The floor near the altar includes inlaid-rock rattlesnakes. Rattlesnakes, says Mary Lou, symbolize protection, wisdom, and defiance. "The whole family had a sense of humor. If you don't have that, you're in trouble."

In spite of its odd appearance, Gulley's castle has proved to be both practical and progressive. The kitchen has an eye-level oven for a quick view of the food baking inside. A central floor drain in the kitchen makes hosing away spills convenient. More emphasis on easy care is evident in the built-in furniture, including a drop-leaf desk, a wine cabinet made with the bottoms of tequila bottles as its border, and many *bancos*, or benches.

One wrap-around window frames an excellent view of Phoenix. Another window features wavy, handmade glass Gulley brought back from Santa Fe, New Mexico; it converts a view of Phoenix's downtown into a shimmering wonderland. Gulley equipped many of the 13 fireplaces with conversation pits to encourage conviviality and storytelling, his version of Western hospitality. The house has an organic feel, melding into the mountain as if it had grown there, like a plant.

Mary Lou and her mother did not learn what happened to her father until after his death at age 62 in 1945. Then his estate's executor tracked down Mary Lou and told her about her inheritance — an Arizona mansion full of secrets.

But the inheritance came with a caveat: Mary Lou must live in the house until the following New Year's Day, and she must NOT open the trap door to a hidden chamber until that time.

This condition was not as easy to fulfill as it might seem. The house contained no running water or electricity — hence no air conditioner — and scorpions, occasional snakes, and other wayward critters inhabited it.

Mary Lou still remained intrigued. She and her mother moved into the house. In the process, she discovered how much her father had loved her: She found stacks of linen embroidered with her initials and a music box that played her favorite song, "Rose Marie."

New Year's Eve, Mary Lou could scarcely sleep, she was so excited. Rising at six o'clock in the morning, she forced open the trap door. Inside she found gold, $74 worth of nickels and dimes, a wallet containing two $500 bills, valentines, and a letter telling her, "I love you."

Mary Lou was hooked. She had fallen in love with Arizona and her very own "mystery castle," just as her father hoped she would.

Then on June 26, 1948, *Life* magazine ran an article featuring her quirky home. The next day, Mary Lou heard a hubbub, looked out the window, and saw the hillside covered with people. "What should we do?" she asked her mother, who replied in a practical vein, "Let's charge $1 a person and maybe they'll go away."

The public did not go away and continues to tour this unusual and fanciful residence to this day. Over the years, the Mystery Castle has been publicized in magazines, newspapers, and on TV programs worldwide.

So, the message displayed at the entrance of the Mystery Castle, inscribed on a rock — naturally — has finally come true for the little girl from Seattle who wished for a sand castle that no tides could wash away: "There Is NO Dream That Is Impossible."

■ **WHEN YOU GO** 800 E. Mineral Rd. Take Seventh Street south to Baseline Road, turn right and go a half block, then turn left and continue south on Seventh Street to Mineral Road. Turn left on Mineral Road and head east to the castle. Mary Lou guides tours personally, October through June, Thursday through Sunday, 11 A.M. to 4 P.M. Entrance fee. (602) 268-1581.

NELSON FINE ARTS CENTER, ARIZONA STATE UNIVERSITY

■ **LOCATION**	Tempe
■ **YEARS BUILT**	1987-1989
■ **STYLE**	Modern
■ **ARCHITECT**	Antoine Predock
■ **SIGNIFICANCE**	Sensory extravaganza in celebration of ASU's centennial

An architect's work is supposed to appeal to our senses.

Antoine Predock, the Albuquerque architect who designed Arizona State University's Fine Arts Center, fulfills this professional obligation with verve:

* The $16.4 million arts complex captivates the eye with its dramatic massing, pale lavender walls, and towering steel-truss "Pharaoh's headdress."

* Gurgling fountains at the entry, bubbling water in a subterranean pool, and footsteps echoing in the flagstone foyer and stairwells intrigue the ear.

* Pockmarked pillars and the aroma of fragrant plants arouse the senses of touch and smell.

The J. Russell and Bonita Nelson Fine Arts Center, which opened in 1989, is the happy result of a design competition launched in 1985 to celebrate ASU's centennial. The university desired a showcase project to represent academic excellence in general, and the arts in particular. It got one: an exquisitely functional complex, filled with intriguing metaphors, which visitors find intellectually stimulating.

Some aspects of the design have been criticized, notably the austere, nearly windowless exterior and its offbeat color. The student newspaper, *The State Press*, described the complex as a high-rise bomb shelter. And some complain the pink-purple hue clashes with the ubiquitous tan-beige color scheme of the campus.

But the unrelieved flat surfaces of the complex were intentional, designed to squeeze as much building into a confined space as possible, reduce energy usage and construction costs, and allow the architect to manipulate pure form.

As for the color, Predock chose it, he says, after cracking open a rock from nearby Tempe (Hayden) Butte. He then integrated the rock's lavender tones into the stucco mix applied to the concrete block walls.

The center is named for former ASU president J. Russell Nelson, who presided over approximately $100 million worth of construction at the university in the 1980s, and his wife, Bonita. The 130,785 square-foot, three-level arts complex contains the ASU Art Museum with five galleries, four open-air sculpture courts, a gift shop, print study room, administrative

▲ The last light of day plays perfect harmony with the Nelson Fine Arts Center's desert-inspired exterior color. ASU's Art Museum, Galvin Playhouse, and University Dance Laboratory are housed within the center.

offices, storage, and supporting services; the Paul V. Galvin Playhouse, which seats 483 and has five attached studio-rehearsal halls; and the 60-by-90-foot University Dance Laboratory, which has a resilient hardwood floor and seating for 200.

Each facility links to the others through imaginative connections. Predock says, "One of my biggest challenges was to bring the arts together in a way that was egalitarian and to symbolically fuse them."

Predock has designed museums in Albuquerque, Tacoma, Skidmore College, and the University of Wyoming, as well as a children's museum in Las Vegas. A visionary, he combines environmentally sensitive structures with a sometimes quirky classicism and a feel for the natural surroundings.

Predock had just returned from a semester as a fellow of the American Academy in Rome when he entered the ASU competition. He won the commission by defeating several other highly regarded architects. The American Institute of Architects favored him with its Honor Award, the profession's highest recognition for design excellence, in 1991.

Visitors to the ASU Art Museum — the largest component of the complex at 119,000 square feet — enter through a phalanx of palm trees, saguaro cactus, turned-concrete columns, and dish-shaped pedestal planters.

Inside the sheltered entry area, triple doorways open. One doorway leads to a plaza and, beyond, to the theater and dance laboratory. The others descend seemingly into the bowels of the Earth.

The concept by which one architectural element invites visitors to investigate the next element is called "processional," the key to Predock's design. He says, "I love the way that many desert temples in certain parts of the world have a processional quality, a feeling of architecture unfolding as you move through it. Rather than an easily comprehensible 'first-take' architecture, I want the architecture to be mysterious and enigmatic."

Predock terms the museum's cavern-like underground entry court a "nymphaeum." Featuring a pool and fountains, low benches, and free-standing sculptures, the nymphaeum leads to the lobby where every giggle and scuffle of touring school children reverberates from the polished sandstone floors and concrete-coffered ceilings. The architect defends this sub-terranean echo-chamber effect: "I want that space to feel hollow and very powerful."

The art museum's lower level holds two galleries, a gift shop, administrative offices, meeting rooms, and research and storage facilities. Art lovers reach upper-level galleries and sculpture gardens either by climbing long, stone stairways, broken by brief landings, or by an elevator. The exhibition halls have hardwood floors and birch millwork, and those on the upper stories receive filtered, natural daylight.

Founded in 1951, the ASU Art Museum houses an extensive early American art collection, craft art, a growing Latin American collection, and prints. Moving on, the playhouse and its adjoining dance laboratory involve still more sensory adventuring. Beyond the triple doorways and the central opening, visitors confront concrete bleachers arranged in the shape of a pyramid, which house an elevator. The grandstands can be climbed, sat upon, or bypassed altogether. The risers allow students to observe performances of music, dance, and theater on the plaza in front of the Galvin Playhouse.

Predock faced a challenge fitting both the art museum and the theater onto a con-stricted site and at the same time blending them with nearby buildings. Tenth Street and a vacant shopping center border the art center on the north, Mill Avenue on the west, the ASU Music Building on the south, and the established campus on the east.

The architect answered the challenge by placing an open plaza between the museum and theater. A curved, arched brick wall outside the entrance to the theater gives a nod to the rounded visage and materials of the music building and nearby Gammage Auditorium. The museum's blank north wall blocks out views of the shopping center and Tempe's downtown.

Not all of Predock's experiments can be judged a total success.

He stretched the theater's fly loft an additional 16 feet — to a total of 98 feet — hoping the museum staff would project films on the elevated surface. "I think of it as a kind of drive-in movie screen. Drive-in movies are an icon of the West, fast disappearing," he says. However, the tall wall mostly anchors banners announcing current shows.

Predock also converted four outdoor landings into sculpture "gardens." But the summer heat converts them into "hot boxes," uncomfortable spaces for contemplating art. But these are insignificant shortcomings.

Overall, the Nelson Center treats visitors to a memorable exercise in design discovery, one that includes tunnels and towers; 2-foot-thick ledges and dramatic drop-offs; pools, patios, and odd projections; glass-block window walls; references to the Sphinx and the great pyramids of ancient Egypt; the play of light and shadow sweeping serene courtyards and secluded passages; and even a stairway leading to nowhere.

■ **WHEN YOU GO** Located on the ASU main campus in Tempe, the center is on the southeast corner of 10th Street and Mill Avenue, one block north of Gammage Auditorium on the northeast corner of Apache and Mill avenues. Open Tuesday, 10 A.M. to 9 P.M.; Wednesday through Saturday, 10 A.M. to 5 P.M.; closed Sunday and Monday. Ground-level parking available north of the building, surrounding the Ceramics Research Center. (480) 965-2787.

ORPHEUM THEATRE

■ **LOCATION**	Phoenix
■ **YEAR BUILT**	1929
■ **STYLE**	Spanish Colonial Revival
■ **ARCHITECT**	Lescher and Mahoney
■ **SIGNIFICANCE**	Only remaining atmospheric-type theater in Arizona; fully restored / National Register of Historic Places, 1985

As the Roaring Twenties came to an end, vaudeville juggler and jokester acts still attracted audiences, but increasingly, fans clamored for talking films featuring glamorous movie stars like Gary Cooper and Gloria Swanson. On Jan. 5, 1929, Phoenix's Orpheum Theatre opened for business with the audience arriving by streetcar, Model T Ford, or on foot to experience the city's newest combination of traveling performances and Hollywood films.

The Orpheum's lavish exterior hinted at the marvels the public would discover inside. An ornate cornice displayed hand-carved statues of Pan and laughing/crying masks of Comedy and Tragedy; busts of Spanish conquistadors adorned its Balcony of the Dons; and a beacon of light from an eight-sided tower beckoned theatergoers.

The first-night crowd at the Orpheum Theatre knew they would be entertained by tap and ballet dancers, a Paramount Pictures newsreel, and 20-minute Movietone talking comedy shorts, along with the big sound of a Meisel-Sullivan organ. But patrons were about to be equally enthralled by an illusionary nightfall projected on the domed ceiling of the auditorium by a hidden magic-lantern machine. The display began with cumulus and nimbus clouds drifting lazily across a blue plaster sky. A golden sunset followed. The light show concluded with a colorful sunset fading gradually to the twinkling of a thousand stars.

The Orpheum is an atmospheric-style theater that surrounds audiences with a fantasy environment as compelling as the performances they come to watch on the stage or screen.

Atmospheric theaters titillated the public's imaginations with more than just cloud and constellation spectaculars. At the Orpheum, walls decorated with trailing vines, wrought iron railings, arched openings, and red-tiled roofs encircled the auditorium. These architectural stage sets promoted the illusion that the audience was participating in an open-air fete in the courtyard of a 16th-century Spanish villa.

Almost every inch of the Orpheum Theatre — from its richly painted and glazed peacock stairway to the carved, three-dimensional birds, grapes, and lizards — conspired to transport viewers from their everyday world to a far-away place where magical moments

▲ Audiences in the Orpheum Theatre watch clouds drifting overhead prior to each performance. The venue's stage, enhanced in the 1990s, can now mount Broadway musicals as well as provide a platform for civic ceremonies.

might unfold any minute. "It was escapism," says Don Stith, chair of the docent program at the theater.

Austrian-born architect-showman John Eberson, who invented the concept for the atmospheric theater, built spectacle houses all across America, including the Majestic in Houston (1923) and the Lowe's Theatre in Akron, Ohio (1929). Eberson said that in these spaces, "our fancy is free to conjure endless tales of romance." He added, "We visualize and dream a magnificent amphitheater, an Italian garden, a Persian court, a Spanish patio, or a mystic Egyptian temple yard, all canopied by a soft moonlit sky."

Lescher and Mahoney, the Phoenix firm hired to build the Orpheum Theatre, sent representatives to visit Eberson's creations so they could adapt his ideas to the theater. After building the Orpheum, their first major commercial commission, Lescher and Mahoney went on to complete more than 2,000 projects in Arizona, including Phoenix's original Good Samaritan, Memorial, and St. Joseph's hospitals and the Veterans Memorial Coliseum.

Theater-chain owners J.E. Rickards and Harry Nace invested $750,000 to build the Orpheum. The men put up the 1,800-seat theater to stage live vaudeville shows as well as to show Hollywood movies.

In late 1929, however, the Great Depression started. Vaudeville began to fade. Families moved from downtown to the suburbs. Eventually, television spelled the doom of large movie theaters as primary entertainment outlets.

The Orpheum Theatre building's gradual physical decline began as a series of well-intentioned owners failed to upgrade the facility for better sound and picture quality. In 1949, the Orpheum was sold and renamed the Paramount. Then, in 1968, James Nederland changed the name to Palace West and used it as a venue for Broadway productions. He put on *Cabaret*, *Annie*, and *The Best Little Whorehouse in Texas*, among others. But Nederland, too, became financially unable to keep the theater going. In 1977, he leased it to the Corona family to show Spanish-language films.

By the early 1980s, the theater faced real trouble. Roger Brevoort, former historic preservation planner with the City of Phoenix, remembers touring the Orpheum. He describes what he saw: "There were only three ropes [ornamental plaster columns framing the proscenium] out of the original seven left in the proscenium. The thing was musty and dingy. The murals had been painted black and everything else was a monochromatic green, so as not to detract from the movies. On the other hand, other than the proscenium, all the details were there. Not missing. Just muted with paint."

Real estate interests suggested demolishing the theater to make way for an office building. At that point, the Junior League of Phoenix inventoried downtown Phoenix's historic buildings and learned that the Orpheum was Arizona's last atmospheric theater and the only Phoenix theater classified as "theater-palace architecture" still left. Theater- (or movie-) palace architecture is ornate, heavily embellished, and very large. Other theater/movie palaces in Phoenix had once included the Rialto, the Palm, the Columbia, and the Fox; all were destroyed by the 1980s. Only the Orpheum remained.

The League deemed the Orpheum worth saving. Their strong support for restoration helped persuade the city to purchase the building in 1984. Listing on the National Register of Historic Places followed in 1985, and three years later, a $7-million bond election authorized enough funds to stabilize the theater and begin its renovation.

In 1990, city officials, in a crucial move, decided to build a new 20-story glass and steel city hall on Washington Street, directly behind the Orpheum Theatre. This meant that the theater could be wrapped, both physically and fiscally, into city hall construction plans, achieving substantial savings. For example, the central plant in the new city hall could supply the Orpheum's electrical, heating, and cooling needs. The two buildings could share a common wall and new loading dock, and each could face onto a common, landscaped plaza after the closing of Second Avenue. In addition, the Orpheum could expand its stage to 4,595 square feet from its original 2,676 square feet, making the stage large enough to mount most Broadway shows.

By agreeing to marry city hall and the theater, the city also quickened the pace of restoring and renovating the Orpheum.

The Cleveland-based firm of van Dijk, Pace, Westlake Architects had earlier drawn up plans

▲ Architectural detailing abounds throughout the theater. Here, a section of one of the decorative bands that arches over the proscenium shows rich patterning.

▲ A winding staircase allows theatergoers the opportunity to descend dramatically to the Orpheum's lobby during intermission.

for a four-phase rehabilitation, to be executed as money became available. Now the architects, who had extensive experience refurbishing historic buildings nationwide, got busy.

They relocated the lobby and box office into space once used for store fronts, added an elevator for handicapped access, enclosed the tower, re-raked the orchestra floor to provide better sight lines, and installed wider seats with more leg room on the first floor — even though this reduced the total number of seats from 1,800 to 1,400. (The original balcony seats have been refurbished.)

New lighting, acoustical, and air-conditioning systems went in. Ironically, in 1929 the theater's air-handling system had been considered state of the art. Huge blowers fitted with 12-foot fan blades pumped in outside air, spray-cleaned it, dried it, and then circulated the air through floor vents into the auditorium. Reportedly, this system changed the air in the audience chamber every three minutes. In the summer, employees placed blocks of ice under the seats so that the air blowing over the ice kept patrons reasonably cool even during the hottest months.

"This whole process has been a nice unfolding of stories," says Joan Weil, executive director of the Orpheum Theatre Foundation. "The Orpheum is really a treasure for the whole community."

The careful restoration and thoughtful rehabilitation of the Orpheum Theatre proved lengthy and expensive, but rewarding.

As might be expected, renovators found a few surprises. They uncovered the foundation for a swimming pool in the basement. Researchers think that perhaps the building initially was planned as an Elks Club. They also discovered an echo chamber in the exact center of the area called "The Room for Young Moderns," under the kissing couple medallions on the balcony level. Tricky acoustics magnify the voice of anyone standing there.

During the renovation, new fiberglass ropes replaced the missing proscenium ropes, which had been removed when the theater housed a Wonderama movie screen. By chance, workers found a scrap of the original, brightly colored carpeting and used it as a pattern for the carpeting now installed throughout the theater. The exquisitely detailed arches, niches, and columns, as well as the zodiac designs in the lobby door panels, all sport their former pristine look. Restorer Conrad Schmitt Studios of New Berlin, Wisconsin, removed the black paint hiding the auditorium's murals. The architects replaced the garish marquee with one consistent with a 1929 movie palace. A computer-controlled Wurlitzer theatre pipe organ, a substitution for the old Meisel-Sullivan organ, has been acquired, and an illusory nightfall once again transforms the ceiling prior to each performance.

Thirteen years and $14 million after the city bought the building, the historic Orpheum Theatre reopened on Jan. 28, 1997, as a multi-use performing arts center. Three entities now collaborate in operating the theater. The Phoenix Civic Plaza manages it with support from the Orpheum Theatre Foundation and Friends of the Orpheum. Bob Allen, general manager for the City of Phoenix theater division, now says, "The stage is one of the best equipped theaters in America."

■ **WHEN YOU GO** 203 W. Adams St. From Van Buren Street, take Central Avenue south to Adams Street; turn west on Adams and travel one block to the theater, which is on the south side of the street. Parking in Wells Fargo garage immediately east of theater; enter from First Street, south of Adams. Free, docent-led tours on Mondays except during the holidays. Meet at the theater under the marquee at 1:00 P.M. Information: (602) 534-5600. Box office (602) 262-7272. www.ci.phoenix.az.us/STAGES/orpheum.html

PINAL COUNTY COURTHOUSE (SECOND)

■ **LOCATION**	Florence
■ **YEAR BUILT**	1891
■ **STYLE**	American Victorian
■ **ARCHITECT**	James Miller Creighton
■ **SIGNIFICANCE**	American Victorian design touched by whimsy / National Register of Historic Places, 1978

Time stands still in Florence's 1891 Pinal County Courthouse. Morning, noon, and night, the clocks on the tower read 11:44. It seems officials ran short of funds when constructing the courthouse, so they cut costs by *painting* clock faces on the cupola rather than installing real timepieces.

The clocks' hands seem to point to 11:44, says John A. Swearengin, former Superior Court clerk and retired manager of McFarland State Historic Park, although a few people see the hands as reversed, which would make the time 8:48. Swearengin says that Phoenix architect James Miller Creighton confessed to setting the clocks at 11:44 so farmers would believe they had just enough time to conduct their business before the courthouse closed at noon for lunch.

Creighton must have had a fine time crafting Pinal County's second courthouse. Cheerful red scrolling contrasts with the flat white paint on the lintels over the windows and on the dormers peeking from the mansard roof. The perky porch repeats the red-and-white motif, and the grand stairway consumes a large portion of the first and second levels.

A closer look at the two-story brick courthouse with its distinctive tower reveals several design deceptions, in addition to the fake clocks. An artist's paintbrush actually created the *trompe l'oeil* curtains on the cupola windows, while green-tinted film applied to the window glass simulates drawn window shades.

Florence leaders decided to build a new courthouse to replace the 1877-78 Sonoran/Transitional-style adobe courthouse, which still stands, primarily because the old courthouse appeared inadequate to satisfy their optimistic view of the future.

Settlers had been flooding west since the Civil War, following the Gila Trail through Florence to seek their fortunes in California's gold fields. In 1875, prospectors discovered silver in the mountains 35 miles northeast of Florence and opened the rich Silver King Mine. Florence became an important supply and shipping center for the mines and the area's agriculture. That same year, Pinal County was named the sixth of Arizona's eventual 15 counties, with Florence selected as the county seat.

In addition, the railroad arrived in Tucson in 1880, introducing Eastern, Midwestern, and Californian building traditions, as well as newer construction techniques and materials. Adobe suddenly seemed outdated and primitive, while brick and the highly ornamented Victorian style looked smart and stylish. (The 1877-78 adobe courthouse, with its pitched, wood-shingle roof, later became a county hospital, from 1892 to 1930, and still stands as part of Florence's McFarland State Historic Park.)

Choosing Creighton as architect for the new courthouse signaled the town fathers' confidence that Florence would continue to prosper into the next century. Creighton was regarded as one of the Territory's premier architects. His projects included Old Main, the first building on the University of Arizona campus in Tucson (1887); the Dominion Hotel in Globe

KERRICK JAMES

▲ The Victorian-style Pinal County Courthouse was built to please townspeople who felt the town was outgrowing the original Sonoran-style adobe courthouse.

(1905); the first Adams Hotel in Phoenix (1896); and the U.S. Custom House in Nogales (1889). Although minimally trained as an architect — his formal instruction consisted of one drafting course — he had worked 12 years in the building trades.

Creighton began working on the design for the courthouse in tandem with two of Arizona's more colorful pioneers. The first, William C. Smith, ran a mercantile business in Florence and owned a local mine and ranch. Smith served as chairman of the Pinal County Board of Supervisors that oversaw the project. The second, A.J. Doran, general contractor with T.A. Adams, had a background that included acting as a millwright and bridge builder. He had also been elected Pinal County sheriff and served six terms in the Territorial legislature, twice as president. Doran built the first railroad turntable in San Francisco, a Florence school, and a mill for the Silver King Mining Co.

Florence's first brickyard had opened in 1886, and Creighton knew that buildings made of brick, rather than adobe, could better incorporate segmental-arched windows and doorways, timber-construction roofs, prefabricated components, and elaborate detailing. Best of all, the Victorian styling he chose would afford psychological comfort to transplants from the East moving to Florence. The Victorian style takes its name from Queen Victoria, who reigned over the British Empire from 1837 to 1901 and who had a fondness for ornate details like turrets, towers, fanciful brackets, and cornices.

In Creighton's design, the courthouse roughly resembled a cross with a modified rotunda at the intersection of the cross and a rounded end, or apse, defining the building's east side at the foot of the cross. The building had a steep, metal mansard roof with projecting gables, and a delicate *fronton*, or sunrise decoration, appeared above the second-story porch. When the 15,300-square-foot structure opened Feb. 2, 1891, it had cost $34,765, including $5,765 spent for the jail.

It housed the offices of the county assessor, recorder, treasurer, and supervisors, as well as the large, second-floor courtroom with the jail below it. Interior features included a redwood staircase, pressed-metal ceilings, wainscoting, hardwood floors, and a judge's bench and jury box in the courtroom. In 1891, wood-burning stoves provided heat, and illumination came from kerosene lights. Bathroom facilities were located outside.

Five additions have significantly altered the shape and functionality of the courthouse, giving the building its current rectangular configuration.

In 1917, workers filled in the courthouse's northwest and southwest corners on the first and second floors, converting it from a cross into a T-shape. The northeast corner was filled in on the first floor in 1933. Workers added in 1975 the rooms that now form the one-story north facade. Six years later, a one-story addition filled in the building's southwest corner and an air conditioner enclosure was added to the original south wall.

Today the courthouse's total area covers about 24,500 square feet, excluding the clock tower and a small basement under the rotunda. The bricks on the addition to the west wall don't quite match the original bricks, and the bricks in later additions differ considerably from those used in 1891 — some are even painted. Fortunately, workmen faithfully copied the building's original detailing in later additions, thereby retaining the courthouse's Victorian character.

Swearengin and others have written several books recounting the colorful early days of the region. The second Pinal County Courthouse often provided a backdrop for much of the drama, especially after the Territorial prison was moved to Florence from Yuma in 1909. It was here flirtatious amateur stage coach bandit Pearl Hart was tried and acquitted in 1899. The not-guilty verdict upset Judge Fletcher M. Doan, since Hart's incompetent partner in crime, Joe Boot, had already pled guilty and received a sentence of 30 years in the Yuma Territorial Prison. Judge Doan believed Hart had unduly influenced the jury with her feminine wiles and impaneled a new jury to try her on the charge of stealing the stage driver's gun. Swearengin writes in his book, *Good Men, Bad Men, Lawmen and a Few Rowdy Ladies*, "This jury, lacking the chivalry of the former and perhaps not wanting to face the contempt of Judge Doan, brought in a verdict of 'guilty.' Pearl was sentenced to five years in the Yuma prison." Hart later received a pardon after becoming pregnant in prison.

Florence's leaders circa 1891 had been overly optimistic in projecting the town's growth. Instead of producing fabulous wealth, as residents hoped, the local silver mines played out. After the railroad arrived in Phoenix and Tucson in the late 1880s, helping create boom towns to the north and south, newcomers began bypassing Florence. Even the weather failed to cooperate during that decade, alternating droughts with floods and making agriculture problematic.

Today's dominant industry in Florence is catering to the needs of between 8,000 and 10,000 prisoners inhabiting the nearby state-run and privately operated prisons, with agriculture ranking second. Tourism ranks third, as visitors enjoy touring the town's historic district with its many old homes, churches, and businesses.

Now that the 1891 courthouse no longer houses the jail or sheriff's office, and no legal proceedings transpire there, government officials ponder new uses for the building.

Happily, Florence's leadership considers the colorful courthouse among the town's most irreplaceable historic properties. A proposal has been made to strip the courthouse of its additions and return it to its original state, but for now, the building doesn't look past 11:44. Or, perhaps, 8:58.

■ **WHEN YOU GO** Twelfth and Pinal streets, Pinal County Complex. In Florence, drive south to East Butte Avenue. Turn west on East Butte Avenue to North Pinal Street, then head north on Pinal Street to 12th Street. Open during regular government office hours. Self-guided tours only. Florence Chamber of Commerce (520) 868-9433 or (800) 437-9433. www.florenceaz.org

ROSSON HOUSE/HISTORIC HERITAGE SQUARE

■ **LOCATION**	Phoenix
■ **YEARS BUILT**	1895-1929; 1980
■ **STYLE**	Rosson House, Eastlake Victorian; Silva, Stevens, Stevens-Haugsten, and Bouvier-Teeter houses, bungalows; other buildings, varied styles
■ **ARCHITECTS**	A.P. Petit, Rosson House; Robert Frankeberger, Lath House Pavilion
■ **SIGNIFICANCE**	Only homes left from the original Phoenix town site / National Register of Historic Places (Rosson House, 1971; Phoenix Town Site Historic District, 1978)

When the handsome Dr. Roland Lee Rosson married beautiful Flora B. Murray in 1880, friends expected big things from the union, and they were not disappointed.

A graduate of the University of Virginia and a former Army surgeon, Dr. Rosson practiced medicine in Phoenix, while Flora Murray belonged to a prosperous family that dealt in livestock. He proved politically astute enough to be elected Coroner, Public Administrator, and Treasurer of Maricopa County and then mayor of Phoenix. She showed a head for business after their marriage by purchasing an entire city block in the original Phoenix town site for $1,000.

On three of the lots, the Rossons built the finest house in Phoenix — a stylish, 10-room Victorian home featuring pressed-metal ceilings, an elaborately carved oak staircase, and elegant parquet floors. The couple lived there only briefly, renting the house during the winter to Whitelaw Reid, editor of the *New York Tribune* and later U.S. ambassador to Britain. Reid needed a dry climate to relieve his asthma.

Reid offered a good firsthand look at Phoenix as it appeared in the 1890s, writing:

"The place is a curious mixture of modern convenience and the crudities of a frontier town. Indians and cowboys pass our doors every hour, and the town has its full share of gambling dens, liquor shops and the other accompaniments of a mining camp. On the other hand, I have rarely been in a community where the churches were better attended, or where there was less public disorder. One policeman serves for a whole town of 10,000 inhabitants, and the [unpaved] streets are much quieter than those of Harlem."

He found the Rosson House pleasing as well:

"We are calmly settled in a brick house two and a half stories high with a basement, extremely well built, and finished as elaborately as such a house would be in Orange or Mt. Vernon, or any of the suburbs of New York. It has hot and cold water, a porcelain bathtub (or an excellent imitation of one), the electric light in every room, a telephone in the back hall, and lines of trolley cars within two or three blocks on either side."

After his first winter in Phoenix in 1895, Reid wrote that his doctors "have given me a clean bill of health." He took the house again in November 1896, complaining only that the kitchen was so small "my cook could hardly get on."

GEORGE STOCKING

▲ Although the carefully maintained house bears the family name, the Rossons lived in the Victorian-era structure only briefly before departing for California.

In 1897, the Rossons sold their home and moved to Los Angeles with their four children. A year later, Dr. Rosson died of gastroenteritis, a stomach disorder, and the story goes that his widow used the insurance from his death and profits from her real estate ventures to build yet another gracious house in California.

Phoenix's original town site included 320 acres bordered by today's Seventh Street, Seventh Avenue, and Van Buren and Harrison streets. Settlers subdivided it into 98 blocks. In 1882, Flora Rosson bought fashionable Block 14, between Sixth and Seventh and Monroe and Adams streets, which contained 10 lots. Sixteen years later, the *1898 Phoenix Directory* estimated Phoenix's population at about 12,800, "exclusive of Chinese and Indians."

Today, all of Block 14 and the northern portion of Block 15 form the Heritage Square Historic District, owned by the City of Phoenix. Heritage Square contains a total of 10 historic structures built between 1881 and 1929, as well as the prize-winning Lath House Pavilion, built in 1980.

The Rosson House serves as the cornerstone of Heritage Square. Designed by Alexander P. Petit, the house exemplifies Eastlake Victorian style, which takes its name from Queen Victoria and English architectural critic and historian Charles L. Eastlake. Eastlake's book, *Hints on Household Taste in Furniture, Upholstery and Other Details,* became a best-seller in the late 1800s, offering homeowners tips for furnishing their homes tastefully.

The Rosson House features a vertical thrust, wrap-around verandah sporting lathe-worked posts and spindles, four main gables with pierced bargeboards and screen work, and a prominent turret.

French Victorian styling influenced the tower, which is octagonal rather than round, with elaborate finial and spool-like decoration. France's Loire Valley chateaux also influenced the metal cresting on the roof ridges, while the home's turret windows, with their hood molds and straight-sided arches, borrow from Victorian Italianate styling. In the interior, the tall ceilings and strong sense of enclosure typify High Victorian design.

Petit, 74 years old when he designed the Rosson House, had established his reputation in San Francisco, where "painted lady" Victorian houses abound. In Phoenix, he chose to build with brick, rather than adobe, the construction material used in earlier dwellings in the area. Petit died around the time of the Rosson House's completion.

After the Rossons left for California, the house went through a succession of owners, finally deteriorating into a rooming house. When Phoenix realized that Block 14 contained the last surviving residences from the original town site, the city acquired the Rosson House in 1974 to turn it into a house museum.

The Rosson House, which took six months and $7,525 to build in 1895, required more than six years and $750,000 to restore. Workers painstakingly scraped off the wallpaper and had fragments from the bottom layer reproduced by Scalamandre and Waterhouse; they lifted the old linoleum to reveal beautiful parquet flooring and restored it; and they repainted the pressed-metal ceilings following a microscopic analysis to discover the original paint colors.

Finally, experts furnished the home with an eclectic mix of furniture appropriate to the period. Objects ranged from fine hair-work wreaths to an Eastlake parlor organ and medical instruments Dr. Rosson might have used to treat patients. Unfortunately, the Rossons' original furniture could not be located.

The other Block 14 houses, most of which offer fine examples of bungalow styling, have been put to good use as restaurants, a coffeehouse, a tearoom, a small museum, the offices of the Rosson House-Heritage Square Foundation, and the ticket office for the Rosson House.

The 22,800-square-foot Lath House Pavilion, built in 1980, provides an open-air community meeting space. Its design combines popular 19-century concepts like a botanical conservatory, gazebo, and beer garden, and it can shelter 1,000 people for sit-down dinners and concerts. Made of wood telephone poles, beams, and lath, it provides welcome shade during Phoenix's hot summers. In 1982, the Lath House won a coveted American Institute of Architects Honor Award.

The Rosson House restoration resulted from a broad community preservation effort. Supporters included the Arizona Society of Professional Engineers, Junior League of Phoenix, Arizona Institute of Architects, American Society of Interior Designers, Heritage Square Guild, and others, including former Phoenix Mayor John Driggs. Block 14's rescued and recycled residences, now part of the city's Heritage & Science Park, give visitors an opportunity to peek into the city's residential past.

■ **WHEN YOU GO** From Seventh and Washington streets in Phoenix, go one block north to Monroe Street. Turn west on Monroe and go a half block to the parking garage on the south side of the street. The Rosson House is just east of the parking garage. (602) 262-5071. Tours Wednesday through Saturday, 10 A.M. to 3:30 P.M.; Sunday, 12 P.M. to 3:30 P.M. Closed Monday and Tuesday. Entrance fee. www.rossonhousemuseum.org

SAHUARO RANCH

■ **LOCATION**	Glendale
■ **YEARS BUILT**	1887-1929
■ **STYLE**	Adobe house, Anglo Sonoran; main and guest houses, Victorian; packing shed, Territorial
■ **ARCHITECTS**	Joseph Lyman Silsbee, guest house; James M. Creighton, packing shed and north wing of main house; adobe house architect unknown
■ **SIGNIFICANCE**	Among the oldest and best-preserved ranches in the Salt River Valley / National Register of Historic Places, 1980

In 1898, 12 years after William Henry Bartlett had filed a claim for land near Phoenix, he brought his family to Arizona in a private railroad car, hoping to save his younger son, William Jr. (known as Willie), from the ravages of tuberculosis. In an era before antibiotics, doctors prescribed bed rest and a change of scenery — often in the Arizona desert — to help TB patients recuperate.

A wealthy Chicago stock and grain trader, Bartlett had homesteaded a 640-acre ranch, dubbed Rancho del Sahuaro, or Sahuaro Ranch after the saguaro cactus, 2 miles north of present-day Glendale. The 1877 Desert Lands Act allowed settlers to file for a section of land (one square mile, or 640 acres), provided they cleared, irrigated, and built upon it. The price was cheap — 25 cents per acre to file a claim, plus an additional dollar an acre three years after the owners had complied with the requirements — a total of $800.

Bartlett filed a claim for Section 30 in 1886 and purchased the water rights in 1887. He knew that the Arizona Canal, which carried water from the Verde and Salt rivers to the vicinity of Glendale, had been completed in 1885. Bartlett persuaded his brother-in-law, Stephen W. Campbell, a banker who suffered from poor health, to travel to Arizona and act as ranch

▲ Thanks to water brought to areas west of Phoenix by the Arizona Canal, successive owners of Rancho del Sahuaro have seen the formerly arid desert land produce a variety of crops.

superintendent. The men thought working outdoors might help Campbell recover. Campbell built a 416-square-foot adobe home that featured low ceilings, a broad verandah, and wood floors. And he planted fig, pear, naval orange, peach, apricot, and olive trees on the property.

With the land cleared, planted, and improved, Bartlett could take title to the ranch and begin turning the desert into a lush, lucrative landscape. Ever the wily businessman, Bartlett planned to ship his fruit back East, beating California growers to the market (their produce ripened later) and realizing a handsome profit on his investment.

First, though, he had to construct a drying and fruit-packing shed, as well as the superintendent's residence. Bartlett chose Phoenix's best-known architect, James M. Creighton, to create a state-of-the-art packing shed made of brick and measuring 40 by 80 feet. Without refrigeration, Bartlett realized, his tree-ripened fruit would spoil unless it could be dried before shipping. Creighton's design for the drying and packing shed called for construction of three air-tight "sweat" rooms, and a "fly-proof" packing area, protected from insects by screens and heavy wooden shutters. An airshaft ventilated the interior, and a wide porch provided space for the employees to gather the fruit and stack the packed boxes awaiting shipment. Workers made and fired the bricks on site, completing the shed in 1891.

In 1895, Bartlett built a one-and-a-half-story brick house for Harry W. Adams, the second superintendent at Sahuaro Ranch; Campbell, the first superintendent, had died at age 36 in 1890. While Adams managed the ranch, it boasted more than 250 acres of orchards, 80 acres of vineyards, and 270 acres of alfalfa and grain. Adams also planted a row of stately palm trees, which lined the ranch's entrance road. The so-called "main house" boasted indoor plumbing, then a rarity. Architect Creighton designed the north wing of the main house, also known as the "ranch office," but researchers are uncertain who designed the rest of the house.

By this time, the Bartlett ranch had become known as a showplace of the valley, and Bartlett and his wife decided to bring son Willie to Arizona because of his TB. The senior Bartlett gave his staff just 72 days to build a guest house to accommodate the family and their servants.

"I think he was a hard-headed businessman," says Carole DeCosmo, executive director of the Sahuaro Ranch Foundation, which manages Historic Sahuaro Ranch for the City of Glendale. "He held the purse strings, and everyone did what he wanted done."

Workmen finished the seven-bedroom, five-bathroom brick guest house, with its 12-foot ceilings and full basement, on time. Designed by Joseph Lyman Silsbee of Chicago who, incidentally, once employed a young architect named Frank Lloyd Wright, the guest house had no kitchen or dining room; the Bartletts planned to use the adjacent main house for cooking and eating.

The Bartletts and their three children moved in — along with Willie's doctor, a Chinese cook, a butler, and several maids, for a total of 13 persons — to spend the winter of 1898-99. The following April, the Bartletts' daughter, Mary, married Charles W. Case Deering in the Sahuaro Ranch rose garden, the social event of the season.

A genial and cultivated host, Bartlett offered guests the use of his library, gramophone, hunting dogs, horses, romantic lily pond with gazebo and bridge, and golf course — with polo ponies substituting as golf carts.

"This was a man who always wore fresh violets in his buttonhole. He had them shipped in," DeCosmo says.

Prominent citizens who visited the ranch during Bartlett's tenure included Robert Todd Lincoln, son of President Lincoln, and Marshall Field, of department store fame.

By late spring, Willie's health had improved enough that Bartlett could switch his attention to other business ventures. He spent from 1900 to 1902 negotiating the purchase of a 205,000-acre ranch near Vermejo, New Mexico. Bartlett may have realized that the prospects for Sahuaro Ranch had dimmed. The ranch suffered a disastrous flood in 1895. Then a drought from 1898 through 1900 killed most of the fruit trees, grapevines, and citrus orchards, causing Adams to change to growing barley, wheat, oats, cotton, and peanuts, as well as to herding cattle.

Bartlett sold Sahuaro Ranch in 1913. He died in 1918 of heart problems in Raton, New Mexico. His older son, Norman Williams Bartlett, died the next September, and Willie succumbed Jan. 5, 1920. A foreman at the Vermejo Ranch mourned, "They had ever'thin' they was to have, and they did ever'thin' they was to do; then they all up and died."

Sahuaro Ranch bounced from owner to owner until 1927, when Richard W. Smith and his wife, Lottie Sands Smith, bought 320 acres of what was left of the original 640 acres. By this time, the Salt River Valley Water Users Association had formed (1903) and built Roosevelt Dam (1911), assuring farmers and ranchers of an adequate supply of water year in and year out. The Smiths farmed Sahuaro Ranch for the next 50 years, planting pecan, citrus, and date palm groves for commercial harvesting and operating a dairy farm of Jersey cows.

"The Smiths were a good, solid Glendale family," DeCosmo says. "They were from Manistee, Michigan, and heard about the availability of the property from her father, Louis Porter Sands, who owned property here in Glendale. They came here to live."

The Smiths made several changes to the ranch buildings, most notably removing a pull-down stairway in the main house, which Lottie Smith disliked so much she refused to view the upstairs prior to buying the house. The Smiths replaced the stairway with a fine staircase, converted the three first-floor bedrooms into a living room, and added a wide, brick fireplace and central heating.

Richard W. Smith died in 1944, leaving the ranch to his son, Richard S. Smith. The younger Smith bred thoroughbred horses and operated the ranch until 1977, when he sold 80 acres to the City of Glendale, which set aside most of it as a park, with 17 acres devoted to Historic Sahuaro Ranch.

The ranch contains 14 old buildings, parts of the original irrigation system, corrals, and portions of the citrus, date, olive, and pecan orchards. Historic Sahuaro Ranch operates a full-blown educational program introducing young and old to some of the life experiences known to central Arizona pioneers — shoeing a horse, stitching a quilt, tasting freshly plucked carrots, and weaving a blanket.

Buildings on view, in addition to the packing shed (now an art gallery), include the restored main house and guest house; a blacksmith shop with a forge; a horse barn and tack house built in the 1890s; a foreman's house, garage, and pump house built between 1900 and 1932; a scale house for weighing cattle; a mill and granary; a hay shed; and an auto-maintenance shed completed between 1930 and the 1970s.

William Henry Bartlett would be pleased to see what has become of his Rancho del Sahuaro. The rose garden displays more than 1,000 rose bushes. And the Sahuaro Ranch Foundation has planted peach, pear, and fig trees. Although peacocks appeared in photographs during the Bartletts' years on the ranch, the two peahens and a peacock that Lottie Smith brought back from the 1933 Chicago World's Fair formed the nucleus of the flock currently roaming the grounds, which at times has numbered 150 birds.

The National Register of Historic Places notation reads, "the structures remaining are all evidences of the settlement pattern of a homestead from its beginning as a desert land to its reclamation as an agricultural ranch."

DeCosmo says, "Everything here is a museum. This is unique. There's nothing else like it in Arizona. And it's all preserved."

■ **WHEN YOU GO** 9802 N. 59th Ave. From central Phoenix, take Grand Avenue northwest to 59th Avenue. Turn north on 59th Avenue to Mountain View Road (halfway between Olive and Peoria avenues. Turn west on Mountain View to the ranch. Grounds open 6 A.M. to sunset daily. Buildings closed end of May to beginning of October. Building tours Wednesday through Friday, 10 A.M. to 4 P.M.; Sunday, 12 P.M. to 4 P.M. (623) 930-4203. www.sahuaroranch.org

SAN MARCOS HOTEL

■ **LOCATION**	Chandler
■ **YEARS BUILT**	1912-13
■ **STYLE**	Mission Revival
■ **ARCHITECT**	Arthur Burnett Benton
■ **SIGNIFICANCE**	Epitome of Dr. Chandler's town plan and site of the state's first all-grass, 18-hole golf course / National Register of Historic Places, 1982

Arizona golfers had two courses to choose from in the early 1900s. They could tee off from a dirt "fairway" and putt on "greens" made of oiled sand and cottonseed meal, or they could play real grass links at the San Marcos Hotel in Chandler.

Dr. Alexander J. Chandler opened Arizona's first 18-hole golf course, seeded with Bermuda grass, in 1914 as part of a posh hotel he built in 1912-13 southeast of Phoenix. Chandler hoped his hotel would attract buyers to a proposed development in what is now the city of Chandler.

Trained as a veterinary surgeon, Alexander Chandler entered the development game by buying 80 acres south of Mesa in 1891 and then expanding his holdings to 18,000 acres. In May 1912, he opened a sales office in the budding community that then consisted of three shacks, a dining hall, and a grocery store. The first day of business, 300 speculators put up $50,000 for small ranch sites.

The entrepreneur chose Californian Arthur Burnett Benton to design the San Marcos Hotel. Considered a prime example of an integrated Mission Revival building — meaning its

MARK VINSON

▲ **The San Marcos Hotel, one of the earliest cast-in-place concrete hotels in Arizona, has arched segmented windows and entries, flat roofs with parapet battlements, and Tuscan columns supporting the heavy timber trellises.**

architectural elements are structural and not "pasted on" for effect — the $250,000 hotel had a lobby, dining room, ballroom, shops, offices, and 35 guest rooms.

Chandler launched his resort with a rooftop dinner party for 500 on Nov. 22, 1913. Notable guests included U.S. Vice President Thomas Marshall, Arizona Gov. George Hunt, and Arizona Congressman Carl Hayden.

The hotel experienced instant success, drawing many of Hollywood's elite, as well as notables like Christian Dior and Herbert Hoover.

The San Marcos later added bungalows and more rooms, shops, and amenities, often enticing visitors to stay for months.

Recent owners, however, bulldozed the 1930s-era bungalows and remodeled the original guest rooms into meeting space and communications centers.

The San Marcos now boasts 30,000 square feet of meeting and banquet space, 295 guest rooms, and a ballroom. A PGA-approved golf course, set amid huge salt cedar trees and ponds, remains the chief lure for players addicted to the sport.

As the good doctor planned, the San Marcos has played a pivotal role in Chandler's development.

■ **WHEN YOU GO** 1 San Marcos Place. Chandler is southeast of Phoenix, via U.S. Route 60 and State Loop 101 (the Price Freeway). Take the Chandler Boulevard exit, drive east to Arizona Avenue, turn south to Buffalo Street, then turn west to the San Marcos entrance. (877) 766-3387 or (480) 812-0900. www.sanmarcosresort.com

TALIESIN WEST

■ **LOCATION**	Scottsdale
■ **YEARS BUILT**	1937-59
■ **STYLE**	Organic
■ **ARCHITECT**	Frank Lloyd Wright
■ **SIGNIFICANCE**	Wright's architectural school, winter home, and testing ground for his theories / National Historic Landmark; National Register of Historic Places, 1974

What makes Taliesin West so special? Why do people from all walks of life and around the world make pilgrimages to see this building complex of rock, concrete, and canvas?

Otto Kort of Breda, Holland, had two personal objectives in mind when he took a business trip to Phoenix: visit the Grand Canyon, one of the world's great natural wonders, and tour Taliesin West.

"I like the architecture of Frank Lloyd Wright," the Dutch business development manager confessed as he waited in line to tour Taliesin West. "To my mind, he's the father figure for modern architecture."

Kort is among an estimated 130,000 people who arrive each year eager to tour Wright's winter home, architectural school, and studio; Taliesin West ranks among the 25 most-visited historic house museums in the nation, according to the *Almanac of Architecture & Design 2001*. While these visitors know Wright as the most famous American architect of the 20th century, their visit may introduce details they didn't know. Wright invented or popularized the carport, desert masonry, organic architecture, the wraparound window, the idea of

▲ At Taliesin West, mature landscaping and a water feature work with the architecture to create a nature-centered environment.

extending the indoors outdoors, and the principle of "breaking the box."

In 1937, when Wright and his third wife moved from Spring Green, Wisconsin, home of his original Taliesin, to winter in the rugged, unspoiled location in the foothills of the McDowell Mountains, he was already architecturally accomplished. The 70-year-old had completed his highly regarded Prairie School designs — the Robie House in Oak Park, Illinois; the Larkin Building in Buffalo; and Midway Gardens in Chicago. He also had conceived a seismic design strategy that allowed the Imperial Hotel in Tokyo, Japan, to survive a severe earthquake (although a wrecking crew later demolished the hotel to make way for economic development).

Wright discovered the desert near Phoenix while becoming involved with the construction of the Arizona Biltmore. Wright met Dr. Alexander Chandler, an Arizona developer, who recruited him to design a resort for Chandler's future namesake city. The 1929 stock market crash ended that prospect, but during preliminary discussions, Wright and his apprentices cobbled together temporary quarters they called the Ocatillo [sic] Desert Camp. Presaging the future Taliesin West, the camp consisted of board and batten boxes roofed with white canvas triangles. Meanwhile, Wright had time to fall in love with the desert.

Then in 1937, Wright announced that he, wife Olgivanna, and his student-apprentices, known collectively as the Taliesin Fellowship, would henceforth winter in Arizona. At Taliesin West, he said, they would build a desert camp to implement his theories of "organic architecture." By organic, Wright meant that each piece of a building should relate to the entire structure and that the architecture as a whole should draw inspiration from its natural surroundings.

A tour of Taliesin West shows how Wright's Western facility stayed true to these concepts. He chose a remote, affordable site — then 13 miles from the nearest town (Scottsdale) — so he and his associates could live close to nature. Earlier, he located the Wisconsin Taliesin in a rural area just below the crest of a hill. He called it "Taliesin," which in Welsh means "shining brow," as a tribute to his family heritage.

Low and unobtrusive, the buildings at Taliesin West have sloping walls and upturned beams that echo the shapes of the mountains behind them, while the wide walkways, open terraces, and vegetation nestled against the buildings mimic the broad swath of desert and streambeds spread across the valley below.

The key building material consists of large boulders that Wright directed his apprentices to drag to the site. Wright showed the students how to assemble wooden forms and set the rocks inside the forms — flat sides facing out — then to secure the rocks with a concrete made of portland cement mixed with the local coarse desert sand. With the forms removed, the rustic results are called desert masonry.

Wright favored using redwood at Taliesin West because of its low cost, durability, and easy availability at the time. Simple white canvas stretched across redwood frames served as roofing, allowing the light to filter inside but eliminating glare and protecting the occupants from occasional rainstorms and the heat of the sun. Canvas also conformed to Wright's image of a camp made of tents pitched in the open. Most of the structures sat directly on the desert floor with the hard caliche surface as a foundation.

In describing his plan for Taliesin West, Wright wrote:

"I was struck by the beauty of the desert, by the dry, clear sun-drenched air, by the geometry of the mountains, the entire region was an inspiration in strong contrast to the lush, pastoral landscape of my native Wisconsin.... The design sprang out of itself, with no precedent and nothing following it."

Wright's philosophy of "breaking the box" meant that a few large, uncluttered interior spaces — as opposed to many small, enclosed rooms — would better accommodate multiple uses in a single area and avoid feelings of claustrophobia. He advocated the easy flow of traffic from one space to another — when possible, eliminating hallways and room dividers. He preferred built-in furnishings, and often attached benches, tables, and storage cabinets of his own design to the wall. When he could find a willing client, Wright even created light fixtures and dinnerware he thought suitable for the project.

Early on, Taliesin West's large, unwalled pavilions, like the drafting room and garden room, incorporated his preference to connect the indoors and the outdoors, both visually and in actuality. Massive stone piers supported the roofs, leaving the space between the piers open, except for canvas flaps. With the flaps tied back, students could walk in and out without obstruction.

Later, Olgivanna persuaded her husband to substitute glass, or layers of acrylic over canvas, for the original fabric panels. Besides the dust, she objected to the rattlesnakes and scorpions that — along with students — felt free to enter and exit at will.

Visually, Wright linked a building's inside and outside by extending the interior flooring through window walls onto the patio and by stretching interior beams to support the outside roof overhangs.

Wright and his apprentices continued tinkering with and remodeling the Taliesin complex until his death in 1959. Improvisation and experimentation were an education unto themselves, he said.

Wright expected fellowship members to design, build, and live in their own primitive habitations in the desert during their first year of residency. Apprentices also learned con-

▲ Rocks, a material favored by Frank Lloyd Wright, figure prominently in the design of a terrace at his formerly isolated desert compound.

RICHARD MAACK

▲"Breaking the box," one of Wright's design tenets, holds that small, enclosed rooms invite claustrophobia, while open, uncluttered interior space accommodates many different uses.

struction skills, farming, gardening, cooking, cleaning, music-making, and even dancing and singing, by doing.

In 1949, Wright wrote in an essay published by *Arizona Highways* magazine, "We've had fun building our unique camp and more than fun living in it. We have found culture by way of it. Meantime — man, boy and girl — we've all learned a helluva lot by practice. . . . We have managed to stay here on the Desert contented for five or six months of every year for 11 years now, planning, playing, working, singing, dreaming — all to pretty good purpose."

Taliesin West encompasses about 45,000 square feet of enclosed or covered areas, divided among some nine buildings, courtyards, and complexes, on approximately 600 acres — for which Wright paid $60 an acre — at the base of the McDowell Mountains.

The first building that visitors usually see on tour is Wright's office. Its translucent roof, supported by deep, exposed beams of wood and steel, rests atop sloping stone and concrete walls. From the office, a broad, concrete terrace fans in a southeast-northwest direction to become the compound's principal axis.

The next group of interconnected buildings forms the core of the complex. It includes a 30- by 96-foot drafting studio with a fireplace at one end and a storage vault for drawings at the other. The building lies next to a pantry, dining area, and breezeway. A second floor above the dining area contains an apartment and other rooms, as well as a terrace that overlooks the valley to the south and west. Another apartment sits a half level down from the dining area.

The sunset terrace steps down gradually to the west in an arrangement of lawn, rock walls, and a pool, with a focal point that Wright described as "the prow of a ship."

On the east, the sunset terrace faces the garden room — the showpiece of Taliesin West — and the Wright family's living quarters. The entrance has a low ceiling with a desert masonry wall leading to a 56-foot-long room dominated by a huge fireplace at one end. A secluded formal dining area at the opposite end of the garden room connects to a bar, bathroom, pantry, and kitchen.

Wright designed all the furniture, except for the grand pianos, including chairs with tent-flap arms, hexagonal tables, and hassocks on rollers. White throw rugs cover the red-stained concrete floor. Light floods into the space by day through a translucent roof and rows of windows. The living quarters that Olgivanna occupied after his death adjoin the garden room at right angles.

Later construction added the apprentice court, with student apartments, a swimming pool, showers, and rest rooms for the apprentices living in the desert.

Taliesin West serves as the headquarters for the Frank Lloyd Wright Foundation, a non-profit corporation that he set up to run both Taliesin properties and his archives. The foundation also runs an accredited architectural school, admitting approximately 35 students who alternate seasonally between the two Taliesin campuses.

Peter Drake, an urban planner from Phoenix, says of Taliesin West: "As a site, [it] demonstrates that architecture can be much more than utilitarian shelter — that it can be a delightful and deeply satisfying interaction of materials, form, space, water, vegetation, and light. Taliesin, possibly more so than any other structure in the American Southwest, grows out of and is an integral part of its desert environment."

■ **WHEN YOU GO** 12621 N. Frank Lloyd Wright Blvd. From downtown Phoenix, take State Loop 202 east to State Loop 101. Go north about 8 miles on Loop 101 to the Shea Boulevard exit, then east on Shea to Frank Lloyd Wright Boulevard, then north on Wright. The entrance is at the intersection with Cactus Road. Open seven days a week; closed major holidays. Numerous scheduled tours available, including special nighttime and apprentice-led tours. Entrance fee. Information (480) 860-8810; reservations (480) 860-2700, ext. 494/495. wwwfranklloydwright.org

TEMPE MUNICIPAL BUILDING

■ **LOCATION**	Tempe
■ **YEAR BUILT**	1970
■ **STYLE**	Modern
■ **ARCHITECT**	Michael & Kemper Goodwin, Ltd.
■ **SIGNIFICANCE**	Emblem of a progressive community; sparked renewal of downtown

Some feared that Tempe's proposed city hall, shaped like an upside-down pyramid, would topple over in the first windstorm. Others worried that maintenance crews couldn't wash the outward-leaning windows and that employees wouldn't be able to hang pictures or drapes on walls made of glass.

But in the late 1960s, with foreign oil-producing countries threatening to turn off their oil taps, Americans had begun to feel a pressing need to save energy. Architect Michael Goodwin, of Michael & Kemper Goodwin Ltd., persuaded a reluctant city council to approve his unusual design because the structure would be self-shading and, therefore, energy thrifty.

Goodwin says he conceived the idea for the design after Mayor Elmer Bradley asked that offices for elected officials and the city manager be located on the top floor, while

▲ A concrete stair tower adjoins the three-story glass polyhedron-shaped municipal building that proclaims Tempe a forward-thinking city.

support staff and people-oriented services occupy the lower floors in order to make them handy to the public.

The inverted pyramid solution occurred to Goodwin when he awoke early and took a shower. Mulling possible building types, he remembered a design that had outward tilted columns at its lower levels because of its restricted site. Goodwin began tracing the outlines of such a structure in the condensation on his shower door. He realized an upside-down pyramid met the mayor's parameters. The next day, Goodwin showed a rough sketch of his concept to an associate architect, Rolf Osland. He says Osland exclaimed, "I think you've done it!"

Sure enough, when the Tempe Municipal Building opened in 1970 on its small (300-square-foot) site, the three-story, glass-and-steel pyramid acted like an umbrella protecting administrators in the main structure, as well as the below-grade courtyard and adjacent offices, from the summer sun. The building's sturdy steel frame supports thick panes of glass engineered for flexibility, heat and cold tolerance, and withstanding the forces of gravity. "You can safely throw a hammer against it," Goodwin says, though he adds that he doesn't recommend that.

At its base, the pyramid measures 45 feet on each of four sides. Walls extend at a 45-degree angle to a roof measuring 120 feet per side. A connecting concrete tower contains a stairway so occupants can escape, smoke-free, in case of fire.

In addition to being environmentally friendly, the building offers political advantages. First, Tempe's council likes to boast of a progressive, forward-looking community; the city hall certainly makes an avant-garde statement.

Second, its location downtown, rather than in the suburbs, sparked an urban renewal effort that transformed the downtown — luring pedestrians by the hundreds of thousands to crowded shops, restaurants, festivals, and street fairs. It serves, in Goodwin's words, as a "lantern to the city."

The architect admits he gave the building its formal name. "You can blame me for calling it the Tempe Municipal Building. I didn't want people talking about fighting city hall."

■ **WHEN YOU GO** 31 E. Fifth St. In Tempe, take Mill Avenue to Fifth Street, then turn east. Open during regular government office hours, Monday through Friday. Tours can be arranged through the mayor's office, (480) 350-8905.

TOVREA CASTLE	
■ **LOCATION**	Phoenix
■ **YEARS BUILT**	1928-30
■ **STYLE**	Vernacular interpretation of a medieval Italian castle
■ **BUILDER**	Alessio Carraro
■ **SIGNIFICANCE**	Eye-catching centerpiece of an unrealized resort development / National Register of Historic Places, 1996

Tovrea Castle, the romantic, wedding-cake-shaped, solitary structure situated on a hill, ringed by stately saguaro cactus has been a Valley of the Sun landmark since its completion in 1930.

But, despite its name, the Tovrea family did not build it, and today, the surrounding garden's abnormally dense forest of mature cactus nearly overtakes the whimsical castle in terms of visual impact.

Retired San Francisco businessman Alessio Carraro designed and built the tiered fantasy form on a flattened knoll north of the Salt River's dry bed. Carraro had made a fortune in the San Francisco sheet metal business when the city rebuilt after the 1906 earthquake. He prospered further in the frothy stock market of the 1920s before the 1929 crash.

On a friend's advice, Carraro had entered the hot Phoenix real estate market. In 1928, he bought 277 acres between Van Buren and the middle of the Salt River east of 48th Street, paying an average price of $245 an acre.

Dr. A.J. Chandler's San Marcos Hotel and the McArthur brothers' Arizona Biltmore north of Phoenix were built by local venture capitalists to advertise their proposed housing developments, and Carraro believed he could construct a signature hotel showcasing magnificent views and perhaps make a second fortune selling home sites. He knew that a former owner of his land, Lillie Warner-Smith, had recorded a 48-lot subdivision called Warner Heights. Carraro decided to name his development Carraro Heights.

After hiring Phoenix architect H.D. Frankfurt to prepare plans for the hotel, the developer ignored Frankfurt's renderings to follow his own vision of a medieval Italian castle. Managing a crew of 15 carpenters, masons, painters, and plumbers (even including his teenage son Olivo, known as Leo), Carraro improvised the castle's design as he went.

Carraro flattened three knolls on the property into building pads. He graded the roads and made cement blocks from granite particles on the site. With his crew, the Italian immigrant hauled 2,600 truckloads of river rock to line the roads, paths, and knolls. They painted the border rocks a bright, reflective white.

After dynamiting a 40- by 60-foot hole in the central knoll, Carraro built a full basement and dug trenches for three arched tunnels connecting the basement to the cactus garden. The tunnels also provided cross-ventilation for the basement. The builder then put up the basement walls with blocks fabricated with his block-making machine. And he built a wine cellar using a vault door and doorframe salvaged from the Phoenix National Bank.

The basement still features an unusual ceiling that looks like meringue whipped into peaks. Dubbed a pulled plaster finish, its stalactite-like qualities contribute to the feeling of living underground.

The castle's basic floor plan forms an elongated octagon. Wooden stairways connect each floor, with stair flights narrowing as they rise higher up the building.

The elaborate first floor encloses a lobby, dining room, kitchen, lavatory, several closets, and a fake fireplace. Imitation stone and brick decorate the non-working fireplace. A large plaster medallion of a 1920s-era dancing flapper girl hangs above the fireplace. Its duplicate can be seen in Phoenix's Orpheum Theatre.

Walls and ceilings textured with layers of ocher-colored plaster and embellished with stenciled borders keep company with Art Deco wall sconces. Carraro strongly believed in recycling, so the kitchen cabinets came from additional salvage — mahogany once used in the Phoenix National Bank's tellers' cages and wainscoting. Maple flooring throughout came from a home being razed in Phoenix.

Following a simpler plan than the first, the second floor includes six guest rooms — each with a sink — and a communal bathroom. Two doors open to a roof deck that encircles the building.

The third floor, with just two bedrooms and a bath, has a single door leading to its own deck.

A narrow stairway leads to the fourth-floor cupola, where a tiny landing offers access to the topmost roof deck and dome with its 8-foot flagpole. The deck affords panoramic views of the Salt River Valley.

Carraro employed an unusual building technology known as platform construction, with each story of his masterpiece built as a separate unit and resting on the roof deck of the story below. Although the basement is block, the upper floors are made of wood frame with stucco over wood and metal lath. Galvanized sheet metal caps the crenellated parapets on the tiered walls that give the building its castle-like appearance. Sheet metal also covers the cupola dome, originally sheathed with copper.

Shortly before Carraro started building the hotel, probably during the summer of 1928, a Russian gardener named Moktatchev arrived on his doorstep and offered to create a unique desert landscape. Carraro accepted, and Moktatchev set to work acquiring cactus from California, Colorado, and New Mexico, adding specimens from Australia, South America, and Africa's Sahara Desert. In all, Moktatchev planted some 300 varieties of cactus, following the land's natural lines. He tagged them with their Latin and popular names and invited enthralled Phoenicians to tour the garden on Sunday afternoons.

Just before Christmas 1930, a joyous Carraro finally finished his dream castle. In celebration, he switched on hundreds of colored lightbulbs outlining the building — the bulbs had been dipped in colored paint. The holiday display peaked in a 10-foot-high, electrically

Although Alessio Carraro envisioned the New World castle he built as the centerpiece of a housing development, his plans were thwarted by a neighbor putting up sheep pens next door.

lit Christmas tree tied to the flagpole on the topmost roof deck. The festive building brightened the night for miles around. As a result, the *Arizona Republican* newspaper awarded Carraro the sweepstakes prize in its "Phoenix Spirit of Christmas" contest.

But Alessio Carraro's plan to launch a resort hotel surrounded by high-priced homes ground to a halt when Edward Tovrea (pronounced Toe-vree) bought 40 acres just west of Carraro's property and introduced sheep pens. Carraro realized that the flies, odor, and bleating of sheep would drive away potential homebuyers. Who would want to live in a house next to a sheep pen?

Carraro thought he had no choice but to put the property up for sale. An attractive offer came through a real estate agent, and Carraro took it. Only later did he discover the buyer's name . . . Della Tovrea, Edward's wife. Within five years, Carraro sold most of his 277 acres to the Tovreas.

Carraro left town to try a new career: water witching. He had a talent for locating potential well sites using a flexible stick. Then he bought 4 acres near Yarnell and worked on a rock wonderland called Carraro's Grotto until his death in 1964.

Tovrea survived only seven months after taking possession of the castle and died on Feb. 7, 1932.

Four years after Edward's death, Della Tovrea married William Plato Stuart, publisher of the *Prescott Courier*. The couple summered in Prescott and wintered at the castle until Stuart died in 1960.

Della Tovrea Stuart made several changes to the castle while she lived there. She installed two concrete patios, one with a firepit; planted a rose garden; added a reflecting pool; scattered concrete urns and benches about; and replaced the original terrace rail fence with a rubble-stone wall. She reportedly kept 75 peacocks as sentries.

Toward the end of her life, Della grew increasingly reclusive, staying mostly in the cool basement. She furnished it with two chairs, reading lamps, piles of newspapers and magazines, and 20 rolltop desks. The lobby became her dining room, and she kept several jigsaw puzzles going at a time there. She slept on a cot in the kitchen, now notable for its bright blue porcelain sink.

Tragically, in 1968, intruders robbed the house and beat Della badly. While Della fought them off, a gun fired, leaving a bullet hole in the kitchen ceiling; it's still there today. Her housekeeper slept through the commotion of the break-in, and the thieves got away with jewels and silver. Della never recovered from the attack; she died the following year of her injuries.

After Della's death, the bank held the castle in trust. Phil Tovrea, Edward Tovrea's great-grandson from an earlier marriage, took on the role of caretaker. The castle and its grounds couldn't escape the inevitable signs of age and lack of use, and many of the garden's exotic cactus have died off. However, the saguaro forest studding the knoll is almost as much of a landmark as the castle itself, both easily visible from nearby State Loop 202. The property now belongs to the City of Phoenix, which plans to have it fully restored and open for public tours sometime in the next few years. Alessio Carraro's dream of creating a signature resort may have died long ago, but the lighted tiers of his castle still illuminate the night with the wonder of what one man with a vision can accomplish.

■ **WHEN YOU GO** 5041 E. Van Buren St. The castle's entrance drive is on the south side of Van Buren, between 48th and 52nd streets in southeast Phoenix, just west of the Loop 202 on-ramp. (602) 262-6412. www.ci.phoenix.az.us/PARKS/tovrea.html

COURTYARD, MISSION SAN XAVIER

RECESSED DOOR, LA CASA CORDOVA

PORTICO DETAIL, AJO TOWN SITE

STOREHOUSE, SLAUGHTER RANCH

PROFILED IN THIS SECTION

- AJO TOWN SITE (AJO)
- ARIZONA INN (TUCSON)
- ARIZONA AND NEW MEXICO RAILWAY PASSENGER DEPOT (CLIFTON)
- BIOSPHERE 2 (ORACLE)
- COPPER QUEEN HOTEL (BISBEE)
- FORT YUMA QUARTERMASTER DEPOT/ TERRITORIAL PRISON (YUMA)
- LA CASA CORDOVA (TUCSON)
- MISSION SAN XAVIER DEL BAC (TOHONO O'ODHAM RESERVATION, NEAR TUCSON)
- NOGALES-SANTA CRUZ COUNTY PUBLIC LIBRARY (NOGALES)
- ODD FELLOWS AND REBEKAHS HOME (SAFFORD)
- OLD MAIN: UNIVERSITY OF ARIZONA (TUCSON)
- OWLS CLUB HOUSES (TUCSON)
- PIMA COUNTY COURTHOUSE (TUCSON)
- ST. PHILIP'S IN THE HILLS EPISCOPAL CHURCH (TUCSON)
- SLAUGHTER RANCH (NEAR DOUGLAS)

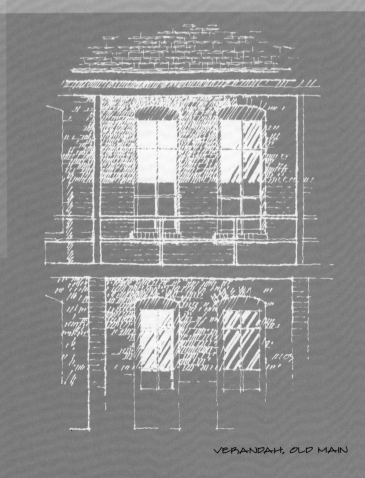

VERANDAH, OLD MAIN

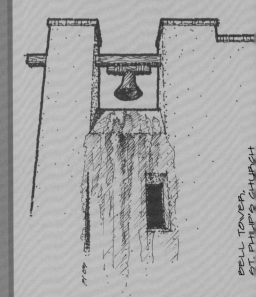

BELL TOWER, ST. PHILIP'S CHURCH

TUCSON AND SOUTHERN ARIZONA

rizona's second-largest city, Tucson, would never be mistaken for someplace in the Midwest. This is definitely a Southwestern city, its arched entries, rough adobe walls, and dusty side streets recalling images of Spanish conquistadors searching for mythical cities of gold, cowboys riding the open range, and sheriffs heading for a shootout.

Tucson began as a walled Spanish fort in 1776, the year America declared its independence from Britain. This small outpost, flanked by the Santa Catalina, Rincon, and Santa Rita mountains and bisected by the Santa Cruz River, joined the United States in 1854 when Mexico ceded the area in the Gadsden Purchase.

Clearly attuned to its Hispanic roots, Tucson offers an architectural heritage rich in Spanish/Moorish/Mexican influences.

The equitable climate — Tucson is slightly higher and somewhat cooler than Phoenix — has made the city a popular tourist destination for those fleeing cold winters, resulting in numerous upscale resort hotels, including the gracious Arizona Inn.

Outside the city, Mission San Xavier del Bac, the restored Spanish Colonial/Mexican Baroque mission built in 1797 by Franciscan friars and Tohono O'odham Indians, is the state's best known and most beloved historic structure.

East and south of Tucson, cattle ranching, scattered farming, and copper mining lured settlers, investors, and adventurers to the region's lush grasslands, craggy mountain ranges, and shady, stream-fed canyons. The San Bernardino (John Slaughter) Ranch near Douglas opens a window to the difficulties ranchers and farmers encountered in Arizona, while the Copper Queen Hotel in Bisbee offers a glimpse of the high life made possible by booming copper mines early in the last century. Among the dangers experienced by those settling the southeast corner of Arizona were Indian raids led by Apache war leader Geronimo, who didn't surrender until 1886.

West of Tucson, the Gila River snakes through the barren region between central Arizona and the Colorado River. The plucky Mormon Battalion crossed this vast desert to defend California in 1847. In Yuma, the bleak Yuma Territorial Prison locked up the Territory's toughest desperados. Also in Yuma, the Army's Quartermaster Depot warehoused blankets and bullets for soldiers protecting immigrants streaming into California. Preserved as a museum exhibit, the commanding officer's quarters allow us a peek at the artifacts of a lifestyle that existed before the arrival of the railroad made Yuma's quartermaster function obsolete, and well before Yuma began channeling Colorado River water onto its rich alluvial plane to grow the melons, lettuce, dates, oranges, lemons, and other produce that provision the nation's grocery stores today.

DAVID H. SMITH

AJO TOWN SITE

■ **LOCATION**	Ajo
■ **YEAR BUILT**	1914-1926
■ **STYLE**	Spanish Colonial Revival
■ **ARCHITECTS**	William M. Kenyon and Maurice F. Maine; others
■ **SIGNIFICANCE**	Company town designed according to City Beautiful principles / National Register of Historic Places, 2001

The Calumet and Arizona Mining Company faced a major problem in 1914. An estimated 40 million tons of copper ore had been discovered in Ajo, and company officials needed men to work the New Cornelia open pit mine.

But Ajo lay in the middle of nowhere, 118 miles southwest of Phoenix in the desert foothills, with little housing, only a few stores, and no entertainment. Worse, summer temperatures sometimes reached 120 degrees, and mining had a reputation as dirty, dusty, hard work. How could the company persuade skilled laborers to move to and live in this uninviting place?

John C. Greenway, the company's dynamic general manager, believed he knew the answer. The socially responsible way was to build a company town.

Greenway hired architects William M. Kenyon and Maurice F. Maine of Minneapolis to design a community based on City Beautiful principles. The City Beautiful movement, a political, cultural, and aesthetic effort rooted in the reform era of the mid-1800s, espoused beautifying cities with lush parks, handsome parkways, and stately buildings, thus fostering pride in the community.

As a model planned community, Ajo provided low-cost dormitories and apartments for single workers, houses for families, a general store, restaurant, bank, post office, movie theater and, later, churches. The company erected and paid for a hospital, public utilities, and a school.

◀ Rows of pale arches roofed with mission tile make up Ajo's downtown plaza. The plaza typifies the Spanish Colonial Revival style found throughout the town.

Greenway insisted that the town center be open to everyone. Housing, however, was separated by race, according to *Ajo: A Model Company Town,* prepared for the Arizona State Historic Preservation Office by Johns & Strittmatter Inc. of Tucson.

The company's American (Anglo) town site placed whites near the town center, with Mexican and Indian town sites located closer to the mine. Streets in the American town site radiated from a central plaza, while the Mexican and Indian town sites followed a grid pattern. Greenway ordered that water, light, and sewer systems be installed before dwellings could be occupied.

Ed Havins, who lived most of his 80-plus years in Ajo and worked as a carpenter's apprentice for the Calumet and Arizona Mining Company, remembers the town's segregated swimming pool. "In the '30s and '40s, whites went to the pool on Friday, Saturday, and Sunday; Mexicans on Monday and Tuesday; Indians on Wednesday, and it was cleaned on Thursday when they changed the water. That old pool was bulldozed in 1947 or '48," he says.

Workers in the American town site could choose from four or five wood-frame home models, each containing approximately 1,480 square feet of living space. The average house featured a living room with a fireplace, two or three bedrooms, a bath, and a kitchen. Sleeping porches let residents sleep in the desert's cooler nighttime air in the days before air conditioning. Most people favored the Spanish Colonial Revival model; others chose Bungalow- or Prairie-style models, or models with no defined style. A one-car, corrugated metal garage opened onto the alley behind each house. Today, the easiest way to determine if a home originated as a company house is to look for a chain-link fence around it and a metal garage out back.

Greenway wanted miners' houses built on alternate lots, with additional homes constructed later as infill. And that's what happened, with occupants personalizing their homes by adding aluminum siding, stucco, and bonus rooms. "People have really, really fancied these houses up," says Bob Boozer, who grew up in Ajo.

Company officials and other important persons received large homes with views. Greenway and Michael Curley, the mine's general superintendent, lived in sprawling hilltop homes overlooking the town and the Little Ajo Mountains, while four comfortable, Spanish Colonial Revival hilltop residences west of the hospital housed the doctors. Less pretentious homes went to foremen, electricians, and master mechanics. In all, an estimated 967 company-owned homes were built in Ajo.

Greenway hoped workers would purchase their homes, but this seldom happened. Rents ranged from a modest $1 to $30 a month for houses valued from $100 to $5,000, according to the Johns & Strittmatter study. Boozer says his family paid $26.50 monthly for a three-bedroom, one-bath house.

With admirable foresight, Greenway avoided the conflict-of-interest problems inherent in company-owned stores by organizing Ajo's general store as a cooperative. Havins recalls, "Workers could charge their purchases using a number you were assigned. Just before Christmas, you got a 6 to 10 percent rebate on everything you bought that year. The store had good quality merchandise and would order what you wanted."

As landlord, the mining company maintained the houses, streets, recreational facilities, and public utilities. It supported public events like an annual Christmas party in the town plaza and provided fire and police protection. It even arbitrated disputes. Asked how the

▲ A stately arcade provides shade for those who have business in the plaza as well as for visitors who want to enjoy a quiet promenade.

company persuaded miners to behave, Havins replies cryptically, "They had their ways." He adds, "This was a good town to live in. They [the mining executives] were damn good to the people here."

The Ajo town site, although no longer company-owned, retains the elements of a company town.

The town center now consists of a business block with a Spanish Colonial Revival-style covered colonnade. Businesses include a restaurant, real estate office, pharmacy, ice cream parlor, and post office. Ajo's city fathers have discouraged highway strip malls in order to keep the downtown alive.

At the closed end of a palm-lined, U-shaped plaza stands the Tucson, Cornelia and Gila Bend Railroad Depot (1917) adorned with arched openings, mission tile roof, and ceramic-tiled dome. An imaginary line drawn from the dome through the plaza ends at the elaborately decorated 1918 Curley School, named for mine superintendent Curley and designed by Lescher and Kibbey, the Phoenix firm which had designed the Douglas Mansion in Jerome and which later became Lescher and Mahoney.

In 1924, Greenway married Mrs. Isabella Ferguson, the widow of a good friend from his Rough Rider days. Isabella Greenway would develop her own sphere of influence in Arizona, but she made some of her first marks here in Ajo by bringing a California architect to build the town's first church. Flanking the axial line connecting the station and the school stand the Immaculate Conception Catholic Church, designed by Santa Barbara architect George Washington Smith (1925), and the Federated Church, designed by Lescher and Kibbey (1926).

Built on a concrete foundation, the white-stuccoed adobe Catholic church, with its graceful dome, has become a town landmark. The non-denominational Federated Church across the street is made of hollow, clay tile.

The American town site still exists, but the Mexican and Indian town sites largely disappeared because mining operations encroached on the land. A few concrete slabs from the dwellings can still be seen at the edge of the open pit that looms above the town.

Among other accomplishments, Greenway patented a process to extract copper profitably from Ajo's low-grade copper ore. The former Rough Rider was so popular with the miners and company officials that, after his untimely death in 1926, more than 3,000 mourners from all over the United States attended his funeral, held in the shadow of the mine's 7-mile-long, 110-foot-tall tailings.

The Phelps Dodge Corp. succeeded the Calumet and Arizona Mining Co. In 1935, its New Cornelia Branch at Ajo ranked as Arizona's leading copper producer. After the mines closed in 1984, Phelps Dodge sold most of the houses and commercial property it owned, reserving only the rights to underground mineral deposits.

Experts estimate that the mine could produce another 17 years' worth of copper if world copper prices ever rise enough to run the operation profitably. In the meantime, Ajo (which translates as either "red-colored ore" in the Tohono O'odham language, or "garlic" in Spanish, for the local garlic-flavored wildflowers) relies on retirees and tourism to produce revenues. In today's Ajo, visitors can readily see what a company town looked like in the early 1900s, while enjoying its current laid-back ambience.

■ **WHEN YOU GO** Follow State Route 85 south to Ajo, heading toward Organ Pipe Cactus National Monument. The road curves east, then south. The plaza is on the east side of the road, across the road from the Catholic and Federated churches. Chamber of Commerce, (520) 387-7742.

ARIZONA INN

■ **LOCATION**	Tucson
■ **YEARS BUILT**	1930-31
■ **STYLE**	Spanish Colonial Revival with Mediterranean, Moorish, and Sonoran influences
■ **ARCHITECT**	Merritt Hudson Starkweather
■ **SIGNIFICANCE**	Enduring resort conceived by Arizona's first U.S. Congresswoman, Isabella Greenway / National Register of Historic Places, 1988

We all wish our grandmothers had had the wit and the wherewithal to create a presence as lovely as the historic Arizona Inn in Tucson. Though they didn't, we can still enjoy this Tucson resort complex with its burnished silver compotes, original Audubon prints, handmade furniture, manicured lawns, and exquisite floral gardens.

Credit for the Arizona Inn, built in 1930-31, goes to socialite, businesswoman, humanitarian, and Arizona's first U.S. congresswoman (1933-36), Isabella Selmes Ferguson Greenway.

The honor of preserving the inn's sterling reputation belongs to Greenway's granddaughter, Patty Doar, president and proprietor of the 86-room in-town resort hotel, who believes in perpetuating her grandmother's legacy of gracious hospitality: "What we try to provide is excellent service. We're like a European grand hotel. You want the guests to feel they can unpack and stay awhile. One of the nicest compliments we've had is that the Arizona Inn is a hotel that does not look like a hotel," she says.

When Isabella Greenway's second husband, John Greenway, died unexpectedly after surgery in 1926, Doar says, "Instead of just collapsing, she started a furniture factory for disabled veterans who had been gassed in World War I." These vets faced poverty because they couldn't work full shifts. The compassionate venture, called the Arizona Hut, succeeded so well Greenway became owner of more tables, chairs, and lamps than could be marketed to stores like Marshall Field and Abercrombie & Fitch.

"Someone told my grandmother she had enough furniture to build a hotel," Doar says. "So she did." Greenway realized that building a resort to use the furniture would bring the added benefit of providing rooms for friends visiting Tucson. "People were beginning to come to Tucson and there was no place to stay," Doar says.

Fortunately, Greenway had the funds and the foresight to fill both needs.

Greenway's father, Tilden Russel Selmes, had been general counsel for the Northern Pacific Railroad in St. Paul, Minnesota. After his death in 1895 when Isabella was 9, she and her mother moved to New York, where she attended the exclusive Miss Chapin's and Miss Spence's schools. Joining the social swirl, she became a life-long friend of Eleanor Roosevelt and served as Eleanor's bridesmaid when she married Franklin D. Roosevelt, later the U.S. President, in 1905.

By the time Isabella built the Arizona Inn, she had supervised the construction of seven homes and outlived two husbands — the dashingly handsome Robert H. Munro Ferguson, one of Theodore Roosevelt's Rough Riders, who died of tuberculosis; and his friend John Greenway, a Rough Rider, decorated World War I brigadier general, and later general manager of the New Cornelia Copper Co.'s mine in Ajo. Fortunately, shortly before the stock market crash in 1929, Isabella Greenway sold her copper mining stock

RICHARD MAACK

▲ Potted flowers and bronze artwork add to the comeliness of Isabella Greenway's hospitable resort. While the inn was being built, Greenway visited each room with a sawhorse and a pillow to ensure that every guest would have a pleasing view.

and purchased government bonds, thus retaining her wealth through the Depression.

Greenway knew just the sort of inn to build.

It would be a home-like haven spread across 14 desert acres 3 miles from the center of what is now downtown Tucson. It would consist of a lushly landscaped complex of cottages, separate buildings, and carefully landscaped open spaces catering to those who desired "privacy, quiet, and sunshine." The only rules, she said, should be those "dictated by good taste and decency."

The buildings would be made of fired clay brick covered by stucco colored the rosy pink of her skin tones, highlighted by cobalt blue awnings and window surrounds. The style would echo the Spanish Colonial Revival look so popular in the Southwest, its red tile roofs,

HENRY FECHTMAN

 The Arizona Inn's library, which houses Greenway's valuable collections of artwork and furniture, makes a comfortable spot for reading or taking afternoon tea.

arched openings, and high ceilings enhanced by Sonoran-style patios.

Greenway spent hours sketching and consulting with architect Merritt Hudson Starkweather of Tucson. "She personally walked to each half-built room with a sawhorse and a pillow to see that each room had a view," Doar says. Closets had to be large enough for a bridge table and a steamer trunk, necessary accessories to affluent travelers during that era.

Phase one of the Arizona Inn opened on Dec. 18, 1930, equipped with furniture from the Hut and Greenway's own antiques. "There are lots of family pieces, from England and Scotland. She was a collector of everything," her granddaughter says. Personal items include a Louis XV walnut armoire, a pair of Edwardian vitrines, an Elizabethan-style trestle table, hand-colored lithographs by artist George Catlin, family oil paintings, and memorabilia from Africa, now on display in the Africa and Safari rooms.

The hotel enjoyed immediate success. It succeeded so well that Greenway felt comfortable sailing to Africa the following summer with her daughter and son, Martha and John Greenway, to see her other son, Robert Ferguson, who was working in Northern Rhodesia's copper mines. She returned in time for the inn's completion in November 1931.

Essentially, the inn appears today as it was then, except for the addition of a pool and clay tennis courts in 1937, and a gift shop, offices and, most importantly, air conditioning, in the early 1970s.

The inn maintains a strict policy of assuring privacy for its guests. However, the word is out that Gary Cooper and Clark Gable did stay there; also Eleanor Roosevelt, singer Marian Anderson, the Duke and Duchess of Windsor, and oil tycoon and philanthropist John D. Rockefeller.

Doar tells how hard her grandmother tried to please her guests. It seems Rockefeller had a standing reservation to visit the inn, but one year, he canceled. Greenway rented his usual quarters to other guests, then learned that Rockefeller would arrive after all, in just three weeks. Without a second thought, Greenway ordered workmen to build a new casita just for Rockefeller, thus satisfying everyone.

The inn's library and dining room set the tone for the gentility and old-money elegance characteristic of the resort. The library has "real" books, not *Reader's Digest* condensations. For example, guests can peruse *The Collected Poems of W.B. Yeats* or *The Complete Works of William Makepeace Thackeray* while waiting for their afternoon tea served in the library. The library's floor has pegged pine and mahogany planks, and the ceiling has hand-hewn wooden beams.

Across the hall, the carpeted dining room space mirrors that of the library, with a light-hued ceiling and decor centered around a palm tree planted in a terra-cotta pot. Hut craftsmen made the tables and ladder-back chairs with rush seats, and now carpenters that Doar keeps on staff make repairs or reproductions when necessary. Leaf-shaped sconces and clerestory windows offer soft illumination.

A third public room, the Audubon Bar, reveals still another dimension to Greenway's personality. As if straight from the movie set of *Casablanca*, it sports a grand piano, bamboo chairs, a giant fishtail palm, and Audubon animal prints. Doar says, "Anything that revolved around my grandmother was fun. My family has always had the ability to make everything a great adventure."

With the inn safely established, Greenway turned to politics. She bought a small airline that served California, New Mexico, and Arizona to aid in her political travels. She gave the first seconding speech for Franklin Roosevelt at the Democratic National Convention in 1932 when he was nominated to run for President. Then she ran for, and won, a seat in congress in 1933, filling the unexpired term of Louis Douglas, who joined the Roosevelt administration. Re-elected in 1934, she promoted Arizona's mining, ranching, and veterans' interests. She refused to stand for office again in 1936.

In 1939, Greenway married Harry O. King, an industrialist who befriended her while she served in congress. From then until her death on Dec. 18, 1953, at age 67, she spent most of her time minding the inn. She once lamented, "I cannot believe that I built an institution in a moment of indiscretion and desire to house furniture made by disabled ex-servicemen, and that it has become so popular that I cannot get my own beloved Aunt and Uncle in on short notice." Her son John managed the inn until his niece, Patty Doar, succeeded him in 1989.

Doar now follows in her grandmother's footsteps. The inn has been made handicapped accessible and its bathrooms updated. "Obviously, people like history, but not in their bathrooms," Doar says. Electronic voice mail and data ports also have been installed.

But the tradition of casual comfort and personalized service still trumps expediency. "When we renovate, we try to restore," Doar says. After all, another generation of Greenways waits in the wings to continue the inn's tradition of graceful hospitality.

■ **WHEN YOU GO** 2200 E. Elm St. The Arizona Inn is located in a residential neighborhood east of Campbell Road, halfway between Grant Road and Speedway Boulevard, near the U of A campus. (520) 325-1541 or (800) 933-1093. www.arizonainn.com

ARIZONA AND NEW MEXICO RAILWAY PASSENGER DEPOT	
■ **LOCATION**	Clifton
■ **YEAR BUILT**	1913
■ **STYLE**	Territorial and Mission Revival with Prairie School influences
■ **ARCHITECT**	Original unknown
■ **SIGNIFICANCE**	Optimistic statement about the mining town's future / National Register of Historic Places, 1990 (part of Clifton Townsite Historic District)

When copper mining arrived in Arizona in the late 19th century, the railroad followed soon after, bringing newcomers of diverse cultures and introducing fresh architectural styles and imported building materials. One of the places that exemplifies the process is the picturesque town of Clifton in Greenlee County.

Bankrolled by investors from Edinburgh, Scotland, the Arizona Copper Co. began purchasing mining claims near Clifton. In 1884, the company financed the Arizona & New Mexico Railway linking Clifton to New Mexico, and brick and mortar began to replace Clifton's adobe buildings. Banks, cafes, hotels, and apartments started to line the town's narrow streets, and passersby could be heard speaking Spanish, Italian, Chinese, and English embellished with a Scottish brogue.

Boosters claimed Clifton's population soon would balloon to 20,000. In anticipation, the railroad built two train depots. First came the freight depot, completed in early 1913; workers completed the more opulent passenger depot a few months later. Combining Territorial and Mission Revival styles with a touch of Prairie School, the two-story, rectangular passenger depot measured 122 by 32 feet with a shortened second floor featuring roof decks and brick balustrades. Double-hung wood windows punctuated the two-toned, pressed-brick walls. Red Spanish tile covered the hipped roof.

Upon dedication on Oct. 21, 1913, *The Copper Era* called the $35,000 building "one of the finest passenger stations in the SW."

Then, during the Great Depression, Clifton shrank to a near ghost town. In 1939, local entrepreneur Frank Martin leased the depot from the railway, converting most of the ground floor to a restaurant and bar, the Coronado Inn, and the upper floor to a social club and meeting hall. A grand re-opening of the refurbished depot was held on Nov. 1, ushering in the second era in the depot's life. Although passenger service was finally discontinued in 1967, the inn remained open until 1982, when it became one of the victims of a bitter copper strike.

In October 1983, heavy rains caused the San Francisco River to roar down the narrow

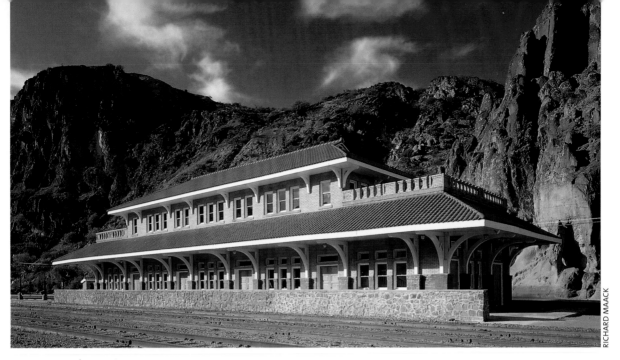

RICHARD MAACK

▲ A corner of the Arizona and New Mexico Railway Passenger Depot had to be clipped off to make room for large trucks negotiating the road that passes between the station and the rock wall facing it.

canyon and deposit 6 feet of silt inside the former depot. Nine years later, native son Charles Spezia and Clifton Town Manager Mark Fooks persuaded the railroad to donate the abandoned depot/inn to the town. Then the two cobbled together close to $500,000 in grants and donations and engaged Phoenix's Ryden Architects for a 1992 rehabilitation.

Today, the reconstituted depot contains meeting space, an art gallery, offices, a restroom/rest area and a pressed-tin replica ceiling. With the exterior restored to its 1913 appearance, the depot once again reflects the glories of Clifton's copper mining past.

■ **WHEN YOU GO** 100 N. Coronado Blvd. Take U.S. 191 to Clifton. The depot is on the east side of the highway (North Coronado Boulevard) north of the San Francisco River bridge and two railroad crossings. Greenlee County Chamber of Commerce, (928) 865-3313. Art Depot, (928) 865-3467.

BIOSPHERE 2

■ **LOCATION**	Oracle
■ **YEARS BUILT**	1988-1991
■ **STYLE**	Futuristic
■ **ARCHITECTS**	Various
■ **SIGNIFICANCE**	Ecological laboratory designed for studying space colonization; now used to study the Earth

Biosphere 2, a $150-million model of the Earth's ecosystems in miniature, began as a first step toward eventually colonizing other planets in our solar system but has since transformed into a school for understanding the Earth.

In the early 1990s, jump-suited "Biospherians" marched purposefully into Biosphere 2, a sealed replica of the Earth's major ecosystems, intent on growing their own food and

▲ From an aerial view, Biosphere 2's white-walled control center appears to snake through its surroundings. The structure, built in three years, was intended as a laboratory for studies on space colonization.

▲ The strong geometry of Biosphere 2 contrasts sharply with the structure's setting in the Sonoran Desert, near Tucson.

recycling their air, water, and waste products in anticipation of someday living on Mars. Two years later, the crew staggered out of the sealed terrarium, haggard, hungry, oxygen-deprived, and angry with their handlers and each other.

Critics termed the project "the fevered dream of a doomsday cult" and "a fraud." As a result, the facility's owner, Texas oil magnate Edward P. Bass, evicted Biosphere's managers and sought a less controversial user for the 250-acre site.

Columbia University saw the possibilities and agreed to convert the Biosphere compound into its western campus, with some 100 students studying there. But Biosphere's connection with Columbia University was discontinued in December 2003, and as this book went to press, its future was not yet settled.

Construction on Biosphere 2 began in the late 1980s as a collaboration between scientists and architects from the University of Arizona. They crafted the futuristic-looking complex on a fast-track schedule. "It was an amazing feat — true design-build," says Clark Reddin, Biosphere 2's director of facilities and engineering. "They finished the project in 1991, or under three years."

The facility consists of some 60 buildings, ranging from a visitors center to greenhouses, a restaurant, gift shop, pump house, residences, and dormitories.

While well-planned buildings in the Sonoran Desert should afford shade, at Biosphere 2, the design challenge was to create the exact opposite: in essence, a working greenhouse. Scientists needed to invite as much sunshine inside as possible so that plants could grow and flourish.

Workers assembled the space-frame complex using hollow connector pipes made of powder-coated mild steel, held together at the knuckles by huge bolts. Windows are double-paned, 3/8-inch tempered glass, and water and air recycle, with the air filtering through two 25,000-gallon airtight "lungs."

Originally the five ecosystems, called biomes, simulated a swamp, ocean, rain forest, desert, and savanna. Visitors entered via air locks to maintain constant air pressure inside.

The most successful biomes, however, turned out to be the rain forest and the ocean. The former, now a steamy tangle of vines and 90-foot trees, thrives, while the ocean — reputedly the world's largest manmade sea — teems with fish and some 50 species of seaweed.

Reddin admits that "Biosphere 2 is not an ecologically friendly place," in the sense that the buildings do not blend into their desert background nor protect inhabitants from too much sun. "But that's the price you have to pay to do the research. There's no other building like it in the world," he says.

■ **WHEN YOU GO** Biosphere 2 is approximately 30 minutes north of Tucson and 90 minutes south of Phoenix on Oracle Road (State Route 77) at Milepost 96.5. Open 9 A.M. to 4 P.M. Guided tours available. Entrance fee. (520) 838-6200. www.bio2.edu

COPPER QUEEN HOTEL

■ **LOCATION**	Bisbee
■ **YEAR BUILT**	1902
■ **STYLE**	Italian Villa
■ **BUILDER**	Van Vleck and Goldsmith
■ **SIGNIFICANCE**	Old-world retreat for the elite in an Old West mining town / National Register of Historic Places, 1980 (part of Bisbee Historic District)

The historic Copper Queen Hotel hosted Territorial governors, mining camp executives, and the Old West's newly rich after the turn of the last century, when Bisbee rivaled San Francisco as a center of culture and wealth with a European flavor.

The 1902 hostelry, recently renovated, still caters to the affluent but, these days, the guests are likely to be business people and their families, retirees, and adventurous singles visiting on holiday.

From the beginning, the Copper Queen Hotel played a significant role in Bisbee's development. Located in the town's center, 95 miles southeast of Tucson, the hotel has long served as a social center for Bisbee residents, while offering reasonably priced, comfortable accommodations and dining facilities for visitors.

With its white-painted, four-story brick walls and its red-and-hunter-green trim, the "Queen" turns a cheerful countenance to the community. Red-capped triple towers top the building in the romantic style of an Italian villa. In its heyday, prominent guests attracted to the turn-of-the-century hotel with its mountain setting included Teddy Roosevelt and Gen. John J. "Black Jack" Pershing.

In recent years, three ghosts have been added to the roster of visitors.

"I had an experience [with a ghost] myself, about a year and a half ago," says Bobbe Hossman, the hotel's special events coordinator. "It was on the second floor, and I smelled lily of the valley perfume. There was something there that you wouldn't expect. I didn't see anyone. But I know it was a ghost."

Hossman describes the hotel's ghostly figures: There's a woman in her late 30s who appears on the hotel's staircase clutching a whisky bottle, wearing a long, black dress and shawl, or, on some occasions, nothing at all; a second spirit, a nondescript older man, rides the hotel's elevator; and a third supernatural visitor appears to be a 5-year-old boy. "Only young children see the little boy," Hossman says. "At Thanksgiving, a little girl kept peeking

▲ Bisbee's Copper Queen Hotel, trimmed with rust-red and green, remains a lodging from another era for visitors. The hotel has 47 rooms, with no two having the same size or shape.

under the table. Her mother asked what she was looking at, and she said, 'That boy.' But there was nobody there, so it must have been the ghost." For those who'd like another type of out-of-the-ordinary experience, the hotel offers Murder Mystery Weekends. Guests dress in period costumes and try to solve crimes based on Bisbee's lurid past.

The Copper Queen Hotel is built as rock-solid as the bedrock on which it stands. One resident notes, "Mining people knew one way to build, and that was hell for stout. I don't think you can find a crack anywhere in those walls."

The charm of the hotel lies, in part, in the fact that no two of its 47 rooms have the same size or configuration. The lobby still uses the massive safe that once stored miners' pay. The oak stair railings and the second-floor lobby, with its gracious brick fireplace, are original, but other facilities have been modernized. An elevator was installed in 1946 and a third tower atop the building was added to accommodate the elevator works. The heated pool is new. Shoe repair and cigar store tenants moved out to allow expansion of the bar, graced by a nude portrait of actress Lillie Langtry. The building has been re-plumbed and the electrical system updated. All rooms have bathrooms, many containing claw-footed tubs, and one room is handicapped accessible, with a roll-in shower. Antiques, like a hat-rack chair, old sea chest, and a shoeshine chair, appear throughout the public areas. Pierced copper light fixtures branded with the letters *CQ*, standing for Copper Queen, illuminate the hallways.

According to local records, in 1875, a silver prospector named Hugh Jones suspected there might be valuable minerals hidden in the Mule Mountains near Bisbee. But Jones, seeing only "copper stains," moved on. Two years later, another prospector, George Warren, staked a claim for what would become the fabulously rich Copper Queen Mine. Then Warren bet it all on a foot race. He lost both the race and his title to the mine. Old-timers say Warren spent the rest of his life telling his story in exchange for free drinks in Brewery Gulch.

With the discovery of copper, first tents, then shacks, and then houses of brick and stone began to sprawl through the canyons and up the gulches of the town. One of them, Brewery Gulch, with 37 bars and 37 bordellos, attracted boisterous miners in the 1920s. The gulch took its name from the Muheim Brewery, built in 1905, which once housed a stock exchange, restaurant, lodgings, and saloon.

By 1910, the mines turned out 3 million pounds of copper a month. The downside of all the mining was the denuding of the once-forested Mule Mountains. The trees were used to

▲ As exemplified in the hotel's burnished barroom, the atmosphere of the Copper Queen is both mysterious and charming.

RICHARD MAACK

stoke the smelters. And the smelters sickened miners with their noxious fumes.

Fortunately, the year before the Copper Queen Hotel opened on Feb. 22, 1902, a new smelter was built 25 miles away in Douglas. Bisbee's air cleared up, and the workers again breathed the crystalline air that is normal in this mile-high city.

Bisbee ranked as Arizona's third largest city, after Phoenix and Tucson, in 1910. Citizens referred to Bisbee as "Little San Francisco," boasting that "It was three miles long, three blocks wide and three acres high." With the population nearing 20,000, residents built in tiers up hillsides so steep that one man's yard stood even with his neighbor's roof. Even today, the U.S. Postal Service refuses home delivery to some because of the many steps and stairways connecting one house to its neighbor.

Over time, the mining companies consolidated, and the Phelps Dodge Corp. emerged as the primary copper producer. In 1951, Phelps Dodge opened the remarkable Lavender Open Pit Mine, now a 300-acre, 1,000-foot-deep crater resulting from the extraction of its copper ore. The mine's name came not from the lavender-colored residue left after the ore was removed, as one might suspect, but from the mine's manager, Harrison Lavender.

Six months after the Lavender Pit finally played out in 1974, the Copper Queen Mine closed, and most of the miners moved elsewhere. Bisbee's population plummeted and now hovers around 7,000.

From 1877 until 1975, Bisbee's mines produced more than 8 billion pounds of copper worth about $2 billion, 3.9 million pounds of lead, 3.8 million pounds of zinc, 1 million ounces of silver, and 2.7 million ounces of gold. It was a great run while it lasted.

Despite the mine's closing and the miners' exit, Old Bisbee today looks much as it did a century ago, although tourism has become the town's main business, and its Victorian buildings house art galleries, antique shops, restaurants, and bed-and-breakfast inns. And in the heart of Bisbee, like true royalty, the Queen presides over the mining town's transformation with *noblesse oblige.*

■ **WHEN YOU GO** 11 Howell St. On State Route 80, after passing through Mule Pass Tunnel in Bisbee, exit to the right and follow the curving road until it becomes Tombstone Canyon; when the road straightens out, it becomes Main Street. Take Main Street for several blocks to Brewery Gulch. Turn left and left again after one block. (520) 432-2216. www.copperqueen.com

FORT YUMA QUARTERMASTER DEPOT/ YUMA TERRITORIAL PRISON

■ **LOCATION**	Yuma
■ **YEARS BUILT**	Commanding officer's quarters, 1859; prison, 1875
■ **STYLE**	Depot, Territorial; Prison, Mission Revival
■ **ARCHITECTS**	Depot, unknown; Prison, A.L. Grow
■ **SIGNIFICANCE**	Supply point for troops prior to arrival of the railroad; the ghosts of Territorial-era penal practices resurrected / National Register of Historic Places, 1966 (both part of Yuma Crossing Historic District)

In the 19th century, it must have been a strange and wondrous sight to watch riverboat captains dropping anchor in the middle of the Sonoran Desert.

Paddle wheelers with names like *Explorer, Esmeralda,* and *General Jesup* plied the swift, cold Colorado River on their three-day run from Port Ysabel, Mexico, at the mouth of the Colorado, to Yuma in Arizona Territory, carrying supplies and passengers. Tall-masted schooners that had set sail from San Francisco or San Diego had delivered the travelers and cargo to the Mexican port. Then the riverboats took them the rest of the way upriver to the Fort Yuma Quartermaster Depot near the confluence of the Colorado and Gila rivers. Once at the depot, the food, clothing, ammunition, and equipment destined for the Southwest's military outposts were hauled up an inclined track into a giant warehouse, across the river from the fort proper. The materiel then was either sent by steamboat farther up the river or transported by mule train to 22 forts in what is now Arizona, Nevada, New Mexico, Utah, and western Texas.

Without the quartermaster depot and its full storehouse containing an ample supply of everything from blankets to bullets, the U.S. Army in the Southwest would have been hard-pressed to maintain its far-flung military outposts. And the steady stream of Civil War veterans, gold seekers, gamblers, and settlers heading to California would have dried up because there were no soldiers to protect them from hostile Indians as they trekked across and settled in Arizona Territory. In 1880, the Army terminated the Yuma depot and moved its supply operation to Tucson, but river steamers continued using Yuma as a port of call until 1916, when a steamboat called *The Searchlight* sank. Before dams were built upstream, the Colorado River could be unpredictable, in some places spreading a mile wide and 30 feet deep and in other locations running shallow. At Yuma, two massive rock outcroppings channeled the flow so ferryboats could dependably transfer people and their wagons and animals across the water — a godsend for settlers following the southern Gila Trail west in the late 1800s.

Today, the Fort Yuma Quartermaster Depot, established in 1864, is memorialized at Yuma Crossing State Historic Park, which also celebrates at least five centuries of Yuma-area river crossings, from the 1500s when local Indians showed Spanish soldiers and missionaries where to swim their horses across the Colorado River, to present-day travelers driving the 667-foot Ocean-to-Ocean Bridge that spans the now-tamed Colorado.

The 20-acre park features four major structures: the office of the depot quartermaster (built in 1872) and the commanding officer's quarters (circa 1859), both now handsomely restored; the corral house (built in stages between 1865 and 1926); the storehouse (also built in stages, then rebuilt after a fire); and a stone reservoir (1864).

The five-room CO's quarters command the most interest. Riverboat captain George Alonzo Johnson, owner of the Colorado Steam Navigation Company, first built the home before the depot was founded. He later sold his house to the Army; now the one-story home with its 2-foot-thick adobe walls is furnished much as it would have been more than a century ago — the parlor equipped with an organ, settee, and rag rug; the dining table set with places for four; and one of the four bedrooms containing a child's miniature hope chest. As was usual at the time, the kitchen occupies a separate structure, reducing the danger from fires.

Both the quarters and the quartermaster's office illustrate the importance of adapting buildings to the Sonoran Desert, where summer temperatures can reach 123 degrees in the shade.

The two structures have roof overhangs, porches, shade trees, and an east-west orientation to avoid the sun's direct rays. Both buildings incorporate 12- to 14-foot-high ceilings to allow hot air to rise above occupants' heads. Twelve inches of dirt in the attic provide insulation, and a special cedar-shingle system permits the roof to breathe. Finally, their 9-foot-tall,

▲ In the late 1800s, men and women prisoners arrived and departed through Yuma Territorial Prison's sallyport.

double-hung sash windows facilitate the chimney effect, with cooler air entering the lower opening and warmer air venting out the top.

The storehouse is a museum today, but in the mid-1800s, the depot's mission required the quartermaster to maintain a six-month supply of food, clothing, ordinance, and other goods at all times in order to provision military posts throughout the Southwest. Memorabilia on display include a stagecoach and a 1909 Model T Ford mounted on a section of the plank road that once snaked across the sand dunes west of Yuma.

The corral house at one time quartered the teamsters who drove mule trains loaded with supplies to the military outposts. Some 900 mules once milled around inside the corral. Part of the corral house is now a community meeting space.

The arrival of the Southern Pacific Railroad in Yuma and completion of a bridge across the Colorado in 1877 foretold the end of the supply facility at Fort Yuma. When the railroad finally reached Tucson in 1880, the depot's function became obsolete, and the Army closed the quartermaster depot in 1883, moving much of its equipment to Tucson's Fort Lowell. The U.S. Customs Service used the commanding officer's quarters for a time, after which they once again became a private home.

A little more than a stone's throw from Yuma Crossing State Historic Park, on a bluff on the south side of the Colorado where the river bends, stand the well-preserved remains of another chapter in Yuma's history.

Arizona Territory's first prison incarcerated 3,069 lawbreakers, including murderers, burglars, bigamists, and those practicing "seduction under the promise of marriage" from 1876 until 1909, when the prison moved to Florence. Twenty-nine of those were women, including notorious stagecoach robber Pearl Hart, who later became a vaudeville actress.

Convicts consigned to the Yuma Territorial Prison wore black-and-white-striped uniforms, lived six to a cell, and spent six days a week quarrying stone and making adobe bricks — the materials used to build the compound. The prisoners built and maintained the prison themselves. They also raised their own food or learned a trade, that is, if they weren't chained in a dark cage, subsisting on bread and water as punishment. Grounds for solitary confinement included passing a note from a male to a female convict. One unfortunate fellow remained in a cage for 105 days.

The 20-foot-tall walls of the prison buildings were made of granite rock, which was plastered and finished with a brilliant whitewash. The cell blocks were open to the elements on the sides. Architect Don Ryden, who helped restore the prison, likened the situation to "being an ant living in a white shoe box with a sky-blue lid."

Today's visitors may wonder if the prison was humane. However, Territorial Gov. Anson P.K. Safford argued in favor of constructing the prison on the grounds that in the county jails — then the only alternative — "Close confinement and idleness often result injuriously to health with scarcely the possibility of moral improvement."

Living up to the governor's hopes, the Territorial prison ran one of the first free libraries in the Territory, and prisoners often learned to read and write there. In fact, medical care was deemed so good that other offenders were transferred to the Yuma prison to recover their health and, presumably, improve their morals.

After its decommissioning as a penal institution, the complex on the hill sheltered homeless people during the Great Depression of the 1920s and 1930s and served briefly as classrooms for Yuma Union High School students before becoming a city museum and then a state park.

The prison's Mission-style sallyport, or entrance gate, once ushered those who violated society's laws into a life of confinement. Twenty-first century visitors can feel only gratitude that, unlike those hapless convicts, they can pass through the graceful-looking portal at will.

■ **WHEN YOU GO** Yuma Crossing State Historic Park: 201 N. Fourth Ave. From Interstate 8 take the Fourth Avenue exit and go south on Fourth Avenue for a half mile. The park is located on the east side of Fourth Avenue. Open daily except Christmas, 9 A.M. to 5 P.M. Entrance fee. (928) 329-0471. Yuma Territorial Prison State Historic Park: One Prison Hill Rd. From I-8 take Exit 1, then follow Giss Parkway, turning north onto Prison Hill Drive and following the road to the hilltop parking area. Open daily except Christmas, 8 A.M. to 5 P.M. Closed at 2 P.M. on Thanksgiving Day and Christmas Eve. Entrance fee. (928) 783-4771. www.pr.state.az.us

LA CASA CORDOVA

■ **LOCATION**	Tucson
■ **YEAR BUILT**	Circa 1848
■ **STYLE**	Southern Arizona-Sonoran
■ **BUILDER**	Unknown
■ **SIGNIFICANCE**	Adobe house believed to be Tucson's oldest residence / National Register of Historic Places, 1972 (part of El Presidio Historic District)

Whoever built Tucson's La Casa Cordova, erected about 1848 in what was then a northern part of Mexico, held a much more perilous view of the world than people living north of the Mexican border.

Unlike most rural Americans, who built in the middle of their farms or ranches in order to watch over their holdings, Mexicans on the remote, northernmost frontier of Sonora arranged their houses in a row, butted against the interior walls of a surrounding fort, or presidio.

The fort was constructed like a medieval town, and the Mexicans living in it adopted this model for good reason. They had to protect themselves and their families against raids by Apache Indians.

The first residents of La Casa Cordova, "the Cordova house," stayed inside the 10-acre fort most of the time. Far from Mexico City and military help, with their supply links to Mexico's southern cities stretched dangerously thin, the residents lived with the threat of Indian assault looming real and often imminent.

Lt. Col. Hugo O'Conor, an Irish expatriate in the service of the Spanish Crown, first laid out the Spanish presidio of San Agustin del Tucson on Aug. 20, 1775, in nearby Tubac. Almost immediately, the facility moved from Tubac to Tucson, occupying the latter site by 1776. When Mexico won its independence from Spain in 1821, the population of the raw frontier community began to grow despite the dangers and hardships. By 1840, nearly 400 people lived in the Tucson presidio, most in crude adobe houses with dirt floors and pole-and-stick roofs, like La Casa Cordova.

The first recorded owners of the land where the Cordova House sits, James Lee and his wife, Maria Ramirez, held a deed to the property at the corner of North Meyer Avenue and Telles Street in 1875. In 1879, Gabino and Carmela Ortega bought the land. No one knows who designed and built the house, but at some point, the structure became L-shaped,

DAVID H. SMITH

▲ The L-shaped adobe house known as La Casa Cordova, believed to be Tucson's oldest residence, lies within El Presidio Historic District.

with four front rooms added to the original two rooms.

La Casa Cordova takes its name from Maria Navarette Cordova, who, with her four children, occupied the home from 1944 until 1973. Born in 1895 in Hermosillo, Sonora, Mexico, Maria and her husband, Raul H. Cordova, co-owned a market in Phoenix until 1930, when she divorced him, they sold the business, and she moved to Tucson.

While living in La Casa Cordova, Maria Cordova ran a smoke shop in the front of the house and lived in the rooms at the rear. Later, the City of Tucson acquired the house for urban renewal. Restored in 1975 with help from the Junior League of Tucson, the house now operates as part of a block of historic houses managed by the Tucson Museum of Art. El Presidio Historic District holds about 90 architecturally or historically significant buildings and claims a place on the National Register of Historic Places.

La Casa Cordova typifies the rudimentary homes of the region built during the mid-to-late 1800s in a style called Southern Arizona-Sonoran. Most of the construction materials came from the surrounding Sonoran Desert.

The walls of Sonoran homes were made of adobe bricks: sand, clay, water, and manure mixed together, molded in an egg-crate-like form, and then dried in the sun. Averaging 22 inches thick, the walls had enough thermal mass to retain prevailing temperatures. Most adobe buildings stood one story high because adobe lacks lateral structural strength. Adobe also tends to dissolve back into mud unless the structure has a stone foundation. Sometimes adobe can be preserved by plastering the walls. Fortunately, the Cordova House rests on a cut-stone foundation. And the walls recently received a coating of stucco.

Sonoran-style homes featured simple entrances — some doors were little more than brush or scavenged saguaro cactus ribs tied together with twigs or rawhide strips. The doors hung flush with the inside surface of the wall, offering some shelter from the sun and rain for those entering the structure. Windows, if they existed, were small and set even with the outside of the wall to form deep interior windowsills. Roofs were flat and supported by beams called *vigas,* which were topped by saguaro ribs, or *savinas.* Adobe mortar mixed with grass "glued" the roof together.

Homeowners kept dust from falling down from the vigas and savinas by hanging muslin cloths, or *mantas,* under the usually high (13-foot) ceilings. Tin troughs, or *canales,* channeled water off the roofs and away from the earthen walls. Family members maintained the floors by sprinkling them with water, then compacting the surface. Of course, the houses had no central heating or cooling, electricity, plumbing, or running water.

Residents of these simple structures spent much of their time in the courtyards, tending vegetable gardens, cooking, eating, entertaining family and friends, playing with their children, and, in the hot summer, sleeping outside under a verdant paloverde, pomegranate, or chinaberry tree.

The Cordova House courtyard had a two-hole privy and a well, although the family used the well water only for washing. Burros transported fresh drinking water in earthenware pots called *ollas,* which were filled from deeper wells near the edge of town.

The arrival of the railroad in March 1880 introduced Tucsonans to new building materials like fired brick and dimensional lumber, as well as more sophisticated construction techniques. People also began to build outside the fort. When Arizona became a territory in 1883, the Territorial style succeeded the Sonoran look. Territorial-style homes feature pitched or hipped roofs, broad verandahs, and setbacks that allow space for lawns.

Today's furnishings in the original two rooms of La Casa Cordova appear much as they were more than a century and a half ago when occupants feared that Apache Indians might breach the walls of the fort, overcome its military defenders, and kill them all. The spartan decor includes a stone bowl, or *metate,* for grinding corn, woven floor mats made of native buffalo grass, a wool *serape,* a prized pair of imported metal scissors, beds with rope "mattresses," and the ever-present chamber pot.

A walk through Tucson's historic El Presidio neighborhood reveals much of Tucson's residential history, of which La Casa Cordova, the early, unadorned Spanish-Mexican Sonoran shelter marks the humble beginning.

■ **WHEN YOU GO** 140 N. Main Ave., in El Presidio Historic District. From Interstate 10 in Tucson, take the Congress/Broadway exit; go east on Congress Street to Granada Avenue and turn north on Granada to the parking lot for the Tucson Museum of Art and the historic district. Open Tuesday through Saturday, 10 A.M. to 4 P.M.; Sunday, 12 P.M. to 4 P.M. Admission to La Casa Cordova is free; museum entrance fee includes admission to all other historic district buildings. (520) 624-2333. www.tucsonarts.com/historic.html

MISSION SAN XAVIER DEL BAC

■ **LOCATION**	Tohono O'odham Reservation, south of Tucson
■ **YEARS BUILT**	1783-97
■ **STYLE**	Mix of Spanish Colonial and Mexican Baroque with Moorish and Byzantine design elements
■ **ARCHITECT**	Believed to have been Ignacio Gaona
■ **SIGNIFICANCE**	Masterpiece of Spanish mission architecture / National Historic Landmark; National Register of Historic Places, 1966

Mission San Xavier del Bac, Arizona's only intact Spanish mission, has it all: an architectural form so strikingly beautiful it overwhelms the senses, religious and secular art ranging from the fanciful to the near fantastic, tales of death and political intrigue surrounding its construction, and an ongoing international effort to preserve the church in its original form.

San Xavier became known as the "White Dove of the Desert" because, when viewed from a distance, its bright white walls shimmer like a hovering bird against the azure sky of the Sonoran Desert. The mission is old by American standards. In 1700, the Jesuit priest and explorer Father Eusebio Francisco Kino built a church at the village of Bac and named it San Xavier to honor St. Francis Xavier, one of the first Jesuits. Nearly a century later, around 1783, Franciscan friars started the present-day church at San Xavier del Bac.

One of the finest examples of Spanish Colonial architecture in the United States, San Xavier functions as a parish church with Mass said daily. Tourists, photographers, writers, historians, and art and architecture buffs, as well as the faithful, arrive daily by the busload to marvel at this church built and embellished by illiterate Indians in the fertile Santa Cruz Valley. In recent years, preservationists also have been found there, working to restore the church.

San Xavier has a fairly straightforward early history. Father Kino, born in a small town near the Italian Alps, declined the offer of a teaching position in mathematics at Austria's University of Ingolstadt to devote himself to converting the "aborigines" of the New World. The priest crisscrossed Baja California, north-central Mexico, and Arizona, preaching, mapping, and founding as many as 20 Roman Catholic missions. He surveyed land in the Santa Cruz Valley for a mission as early as 1697 and, in 1700, set the cornerstones for what was to be San Xavier, in the Indian village of *Bac* (meaning "where the waters gather" in Tohono O'odham).

Kino traveled almost incessantly through the rugged Sonoran Desert until his death in 1711 at age 65 and established conclusively that Baja California was a peninsula and not an island. In addition to laying the groundwork for San Xavier, he founded Tumacacori, a sister mission near Tubac that now lies in ruins and is a national historic monument. A companion once said of Kino, "He died as he had lived in the greatest humility and poverty. . . . He was merciful to others but cruel to himself."

After King Charles III expelled the Jesuits from the Spanish empire in 1767, the Franciscan order took control of the Mexican missions. Between 1783 and 1797, the Franciscans built San Xavier under the direction of Fathers Juan Bautista Velderrain and Juan Bautista Llorens. Researchers believe Ignacio Gaona, a trained architect, designed the church in the shape of a cross on the site Kino had designated. San Xavier is distinguished by a massive, 52-foot-high,

Mission San Xavier del Bac is a marriage of Spanish Colonial and Mexican Baroque styling.

RICHARD MAACK

▲ **Appearing as a bright wash of white against the blue Arizona sky, the mission has earned the appellation, "White Dove of the Desert."**

flattened dome with a lantern on top and two 80-foot bell towers supported by flying buttresses. The walls, constructed of parallel rows of fired adobe brick, sometimes 6 feet thick, have rubble rock filling the cavities, a technique known to the ancient Romans, and limestone plastering.

San Xavier's style combines Byzantine, Moorish, late Mexican Baroque, and native motifs, blending them all together so well that one look flows into another.

Life at the San Xavier mission was never easy. Apaches often attacked the peaceful farming villages of the Tohono O'odham. Earthquakes, rainstorms, and drought afflicted the area. The mission remained abandoned from 1828 to 1850 after Mexico won its independence from Spain. Before retreating, the padres gave the sacramental silver and valuable vestments to the Indians to hide. When, as part of the Gadsden Purchase, the United States bought the territory south of the Gila River from Mexico in 1854, priests began visiting the mission again, and some of the church's treasures reappeared.

Mission San Xavier del Bac, actually a complex of buildings, includes a small, white mortuary chapel; monastery buildings; an enclosed patio; and the church. The church's façade has three parts. The two outer thirds, which are white, have relatively few decorative elements, while the central portion bursts forth in a rusty rose (sandstone) effusion of swirling volutes, shells, bas relief figures, and arabesques of Moorish and Mexican Baroque derivation.

Entering the church is like stepping into an earlier and more imaginative time period. Flamboyant frescoes, colorful stenciled imagery, more than 50 statues of Jesus, the Twelve

Apostles, the Virgin Mary, St. Francis Xavier (the patron saint of the mission), and other representations fill the interior.

Indian artisans communicated their own idea of heaven in vivid scenes featuring clouds and flights of angels — in all, some 300 angels have been counted clinging to pillars and peeking out from within portraits. Schooled in the bloody lore of Christianity's early saints and martyrs, the Indians crafted scenes gory enough to thrill an 8-year-old.

For example, the figure of St. Fidelis stands with a knife implanted in his chest, a raw, red wound visible near his temple. Satan glowers half-hidden in a scene from the Last Supper, while Judas clutches the 30 pieces of silver he received for betraying Jesus. Handles on the sanctuary doors look like rattlesnakes posed to strike, while more serpents writhe around niches in the walls.

Much of the ornamentation is *trompe l'oeil*, or "fool the eye." For instance, the blue and white tiles on the nave's walls are painted there, as is a fake door that symmetrically matches a real door on the opposite side of the altar. A pretend cord supports a framed painting that is actually a fresco. The ribbed domes in the nave imitate folds of cloth.

Birds and animals show up with apparent randomness. A cat above the west exterior volute forever threatens a mouse on top of the east volute above the entrance. Grapes, wheat, watermelon, and flowers rise in high relief. Lions guard the sanctuary. And every possible color available at the time pulses with restless energy — the brilliant reds made from the root of the ocotillo, blues contrived from the pulpy sap of the saguaro, brown and yellow taken from beneath the bark of the palo verde tree, green made from sage, and black from mesquite beans. Workers created a curious pattern of blue dots by dipping their thumbs in vegetable dye and pressing them onto the plaster. No one knows exactly what the dots signify.

Of necessity, the Franciscans and their laborers used the building materials they had at hand. They mixed boulders and cement on site to form foundations extending 5 feet below ground level and 2 feet above. Stones were collected and transported from the neighboring hills. Workers extracted lime from local limestone deposits to use in making the plaster, which consisted of a secret mixture of lime, milk, caliche, and animal blood. Pine used to form the woodwork originated in the forests of the Santa Catalina Mountains, as did oak for the entry doors and mesquite for the altar railing and pulpit. Records indicate mesquite trees sometimes grew 40 feet high in the late 1700s.

By the 1950s, though, the exuberant colors animating the artwork had begun to fade. A local artist over-painted some of the original decorations with oil-based pigment, topped with varnish — a no-no from a restorer's point of view. In the late 1980s, pieces of plaster started dropping into the sanctuary. It seems that patches of portland cement had trapped moisture inside the walls and prevented the surfaces from breathing, causing the plaster to crack and fall.

Concerned citizens met to form a non-profit organization to address the deterioration. The group, Patronato San Xavier, retained Paul Schwartzbaum, chief conservator of the Solomon P. Guggenheim Museum of Art in New York City, and hired an international team of conservators to rescue the church. Schwartzbaum reportedly was thrilled with the opportunity and praised San Xavier as "the Sistine Chapel of the United States."

To save the art painted on the walls, the experts applied Japanese rice paper soaked in denatured alcohol to release the dirt accumulated through the ages. They removed the non-conforming oil paint and varnish with lacquer thinner and erased layers of dust, candle soot, and bird excrement with clear water or special dry sponges. Then they injected an adhesive through syringes to reattach any loose plaster.

Preservationists replaced the offending cement patchwork by applying a new "skin" made of traditional lime, sand, and a "glue" produced from the lobes of the prickly pear cactus. Finally, they burnished the roof with river rock to slow water absorption.

The restoration proceeded as money became available. Meanwhile, several Tohono O'odham tribal members have learned conservation techniques through practice and devotion. And the Patronato is attempting to raise an endowment fund to complete the restoration and to maintain the mission forever.

San Xavier del Bac, Arizona's most famous church, visibly acknowledges southern Arizona's close relationship to the art, culture, and architecture of Mexico and symbolizes the significant role religion and spirituality have played in the development of the Southwest.

At San Xavier, the Tohono O'odham agreed to adopt the Catholic faith of their Spanish conquerors, but they did so on their own terms. Mission San Xavier del Bac and its art and architecture embody the meshing of two cultures — sometimes fractious, but mostly peaceful and harmonious.

■ **WHEN YOU GO** 1950 W. San Xavier Road, in the community of Wa:k. From Tucson, follow Interstate 19 south toward Nogales. Take Exit 92 to the right and continue a mile or so to the mission. San Xavier is an active church that is open every day, 8 A.M. to 5 P.M. Admission is free, but donations are appreciated. (520) 294-2624. www.sanxaviermission.org

NOGALES-SANTA CRUZ COUNTY PUBLIC LIBRARY

■ **LOCATION**	Nogales
■ **YEAR BUILT**	1962
■ **STYLE**	Southwest Modern
■ **ARCHITECT**	Bennie M. Gonzales
■ **SIGNIFICANCE**	Architectural triumph over space and budgetary constraints

The test of a true architect is to create a beautiful and beloved building on a difficult site, constrained by a tight budget.

Bennie M. Gonzales faced just such a challenge in 1960 when the City of Nogales asked him to design a small public library on land wedged between railroad tracks and an open canal and to do it at the lowest possible price.

Gonzales took the job, in part because he had spent many happy summers visiting his grandmother in the town on the Mexican border.

The architect, then living in Phoenix, kept costs down by using locally available building materials.

"I used adobe fired in Mexico. Then the wood, I think, we got from the Apache Indian reservation," he says. He cut heating and cooling expenses by shading the openings. "An extension over the patio kept the east sun from hitting the patio windows." And his design captured the look and feel of Nogales' Hispanic culture and history. "The arches and the roofline are in harmony with the architecture in Mexico," he says. "I think the library cost $14 a square foot. "The same library today would cost $100 a square foot or more," he says.

▲ Architect Bennie Gonzales emphasized openness and flexibility in the library he designed in Nogales. High arches allow light to reach the building's interior while shielding an outdoor reading patio.

In 1962, the American Institute of Architects, Central Arizona Chapter, honored Gonzales' work on the Nogales Public Library with its top award. Subsequently, clients rewarded Gonzales' talent with important commissions, including the Scottsdale Civic Center; a Bank One branch in Phoenix; a Sun City church and community center; hotels in Mazatlan and Cabo San Lucas, Mexico; homes for Randolph Hearst and Dick Van Dyke; and a $1-billion-plus palace for the king of Saudi Arabia. His peers recognized Gonzales, born in Phoenix in 1924, by naming him a Fellow of the American Institute of Architects.

The library has been altered as Nogales has grown, but the building retains its optimistic arched openings, Mexican-style heavy beams, and modern, minimalist ornamentation — well suited to a library in the American Southwest.

"The main thing is, the kids are still using it," Gonzales adds.

■ **WHEN YOU GO** 518 N. Grand Ave. In Nogales, Interstate 19 becomes Grand Avenue, and the library is four blocks north of the Arizona-Mexico border. Open Monday and Wednesday, 9:30 A.M. to 6 P.M.; Tuesday and Thursday, 9:30 A.M. to 7 P.M.; Friday, 9 A.M. to 5 P.M.; Saturday, 9 A.M. to 4 P.M. (520) 287-3343.

ODD FELLOWS AND REBEKAHS HOME

■ **LOCATION**	Safford
■ **YEAR BUILT**	1922
■ **STYLE**	Tudor Revival
■ **ARCHITECT**	William Bray
■ **SIGNIFICANCE**	Best-case example of society providing housing for the needy / National Register of Historic Places, 1988

By the end of the 19th century, fraternal organizations had become the centers of social and political life in Arizona Territory. Men established the Masons, Knights of Pythias, and Odd Fellows. Women joined auxiliaries like the Order of the Eastern Star, Pythian Sisters, and Rebekahs.

Beyond mere socializing, these groups provided for the welfare of needy members when there was no government "safety net."

In 1897, the Arizona Jurisdiction of the International Order of Odd Fellows organized an endowment fund to construct a fraternal home for aged members, widows, and orphaned children, with the Rebekah branch of the order assisting. After raising funds for 20 years, the order settled on a site in Safford, a Gila Valley farming community and the Graham County seat.

Construction began in January 1921, with the building dedicated April 25, 1922. The two-story Tudor Revival structure had a hipped, wood-shingled roof and partial basement. Workers fabricated its clay bricks and pre-cast concrete components on site. The style probably reflected the English heritage of its architect, William Bray. A 1920's-era Odd Fellows guidebook described the home:

"On the main floor are the Office, Superintendent's and Matron's quarters, and a large living room, reception hall and dining room. Also a large and well-equipped kitchen, pantry and store room. The upper floor has eight large sleeping rooms and three baths, equipped with tub and shower. The four rooms on the rear each have a screen sleeping porch, which makes it most attractive in the summer. The Home has a beautiful lawn attractively laid out in flowers and shrubbery. In the rear is located the orchard with about sixty assorted fruit trees, a large vineyard with different varieties of grapes, a large chicken yard and about eight acres devoted to garden and grain."

When residential operations ended in 1953, 18 elderly convalescents and 33 orphans had called the handsome building and lovely grounds home. In 1963, the city of Safford bought the property, renovated it, and turned the first floor into the Safford Public Library, with the Graham County Historical Museum housed upstairs. By the mid-1980s, however, the structure

▲ Fraternal organizations became the center of social life in Territorial times. The Odd Fellows and Rebekahs used their joint resources to sponsor a comfortable home in Safford for aged, widowed, and orphaned members of society.

began displaying leaks and cracks. After the library moved across the street in 1991, the city began a repair and reconstruction effort with assistance from two Arizona Heritage Fund grants, the Phelps Dodge Corp., and Graham County, as well as contributions from private citizens. Although the grand old building no longer houses the oldtimers and orphans for whom it was designed, in its current incarnation as home to several city of Safford offices, it is once again a Gila Valley architectural gem.

■ **WHEN YOU GO** 808 S. Eighth Ave. From U.S. Route 70 in Safford, turn south on Eighth Avenue and cross the irrigation canal. The city of Safford Planning and Community Services offices are located in the building, which is open Monday through Friday, 8 A.M. to 5 P.M. (928) 348-8514. The Graham County Historical Museum, located at 3430 W. U.S. 70 in Thatcher, has mapped a walking tour of Safford that includes the Odd Fellows and Rebekahs Home. Displays in the museum include an ancient clay duck effigy that was unearthed when the site for the home was excavated and the guestbook showing names and dates when orphans checked into the home. Open Monday, Tuesday, and Saturday, 10 A.M. to 4 P.M. (928) 348-0470.

OLD MAIN (UNIVERSITY OF ARIZONA)

■ **LOCATION**	University of Arizona, Tucson
■ **YEARS BUILT**	1887-1891
■ **STYLE**	Territorial Victorian
■ **ARCHITECT**	James Miller Creighton
■ **SIGNIFICANCE**	First permanent structure built at the University of Arizona / National Register of Historic Places, 1972

The University of Arizona could hardly have opened its doors under less auspicious circumstances.

In 1885, the so-called "Thieving 13th" Arizona Territorial Assembly awarded a hefty $100,000 to rival Phoenix for the construction of the coveted insane asylum, while Tucson, then Arizona's largest city, received just $25,000 to establish the first university in the Territory. What's more, the Assembly attached strings to the award. The bill said that Tucson must somehow obtain 40 acres within a year to build a campus; otherwise, the Assembly would withdraw the funding.

But there were no volunteer donors in sight.

Fortunately, Prussian-born emigrant Jacob S. Mansfeld believed in the university concept enough to search for a site. A member of the university's Board of Regents, he hiked the Tucson area until he found a barren, rocky mesa that he thought suitable. For months, he pleaded with the landowners — E.C. Gifford, Ben C. Parker, and William S. Read — until they reluctantly agreed to donate their land. A groundbreaking party for the new university, held on Oct. 27, 1887, drew some 600 Tucsonans.

Once they had the land on which to build, the university's backers faced another daunting challenge: Few settlers could attend. Since the Territory had no high schools, there were no recent graduates ready for higher education; old-timers, busy scratching out a living, had precious little time for study; and newcomers often stopped in Tucson only briefly before moving on to California. The regents chose James Miller Creighton, born in New Brunswick,

RICHARD MAACK

▲ A hybrid style known as Territorial Victorian accounts for the architecture of Old Main, the first building erected at the University of Arizona.

Canada, of Scottish parents, as the architect to design the university's first building. Creighton had studied design in Denver, worked in the contracting business in Tucson, and then operated an architectural office in Phoenix. He soon became the Territory's best-known architect, designing the Pinal County Courthouse in Florence, the Old Dominion Hotel in Globe, buildings at Fort McDowell and Fort Huachuca, and the first Adams Hotel in Phoenix, among others.

Newspaper ads had invited architects in the Tucson and San Francisco areas to submit plans and specifications for a school of mines at the new university. The regents accepted Creighton's plans, for which he received the munificent sum of $500. Before it could be completed, the university's first permanent building ran out of construction funds. The building sat vacant, without a stairway or a porch railing. Fortunately, the regents learned of federal money available for schools of agriculture, and the school of mines conveniently became an agricultural college. Called simply the University Building, the two-story brick, wood, and stone structure opened Oct. 1, 1891, with six faculty and 32 students. Only six young people actually qualified for university-level instruction, but the rest signed up for remedial courses.

Officially dedicated to educating agricultural students, the University Building actually served a hodge-podge of purposes, housing classrooms, chemistry and mineralogy laboratories, offices for faculty and staff, temporary sleeping quarters for male teachers and students, a kitchen, dining hall, Territorial weather bureau, photographic darkroom, and a library.

No one seemed to know what to call it. In 1893, the University Building became known as the Main Building. In 1901, the name was changed to University Hall. And in

1927, it gained the title "Old Main," which has stuck to this day.

The building turned out to be surprisingly energy efficient. More than a half-century later, in 1945, university President Alfred Atkinson remarked, "We are going to put a good many summer classes in Old Main. It is the coolest building on the grounds."

Partially earth-integrated, Old Main's first floor is a sort of raised basement with the earth piled around it to moderate temperatures. An encircling porch shaded by a 12-foot overhang protects the first and second stories from the sun's direct rays. High ceilings (12 feet downstairs and 17 feet upstairs) allow the heat to rise, which helps occupants stay cool in the summer. Tall, double-hung windows foster air circulation. Finally, stone walls on the first floor and brick walls with stone lintels spanning the doors and windows on the second floor increase the mass and help sustain constant temperatures.

Built symmetrically in the shape of an elongated cross with entrances facing all four directions, Old Main extends about 195 feet on the long, or north-south axis, and 120 feet on the short, or east-west axis. Four 50-foot-high towers with pyramid roofs indicate the entries, which are further distinguished by arched openings. The roof is a variation on a French mansard roof, and the porch has a sloped-shed roof.

In 1940, when asked what style characterized Old Main, Creighton replied, "We had to cut corners in those days. We sank the structure 6 feet below the surface so the ground itself would help support the building. . . . I used the small towers outside to indicate the heights to which education might rise, and the whole building is an European adaptation, even to its curved French mansard roof."

Most architects call Old Main's hybrid design Territorial Victorian.

Begun so tentatively, the University of Arizona quickly grew in size and reputation, regularly adding new buildings and educational disciplines, with red brick as the unifying building material. In the case of Old Main, the brick was fashioned on site from dirt dug for the below-grade first floor. The university's newer buildings did not echo Old Main's simplicity. As more and more revivalist-style buildings appeared, the university gradually came to view Old Main as a non-conforming relic. A 1919 university master plan showed the building already replaced. In 1938, authorities declared Old Main unsafe, and the *Arizona Daily Star* called the building "too shabbily constructed to endure." In 1940, critics proposed making over Old Main into a Spanish Colonial structure. They wanted to stucco its walls, re-roof it with mission tile, and add wrought-iron decoration.

The U.S. Navy came to the rescue in 1942. Intent on rehabilitating the building as a training school during World War II, the Navy contracted to have Old Main's beams, trusses, and joints repaired or replaced, new floors laid, a new roof installed, and the heating, lighting, plumbing, and cooling systems updated.

But by 1947, agitators urged tearing it down to make room for a student union. The building was even referred to, in 1962, as "a monstrosity" that should be removed to "make way for progress."

Happily, Old Main survived. And in 1972, Creighton's design gained recognition on the National Register of Historic Places, the first U of A building to receive that designation. Nomination papers praised Old Main as "a well preserved gem of the Territorial period of Arizona's history. . . . Its exterior, especially, possesses an architectural integrity found all too seldom in the Southwest of today, for structures of this vintage have all too often been badly altered or even destroyed."

Old Main remains basically intact despite the discommodious events of its long life, including anti-Vietnam War demonstrations, over-enthusiastic victory celebrations, and the seemingly unending remodeling of its interior. At various times, the building has housed a radio-TV studio, French classes, the Graduate College, the Alumni Office, and the R.O.T.C. Today, awkward partitions accommodate its many users.

But the building has earned the respect of faculty, students, and alumni who see the facility as an icon that stands for the university's indomitable spirit over the course of more than a century. Architecturally, Old Main represents the triumph of good, sound design over stylistic pretension.

■ **WHEN YOU GO** Old Main lies directly east of the main gate of the University of Arizona campus, astride the east/west mall in the historic district of the campus, south of Speedway, between Euclid and Campbell avenues in Tucson. (520) 621-2211.

OWLS CLUB HOUSES

■ **LOCATION**	Tucson
■ **YEARS BUILT**	1900; 1901
■ **STYLE**	Mission Revival with Sullivanesque and Prairie-style elements
■ **ARCHITECT**	Henry Charles Trost
■ **SIGNIFICANCE**	Gentlemen's quarters for upwardly mobile Tucson bachelors / National Register of Historic Places, 1976 (part of El Presidio Historic District)

Many of the young bachelors arriving in Tucson near the turn of the 20th century were well educated, sophisticated, ambitious, and adventurous.

But Tucson, like most frontier towns at the time, contained a profusion of saloons and gambling houses, relegating the young men to dreary boarding houses to consume barely edible meals. Even worse, from the viewpoint of one group of bachelor-newcomers committed to taking over the business and financial leadership of Tucson, marriageable, single women of high social status were few and difficult to meet.

So in 1886, 13 high-spirited, enterprising "gentlemen" banded together to form the Owls Club, an elite male group devoted to fun and festivities. They hired a cook and proceeded to throw galas, masked balls, and fetes that quickly became the talk of the Tucson social scene. Club members even printed stationery embossed with their seal, a royal blue owl.

Then Levi Manning, on his way to becoming a prosperous rancher and real estate developer, hatched an idea. He would commission well-known architect Henry C. Trost to design an Owls Club "nest" where members could live and entertain in the style to which they hoped to become accustomed.

The building, which measured 110 feet long and 72 feet wide and cost $10,000, was stuccoed brick done in the Mission Revival style, with arcades and a hipped roof covered with red tiles. Four bachelors lived there in elegant, high-ceilinged suites and dined or received guests in double parlors on the top floor. Servant quarters and storage occupied the more confined lower level. The sloping site with its U-shaped structure provided sufficient space for a dramatic, open-air palm garden-courtyard with lush landscaping, paired stairways, and a fountain supplying ambience for romantic events in the evenings.

Architect Henry Trost was born in Toledo, Ohio, on March 5, 1860, the son of a carpenter-contractor. He studied art before evolving into something of an itinerant architect,

RICHARD MAACK

▲ Once used as a "nest" for sophisticated bachelors, the Owls Club houses were designed by
Henry C. Trost in the Mission Revival style.

practicing his skills in Denver; Pueblo, Colorado; Galveston, Texas; New Orleans, and Dodge
City, Kansas. Trost then moved to Chicago. Between 1888 and 1896 he probably worked in the
Chicago office of the great Louis Sullivan and most likely knew Frank Lloyd Wright.

Trost arrived in Tucson in 1899 — just in time to gain the Owls Club commission. Not

surprisingly, he incorporated the stylized embellishment typical of Sullivan's work in the design of the first Owls Club building. He also placed the statue of an owl in a niche on the building's facade and added more owl insignia in the spandrels between the arches. Many believe Trost's playful birds reflect his acquaintance with and appreciation for Tucson's Mission San Xavier del Bac, where images of animals appear throughout the decoration.

Not only did Trost's choice of the Mission Revival style fit with Tucson's architecture, it suited the hot climate as well. For example, oval openings ringing the space beneath the roof of the first Owls Club structure helped vent hot air, and exterior walls with their arched openings protected interior patios from the direct sun. The courtyard's verdant growth also provided an evaporative cooling effect.

When Owls Club member Levi Manning married, he and his new wife decided they would like to live in the Owls Club house. To provide new accommodations for his Owl friends, Manning commissioned Trost to design a second Owls Club building two lots away.

In some ways, the second Owls "nest," often lauded as a Trost masterpiece, shows more influence of San Xavier than the first because of its ornate central entrance portal and second-story balconies. The owl figure from the first Owls Club house was moved to a round niche in the second. Additional festive decorations in the new house included a symmetrical arrangement of Southwestern flora and fauna — like carved horned toads, saguaro cactus, and mice, mixed with classic motifs like strapping, laurel leaves, C-scrolls, spindles, and linked rings. Equally attention-getting, over-sized *canales*, or rain spouts, culminated in giant squash blossoms. Trost obviously expanded upon the Sullivanesque decorative embellishment he had used in the original Owls Club house and added spice to give it a distinctly Arizona flavor.

Manning and his wife lived only briefly in the original Owls Club. Albert Steinfeld and his wife, Bettina, bought the property in 1908, furnishing it with Chinese teakwood antiques, massive mahogany pieces, and Oriental rugs, and enriching the interior surfaces with parquet floors, tile-framed fireplaces, and the finest wood trim. Contemporaries called Steinfeld, the wealthy owner of a dry goods store, the "merchant prince of the Southwest."

Over time, other bachelor members of the Owls Club married, one by one. Many built their own sumptuous mansions on what is now Main Avenue. Frank Hereford, later a distinguished attorney, moved into the Trost-designed Hereford House (1902) between the two Owls Club houses, and Leo Goldschmidt, the last Owls Club bachelor, bought out the interests of his fellow Owls and moved into the second Owls Club. He and his sister, Eva Mansfeld, lived there for years with her two daughters, her widowed son, and his two daughters. During the family's tenure there the house rang with the sounds of young people, making the household one of the liveliest on Main Street.

Eventually, the first Owls Club house (now known as the Steinfeld Mansion), as well as the second Owls Club house, succumbed to the effects of time and neglect. The original Owls Club became, in succession, a convent, an American Legion hall, and art studios. The exterior ornamentation disappeared. Then in 1977, an application was made to demolish the building. Fortunately, a Tucson construction company purchased the first Owls Club house and, benefiting from federal tax incentives and using old photographs, restored the outside and renovated the interior for use as professional office space.

The second Owls Club house also suffered before being rescued. In the 1960s, the Loyal Order of the Moose bought the building and stripped it of its ornamental plaster, *canales*, and balconies. Later, the building stood vacant, and transients camped in its hollow shell.

In 1985, Collier-Craft Development Company bought what was left of the 9,000-square-foot second Owls Club for $125,000 and restored the exterior to its original splendor. Artist Robb Boucher reproduced the decorative elements from molds made according to images he discovered in an early glass negative showing the facade. The owl statue was replaced, and neon lighting strung around it. The building is now an office building with a contemporary interior.

Trost moved to El Paso in 1903 but continued designing buildings in Arizona almost until his death in 1933 at age 73. His other Arizona projects include Phoenix's Luhrs Tower, Prescott's Hassayampa Inn, and the Gadsden Hotel in Douglas.

He mastered every architectural style then current in the United States. His prodigious output over a 55-year career ranged from theaters to department stores to hotels, with more than 200 designs in Arizona alone — and the quality of his work consistently rated as excellent. The two restored Owls Club houses provide ample evidence of the importance of Henry Trost's architectural legacy in Arizona.

■ **WHEN YOU GO** 300 and 378 N. Main Ave. In Tucson, from East Speedway Boulevard, go south on North Granada to East Sixth Street, then east on East Sixth Street to North Main Avenue and south to both addresses. Walking tours of the downtown area are available through the Metropolitan Tucson Convention and Visitors Bureau, (520) 624-1817.

PIMA COUNTY COURTHOUSE

■ **LOCATION**	Tucson
■ **YEAR BUILT**	1928
■ **STYLE**	Spanish Colonial Revival
■ **ARCHITECT**	Roy W. Place
■ **SIGNIFICANCE**	Outstanding example of Spanish Colonial Revival style in Arizona / National Register of Historic Places, 1978

Tucson's Pima County Courthouse is an unusual downtown landmark. In the first place, the handsome, blue-domed icon is not a high-rise commercial office building like Chicago's Sears Tower or New York's Empire State Building, but rather a government structure; and secondly, the architect who designed it chose to disregard the convention of the day, which was to design county courthouses in the Neoclassical style.

As the architect, San Diego native Roy W. Place chose the Spanish Colonial Revival style, partly because it was the design theme for the 1915-16 Panama-California Exposition in San Diego, which celebrated the completion of the Panama Canal, and partly because he believed the style paid homage to Tucson's Spanish heritage.

The beautiful ceramic-tiled dome makes a dramatic statement about the building's Hispanic origins. A close look at the dome reveals a mosaic of blue, green, yellow, and red tiles that, from a distance, appears all blue.

One interesting note about the tiles: When the bids for the plumbing, heating, and electrical contracts came back, they were *lower* than the County Board of Supervisors had expected. Delighted, the supervisors spent the surplus funds on tiling the dome. The massive concrete dome measures 32 feet in diameter and towers 100 feet above Tucson. Illuminated at night, the dome and arcade add romance to Tucson's downtown profile.

Other Spanish Colonial Revival characteristics evident in the Pima County Courthouse,

An excellent example of Spanish Colonial Revival architecture, the Pima County Courthouse design countered the Neoclassical trends of the 1920s. A mosaic of blue, green, red, and yellow tiles caps the building's dome; from afar, the dome appears completely blue.

completed in 1928, include a low-pitched, red-tiled roof; pink stuccoed walls; arched windows; elaborate churrigueresque carvings; pilasters near the doorways; ornate balconies; and arcaded post-and-lintel-type entries opening to an interior courtyard.

The U-shaped structure has a three-story-high central portion and two wings, each two stories tall. The arcade connecting the wings borders a pleasant, lawn-covered courtyard cooled by a fountain. Sharp-eyed visitors will notice a thin strip embedded in the walkway extending the width of the courtyard. This band of granite indicates where the walls around the old Tucson Presidio once ran.

Although workers dismantled El Presidio years ago, a portion of the adobe wall — crumbling but recognizable — was salvaged and is displayed behind glass in the county assessor's office. The county courthouse also houses the offices of the county recorder, the county treasurer, and the consolidated justice courts.

Courtroom F is an opulent space filled with heavy molding, carved scrolling, extensive wainscoting, and fluted Corinthian pilasters next to dark-stained oak doors. The judge's raised dais, witness stand, and jury box are trimmed with the sort of turned balusters, rich paneling, and denticulated molding associated with TV dramas. The other courtrooms don't compare in elegance.

When Arizona became an American territory in 1863, Tucson was the seat of Pima County. At first, county officials rented office space, but in 1868, they decided to build a simple, Sonoran-style courthouse with a flat, unadorned exterior and deep-set windows and doors, costing $15,500. Specifications called for a rock foundation with "walls of adobe made of good dirt well mixed with straw" plus a step placed in front of each doorway to be "made of good sound mesquite timber." This was the first of the county's three courthouses.

By 1880, the year the Southern Pacific Railroad reached Tucson, the commissioners wanted a larger county courthouse in keeping with Tucson's more exalted status. The second courthouse was a two-story brick building laid out in the shape of a cross with a cupola topping a central tower. At the time, it was "the pride and joy of the Territory," clippings stated.

After Arizona became a state in 1912, the commissioners wanted an even grander county courthouse. They had the Territory's former pride and joy demolished and erected on its site the third and current Pima County Courthouse using Roy Place's design. The new courthouse cost about $350,000.

In 1917, Place and fellow San Diego architect, John B. Lyman, had won a competition to design the mines and engineering building for the University of Arizona. They moved to Tucson, founded Lyman & Place, Architects, and designed Tucson High School, Casa Grande High School, and the Yuma City Hall. They also collaborated on other U of A buildings until Lyman returned to San Diego in 1924.

Place then ran the firm under his own name and designed many more buildings on the U of A campus, in Tucson, and throughout southern Arizona. Roy Place died Sept. 23, 1950, praised for his careful attention to detail and expertise in a variety of styles.

The Pima County Courthouse has aged well. An expansion of the south wing in 1956 added more courtrooms, then the jail was removed from the north wing in 1965. Other renovations included restoring the 1928 courtyard fountain and adding sprinklers and fire alarms, says Bill Clarke, Pima County's downtown maintenance supervisor, who knows every inch of the structure, including its two underground tunnels and basement safes and vaults.

Clarke notes that the original steam boilers remain in the basement, although a central plant supplies the facility with heating and cooling. "It was easier and cheaper to leave them," he explains.

Clarke has an obvious fondness for his architectural charge. "The building is so unique and springy," he says.

■ **WHEN YOU GO** 115 N. Church St. From West Congress Street in Tucson, go east to North Church Avenue, then north to the courthouse. Walking tours of the downtown area are available through the Tucson Metropolitan Chamber of Commerce, (520) 624-1817.

ST. PHILIP'S IN THE HILLS EPISCOPAL CHURCH

■ **LOCATION**	Tucson
■ **YEAR BUILT**	1936
■ **STYLE**	Mission and Spanish Colonial Revival
■ **ARCHITECT**	Josias Thomas Joesler
■ **SIGNIFICANCE**	Harbinger of an architectural look still popular in Tucson / (Nomination to National Register of Historic Places in process)

St. Philip's in the Hills Episcopal Church, a Tucson landmark, looks like an 18th-century mission church in Mexico. The resemblance was intentional.

In 1936, real estate developers John and Helen Murphey decided that a good way to sell houses in the then-remote desert 4 miles north of Tucson was to appeal to the romantic inclinations of potential buyers. The Murpheys teamed with architect Josias Thomas Joesler, well known for his "period" designs, to draw up the plans for a housing development with a Spanish Colonial church as an amenity.

The result was a theme-oriented, master-planned community, says R. Brooks Jeffery, coordinator of preservation studies in the University of Arizona's College of Architecture. The Episcopal church became to the Catalina Foothills Estates what a cathedral is in a Mexican village — the center of community life.

"In the Catalina Foothills Estates," Jeffery wrote in his book, *Joesler & Murphey — An Architectural Legacy for Tucson* (1994), "the vision was ... focused on creating a Mexican village, complete with a church and plaza. As development of the residential community grew, St. Philip's Plaza evolved into [a] Mexican plaza as envisioned by the Murpheys."

The Murphey-Joesler housing development proved successful. The 200-some homes, many also crafted in the Spanish Colonial Revival style, complete with arches, ceramic tile roofs, covered patios, and wrought iron ornamentation, set the tone for an architectural look still popular in the Tucson area. Jeffery wrote, "The romanticism of Tucson's Hispanic past strongly defined its architectural identity through World War II, and continues to define its cultural identity today."

John Murphey, a native Tucsonan born in 1898 and one of eight children, studied engineering and geology at the University of Arizona. While in school, he met Helen Geyer, who had moved to Tucson from Massachusetts with her mother, who came for arthritis relief. Murphey fell so deeply in love with Helen that, in 1920, he gave up a Rhodes scholarship to marry her. Through their first years together, the couple lived in a tent in the desert to maintain a claim to the homestead that would became part of the Foothills Estates.

Helen Murphey, artistic by nature, collected photographs and drawings of Mexican

▲ Lush desert vegetation surrounds St. Philip's in the Hills Episcopal Church, which is part of the 7,000-acre Catalina Foothills Estates.

▲ **Dark wooden doors and elaborate metalwork are characteristic of the church's Old Mexico detailing.**

architectural elements in scrapbooks. Later, she used these motifs on the painted shutters, lintels, and beams that decorated her husband's projects. The two became partners in The John Murphey Building Co., which, in addition to developing homesites, bought and sold land, insured property, and rented and stored furniture.

The Murpheys hired Joesler because the architect had built a reputation designing exotic Old World-type homes. The Murpheys believed houses of this kind would attract affluent buyers to their subdivision. Swiss-born, cultured, and well-educated, Joesler had studied architecture in Bern, Switzerland; engineering in Heidelberg, Germany; and history and drawing at the Sorbonne in Paris. He had visited north Africa and Latin America and practiced architecture in Los Angeles.

Joesler designed subdivisions that avoided the grid-like layouts usual in the West, instead featuring curving streets, landscaping that followed the contours of the land, and rustic building materials.

The Catalina Foothills Estates became the Murpheys' and Joesler's signature collaboration. It centered on a "Mexican" plaza with a tearoom, artist's studio, offices, a large courtyard, and, of course, St. Philip's in the Hills Episcopal Church. Three of Joesler's buildings there, as well as the church, still stand, although recent street widenings and nearby development have altered the character of the area.

Spread over approximately 7,000 acres, the homes radiate from the central plaza and St. Philip's. According to parish records, well-known early homebuyers included author Erskine Caldwell, Mrs. Will Mayo of the Mayo Clinic family, Louise Grace of the Grace shipping lines family, and the Drexels of Drexel University in Philadelphia.

St. Philip's in the Hills occupies the corner of Campbell Avenue and River Road. Its 3- to 5-foot-thick adobe walls have a stucco coating, and a row of burnt-adobe bricks outlines the

▲ Josias Thomas Joesler designed the church with deep recesses in the windows and doorways. He wanted the building to resemble a mission but have a cool, airy feel throughout.

mission-shaped parapet. The deeply recessed entry doors typify old Spanish design with small pilot doors.

Joesler wanted to design a church that would look like an authentic Spanish mission but feel light and airy. He accomplished this by focusing the nave on a 12-foot-high arched window, through which parishioners can view the Santa Catalina Mountains and the surrounding desert landscape. Colored warm white inside and out, the church has a dozen stained glass windows created by Francisco Garduno Cañedo, which project additional color and light into the interior. Three chandeliers illuminate the dark, carved-wood beams in the flat ceiling overhead.

Beams, pews, and an altar made from cedar logs grown on Mexico's southwest coast and carved by a Mexican artisan reinforce the mission concept. Aisles connect to the central nave through turned cast-stone pillars and arched arcades, and the pillars, which march the length of the church, have Corinthian capitals.

The congregation celebrated the church's completion with a midnight eucharist on Christmas Eve, 1936. Some 235 people crowded into a facility designed to seat 200. The glow of *luminarias* beckoned worshipers to the over-sized entry doors, and joyous organ music urged congregants to come inside to worship.

The Murpheys gave the land for the original chapel-sized church and later donated much of the cost of the building. But visitors today will see a considerably expanded facility.

Remodeling in the late 1950s and early 1960s included moving the original 12-foot plate-glass window behind the freestanding altar 52 feet north, doubling the size of the sacristy and widening the nave with the addition of a bay. Later additions included a baptistery, three cloistered gardens, classrooms, offices, and a nursery — all done in the Spanish

Colonial Revival style. In 1986, workers stabilized the structure, installed a three-manual pipe organ, and added a campanile tower.

Over the years, parishioners contributed art objects of great beauty and significance as an expression of their love for the church. These include a 17th-century painting of Saint Philip, one of the Twelve Apostles and the church's patron saint; a 16th-century carved, gessoed wood statue of St. Anthony of Padua; and a 14th-century painted crucifix by an unknown artist from the School of Giotto.

"As the congregation grew, the whole complex grew with it," wrote Jeffery. "It was so successful, it drew development north from Tucson.... Their [The Murpheys' and Joesler's] work successfully promoted Tucson as a resort destination and, subsequently, fostered America's romance with the Southwest."

■ **WHEN YOU GO** 4440 N. Campbell Ave. From downtown Tucson, go north on Campbell Avenue to just beyond East River Road. Open from 8 A.M. to dusk most days. Call for information about free concerts, lectures, and art shows. (520) 299-6421. www.stphilipstucson.org

SLAUGHTER RANCH

■ **LOCATION**	East of Douglas
■ **YEARS BUILT**	1887-88
■ **STYLE**	Transitional (adobe/rock buildings combined with mail-order add-ons)
■ **BUILDER**	John Slaughter
■ **SIGNIFICANCE**	Testimony to the rigors of pioneer ranch life near the border with Mexico / National Historic Landmark; National Register of Historic Places, 1966

John Horton Slaughter was 74 years old when he heard that the bandit Pancho Villa was butchering his cattle. Calmly, the rancher placed a shotgun in the scabbard of his saddle and swung up on his horse. Alone, he rode south into Mexico to face the guerrilla fighter. Soon afterwards Slaughter returned home, bringing back both an apology and a bag of $20 gold pieces — ample payment from Pancho Villa for the cattle he had stolen.

This story — one of many — illustrates John Slaughter's bravery and determination. A former Confederate soldier and Texas Ranger, Slaughter moved to Arizona and eventually served as Cochise County sheriff from 1887 to 1891. He admitted to "disposing of" at least 12 thieves, rustlers, or murderers. (In those days, sheriffs acted as judge, jury, and executioner.) The cowman also served in the Arizona Territorial Legislature from 1906 to 1907 and helped found the town of Douglas.

But Slaughter's main interest was his vast ranch, which extended on both sides of the U.S.-Mexico border near Douglas. There he raised cattle, branded with the letter Z, that fattened on the lush waist-high grass of the San Bernardino Valley. Slaughter also profitably cultivated wheat, barley, beans, and cotton in the marshy lowlands of the ranch. At one point, as many as 500 people, including 200 Chinese vegetable farmers, lived on Slaughter's spread.

Known for his mild-mannered ways and love for children, the fearless gunslinger with the piercing eyes and quick draw stood just 5 feet, 6 inches tall. When possible, he avoided confrontation. As sheriff, he gave the bad men of Cochise County time to buy a suitcase, then he'd set a deadline, saying, "If you're here past that deadline, I'll come looking for you, and you'll stay here as a permanent resident," in other words, 6 feet underground.

Slaughter the lawman wore a pearl-handled Colt revolver, a diamond ring, and fancy boots. But off duty he might be found walking hand in hand with the children on the ranch, particularly Apache May, an Apache tyke Slaughter adopted. He brought her up as his own daughter until her tragic death from fire at age 6. Slaughter, distraught over the accident, refused to play cards for six months.

Slaughter bought his original 65,000-acre holdings, extending on both sides of the border, in 1884. After finishing his second term as sheriff in 1892, he started building the compound that included a five-bedroom ranch house, granary, commissary, wash house, and ice house. Slaughter and his second wife, Viola, lived in the main house of the compound for almost 30 years, until 1921, when a treacherous employee killed Slaughter's best friend and nearly murdered him. This persuaded the aging Slaughter to move to the safety of Douglas, where he died a year later at age 80. Before she died in 1941, Viola sold the Mexican portion of the ranch to a Mexican citizen and the American acreage to Marion Williams, another rancher.

A 16-mile dirt road east of Douglas leads to the 142-acre Slaughter Ranch, also known as the San Bernardino Ranch. The ranch house compound has been restored, as much as possible, to its condition when Slaughter lived there with his family. The remainder of the U.S. portion of the ranch is a wildlife refuge, administered by the U.S. Fish & Wildlife Service. The Johnson Historical Museum of the Southwest now takes care of the ranch house and other ranch buildings, which are set amid carefully mowed lawns adjacent to a tree-shaded pond. Visitors to the ranch house can't help but imagine the self-effacing John Slaughter and his much younger wife exchanging verbal parries on their wrap-around front porch — she explaining heatedly why she should accompany him on their next buying expedition to Bisbee, and he pointing out mildly why she should not take the four-day, roundtrip journey. Slaughter, or his ranch manager, regularly traveled the dangerous backcountry route by

DAVID W. LAZAROFF

▲ In Slaughter Ranch's heyday, hands transported 300-pound blocks of ice from Douglas to the icehouse to cool perishable meats and vegetables. Today, the ranch serves as an example of a lifestyle hardly remembered.

BERNADETTE HEATH

▲ The ranch's sprawling design, complete with shaded benches on the porch, conveys a lazy feeling. History contradicts: in the late 19th century, the ranch employed as many as 500 people at one time.

horse and wagon to purchase staples like sugar, flour, and salt, or treats like cloth and candy, which they then sold to workers and their families in the ranch store. Although Geronimo, the Apache war leader, had been captured, renegade Indians still presented a threat to settlers traveling alone across the desert.

In the evenings, one can envision Viola serving guests homemade ice cream made with ice from the icehouse, built in 1903. Every few days, the ranch hands brought 300-pound blocks of ice, wrapped in burlap and sawdust, by wagon from Douglas and dropped them down a chute in the icehouse to cool the milk, cheese, meat, and vegetables. Most of the ranch buildings were built with locally available materials, like adobe and the black rocks spewed long ago from a nearby now-dormant volcano. The restoration shows that the Slaughters were aware of current fashion. For the living room, they ordered a built-in china cabinet and a diamond-paned window adorned with a classical cornice from Sears, Roebuck and Co.

Gerald Doyle, of Gerald A. Doyle & Associates in Phoenix, spent three years restoring the Slaughter house and out-buildings. Doyle says his toughest task was making new adobe bricks to replace those that had been damaged. He placed new cedar shingles on all the roofs except for the icehouse, which had a metal roof. He removed the ragged screening from the porch, and erected a white picket fence to replace the anachronistic stone wall. "We attempted to be faithful even to the details on the screen doors," Doyle says.

Doyle assesses the Slaughter Ranch: "It's really a good example of a lifestyle of more than 100 years ago. The Mormon Battalion went through there and so did prospectors on their way to California's gold fields. You really feel you're going back in time."

■ **WHEN YOU GO** From Douglas, follow the Geronimo Trail east 16 miles to the ranch. The road is partially dirt, but passable for passenger cars. Open Wednesday through Sunday, 10 A.M. to 3 P.M. Closed Monday and Tuesday, Christmas and New Years. Entrance fee. (520) 558-2474.

GAMMAGE AUDITORIUM

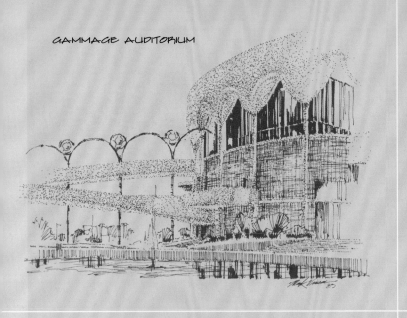

STAIRWAY, MYSTERY CASTLE

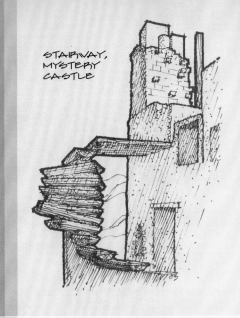

DECO WINDOW DETAILS, LUHRS TOWER

PARAPET VOLUTE, SAN XAVIER

■ ■ ■ ■ ■ ■
GLOSSARY OF ARCHITECTURAL TERMS

ART DECO: design style of the 1920s and '30s that took its name from the 1925 Exposition International des Arts-Décoratifs et Industriels Modernes held in Paris. Characterized by linear, hard-edged, or angular compositions with stylized, geometric motifs.

ATMOSPHERIC THEATER: performance venue, popular in the 1920s and '30s, that surrounds audiences with a fantasy environment, such as clouds and constellations projected on the ceiling, or walls decorated as stage sets promoting the illusion that viewers are in a faraway, romanticized location.

BALUSTER: one of several short, vertical posts, often shaped on a lathe or otherwise detailed, that supports a stair railing.

BARGEBOARD: trim board, often ornately carved, used on the edge of a gable to hide the end of the rafter.

BATTERED: describes a building element, such as a wall or column, that is wider at the bottom than at the top.

BOARD AND BATTEN: sheathing used on wood-frame buildings consisting of wide, abutting boards with the joints hidden by narrow strips of wood called battens; simple wood-frame structures sheathed this way were sometimes called "board-and-batten boxes."

BUNGALOW: one-story, usually wood-frame, house that includes a covered front porch with a gable usually supported by battered piers at the corners. The exterior walls are often covered with wood shingles or stucco; the windows usually contain several panes. Comes from a Hindustani word meaning "belonging to Bangal," referring to India's simple roadside rest houses surrounded by verandahs, a concept the British brought to the New World.

BUNGALOW, CALIFORNIA: often used as a generic term for any small, one-story frame house with a gently sloped gabled roof, shingled siding, covered front porch with its own gabled roof, exposed rafters that extend beyond the roof (sometimes supported by brackets), multipaned windows, and sometimes a cobblestone chimney. An offshoot of the Arts and Crafts Movement, the style became popular in early 20th-century California because of that state's mild climate.

CEMENTITIOUS PLASTER: lime, gypsum, sand, portland cement, and water mixed to form a paste-like material that, after being applied to a wall or ceiling, dries as a hard surface.

CHURRIGUERESQUE: elaborate Baroque-style architectural design most often found in Spain and Latin America in the late 17th and early 18th centuries. Derives from the Churriguera brothers — José Benito (1665-1725), Joaquin (1674-1724) and Alberto de Churriguera (1676-1750) — three Catalan architects known for richly ornate churches and plazas.

CLADDING: building's visible, non-structural, external sheath.

CLASSICAL ARCHITECTURE: ancient Greek and Roman architecture, characterized by the temple form with a portico running across the entire front, low-pitched or flat roofs, bilateral symmetry, smooth-surfaced walls, and columns with decorative capitals.

CLASSICAL REVIVAL STYLE: based on ancient Roman and Greek architecture, its simple, symmetrical shapes developed as a reaction to ornate styles such as Rococo and Baroque.

CLUB-FOOTED COLUMN: column with a base shaped like the end of a club.

CORNICE: uppermost portion of the molding that crowns a building or wall.

CRENELLATED PARAPET: low wall or railing along a roof's edge with a repeating pattern of squared-off notches alternating with rectangular projections, as along the top of a fort or castle.

DESERT MASONRY: construction method that involves mounding large rocks from the surrounding desert within wooden forms; pouring mortar in; then, once the mortar is dry, removing the forms so the rocks become prominent features of the structure.

DESIGN-BUILD HOUSES: homes designed and built by the same person or firm.

DOUBLE PYRAMIDAL ROOF SYSTEM: two roofs hipped equally on all four sides, with one placed above the other to add insulation or protection.

FLOOR WELL: recessed portion of an earthen, stone, or concrete floor, usually covered and used for storage.

GABLE: triangular upper portion of a wall at the end of a pitched roof that mimics the slope of the roof it supports.

HIPPED ROOF: roof with slopes on all four sides.

I-BEAM CANOPY: roof-like structure composed of rolled or extruded metal beams that, in cross section, resemble the capital letter *I*.

ITALIAN ROMANESQUE REVIVAL: Romanesque Revival style modified with the addition of decorative "eyebrows" above the windows, recessed entryways, gently pitched roofs resembling classic temple pediments, and windows grouped in threes or placed within arcades.

KNITLOCK BLOCK: concrete blocks, hollow in the center and grooved at the perimeter; the grooves can be linked, or "knit," together to provide structural stability and allow both inner and outer walls to be constructed simultaneously.

MANSARD ROOF: named for French classical architect François Mansart (1598-1666); has two slopes on all four sides, with the lower slopes steeper than the flatter, shorter, upper ones. Almost always contains dormer windows.

MARBLECRETE: concrete embedded with tiny, sparkling marble chips.

MISSION REVIVAL: California regional style that loosely resembles the 18th-century missions of Mexico and the American Southwest, characterized by simple forms and sparse ornamentation, semicircular arches, tiled roofs, smoothly plastered walls, balconies, and sometimes towers or turrets capped by domes or pyramidal tiled roofs.

MISSION REVIVAL, INTEGRATED: building done in the Mission Revival style in which the style components, like arches and balconies, are functional, not mere decoration.

MODERNISM: current architectural movement (from 1895 to the present) in which architects tailor designs to their times, rejecting applied styles, moldings, and ornament, but showcasing manufactured materials like concrete, steel, and glass and making clear a building's construction methods and intended functions.

MODERN, HIGH TECH: architectural style emphasizing the newest in building materials, construction systems, and technology.

NEOCLASSICAL REVIVAL: style similar to Classical Revival; based on ancient Greek and Roman designs, produces symmetrically arranged buildings of monumental proportions that are distinguished by smooth surfaces and simple geometry.

ORGANIC ARCHITECTURE: concept advanced by Frank Lloyd Wright that attempts to connect a building's form with its function; relate the whole to the parts; bring the outdoors inside; employ natural materials like wood and stone; and integrate a building with a site's natural terrain.

PEDIMENT: low-pitched, triangular gable above a façade or over porticos above a doorway or a window, often featuring Greek-inspired detailing at the perimeter.

PIER: upright structural element, typically of masonry, which serves as a main support, often for an arch. May be separate from or part of a wall.

PILASTER: pier or column set into or projecting slightly from a wall.

PILOT DOOR: smaller door, within a much larger door, allowing people to enter an enclosure separately. The larger opening often accommodates horseback riders, wagons, or carriages.

PORTE COCHERE: projecting roof at a building's entrance that shelters disembarking coach or automobile passengers from the elements.

PORTICO: covered porch or a walkway with a roof supported by columns.

POST-AND-LINTEL: simple form of construction characterized by vertical posts or columns supporting horizontal beams (or lintels) to carry a load across an opening.

PRAIRIE STYLE: architectural look, originating in the late 1800s, associated with Frank Lloyd Wright and other Midwestern designers, that emphasizes the horizontal, extends the eaves of low-pitched roofs well beyond their walls, groups clerestory windows in horizontal bands that often continue around corners, and attempts to integrate the building and its site.

PRAIRIE STYLE, LATE: later expression of the Prairie Style affected by Modernism.

PROSCENIUM ARCH: space in a theater between the curtain and the orchestra that includes the entire span of the stage opening.

PUEBLO, PUEBLO REVIVAL: style based on communities built by Pueblo Indians; characterized by a massive look, stone or adobe construction, battered walls, flat roofs, rounded corners, deep-set windows, projecting roof beams, and terraced upper floors.

PUEBLO DECO: Art Deco style adapted to the Southwest and featuring indigenous plants, animals, and symbols as decorative motifs.

PUEBLO MODERN: architectural look that combines contemporary building methods and technology with forms and materials that recall the buildings of the Pueblo Indians.

REVIVAL STYLE: use of an older architectural style in new architecture, most often referring to the Egyptian, Greek, Roman, Gothic, Renaissance, or Colonial styles of the 18th, 19th, and early 20th centuries.

ROMANESQUE REVIVAL: style characterized by monochromatic brick or stone buildings featuring semicircular arches above the windows and doors. Arches and column capitals are carved with geometrical medieval moldings, and façades are flanked by polygonal towers.

ROTUNDA: circular building element covered by a dome, or a large room with a high ceiling.

RUSTICATED: made to look rustic; usually pertains to rough-surfaced exterior walls consisting of quarry-finish stone or heavily textured concrete block laid with deep joints.

SPANDREL: triangular space formed between the sides of adjacent arches and the line across their tops; in modern glass curtainwall construction, the space between floors covered by obscure glass panels.

SPANISH COLONIAL REVIVAL: style derived from the missions and haciendas in northern New Spain and popularized by the 1915 Panama-California Exposition in San Diego. Notable for ornate, low-relief carvings highlighting arches, columns, cornices, and door and window surrounds. Characteristics include iron window grilles and balconies, red-tiled hipped roofs, decorated parapets, arcaded porches, and, often, a bell tower.

SPANISH ROMANESQUE REVIVAL: variation of Romanesque Revival style that features ornate, low-relief carvings that highlight arches, columns, window surrounds, and cornices. Red-tiled hipped roofs, arcaded porches, and wrought-iron window grilles and balconies are also typical; exterior walls finished with plaster or stucco or left exposed.

SYSTEM HOUSE: home built of pre-engineered, prefabricated components according to a predetermined plan.

TECTUM: material made of compressed wood fibers and a cementitious bonding agent formed into panels and used for sound and thermal insulation and, in some cases, structural sheathing in roof and wall assemblies.

TERRA-COTTA: hard fired clay used in pottery and, decoratively or structurally, in construction.

TERRITORIAL STYLE: architectural style popular when Arizona was still a territory. Buildings are typically long, low, and rectangular with a gentle slope to the gable roof and a wide roof overhang. A wide verandah often encircles the building or runs its length. Windows are double-hung, and ceilings are high to allow heat to rise and enhance air circulation.

TOMBASIL: silvery-gold alloy of bronze commonly used to make boat propellers.

VENEER: thin finishing layer bonded to an inferior substrate; for example, a thin facing of walnut or cherry wood glued to a plain pine plank, or a non-structural layer of brick or stone applied to a frame or concrete block wall, enriching the look of the object underneath.

VENETIAN PLASTER: special imported Italian plaster mix applied to walls in several layers to achieve the effect of an aged oil painting.

VERNACULAR: native to a particular region or locale; also ordinary or practical buildings not designed by trained architects.

VICTORIAN ARCHITECTURE: from the period when Britain's Queen Victoria reigned (1837-1901; especially after the celebration of her Golden Jubilee in 1887); known for wooden "gingerbread," or heavily ornamental elements such as curved brackets, extensive latticework, and round perforations. Characteristics also include fish-scale shingles; small porches; pointed turrets; tall, thin windows; and impressive chimneys.

VICTORIAN, EASTLAKE: named for English architect Charles Locke Eastlake (1836-1906), this generally massive, overly decorated style can be recognized by its many posts, railings, and balusters turned on a mechanical lathe; multiple spindles and latticework attached to the porch eaves; and scrolling and curved brackets at almost every corner or projection of the façade.

VICTORIAN, FRENCH: Victorian look featuring distinctively French design motifs, like the fleur-de-lis.

VICTORIAN, HIGH: Victorian architecture carried to excess, most notably in the latter period of the style's popularity.

VICTORIAN, ITALIANATE: Victorian architecture with an Italian twist; for example, arched windows with decorative "eyebrows," and cast-iron façades.

VICTORIAN, PAINTED LADIES: vibrantly painted Victorian houses, with a different color for each architectural detail; much-photographed examples found in San Francisco and, more locally, in Prescott.

REFERENCES:

Burden, Ernest (1998), *Illustrated Dictionary of Architecture* (USA: McGraw-Hill).

Curl, James Stevens (2000), *Oxford Dictionary of Architecture* (Oxford: Oxford University Press).

Fleming, John; Honour, Hugh and Pevsner, Nikolaus (1999, Fifth Edition), *Architecture and Landscape Architecture* (London, New York et al: Penguin Group).

Saylor, Henry (1952), *Dictionary of Architecture* (New York, Toronto, et al: John Wiley & Sons).

Whiffen, Marcus (1988), *American Architecture Since 1780* (USA: Massachusetts Institute of Technology).

INDEX